PRAEGER LIBRARY OF U.S. GOVERNMENT DEPARTMENTS
AND AGENCIES

The Department of Defense

The Department of Defense

C. W. Borklund

FREDERICK A. PRAEGER, *Publishers*
New York • Washington • London

FREDERICK A. PRAEGER, PUBLISHERS
111 Fourth Avenue, New York, N.Y. 10003, U.S.A.
77-79 Charlotte Street, London W.1, England

Published in the United States of America in 1968
by Frederick A. Praeger, Inc., Publishers

Library of Congress Catalog Card Number: 68-16080

This book is No. 11 in the series
Praeger Library of U.S. Government Departments and Agencies

The author is grateful for permission to cite from:
Can Democracy Survive Cold War?, by Harry Howe Ransom.
Copyright © 1963 by Harry Howe Ransom. Reprinted
by permission of Doubleday & Company, Inc.
The White House Years: Mandate for Change 1953–1956,
by Dwight D. Eisenhower. Copyright © 1963 by
Dwight D. Eisenhower. Reprinted by permission of
Doubleday & Company, Inc.
The White House Years: Waging Peace 1956–1961.
Copyright © 1965 by Dwight D. Eisenhower. Reprinted
by permission of Doubleday & Company, Inc.

Printed in the United States of America

Preface

The United States Department of Defense celebrated what is generally considered its twentieth birthday in 1967. Its senior military and civilian leadership can still recall the sometimes bitter wrangling over passage of the National Security Act of 1947 that brought "the three military Departments of the Army, the Navy (including naval aviation and the United States Marine Corps), and the Air Force under the general direction, authority, and control of the Secretary of Defense."

This new supervisory organization forced an immediate redirection of effort, behavior, and thinking on those who had formerly run the military forces, and the change in attitude and activity was spurred even more in later years as the Office of the Secretary of Defense was given increasing authority over those forces.

Complainers called the change a "radical departure" from tradition; yet, in fact, the nation has always had a single authority in control of its armed forces. Since 1789, in accordance with Article II, Section 2, of the Constitution, one person, the President of the United States, has been "Commander-in-Chief of the Army and Navy of the United States, and of the Militia of the several States, when called into the actual Service of the United States."

The concept of single authority has never changed. As the course book on national security management of the Industrial College of the Armed Forces concludes:

v

America's organization for national security has evolved within
the framework of its Constitution, its customs, and its traditions.
Powers bearing on national security are vested by the Constitution in the Government as a whole, and are shared primarily by
the President and the Congress. Under a system of checks and
balances, these . . . elements have developed distinctive patterns . . . in their concern with the national security.

In the last thirty years, however, several factors have pro-
foundly influenced those distinctive patterns, especially in the
executive branch of government. New pressures have resulted
from the shift in the world balance of political power that
placed the United States in a position of world leadership,
from U.S. pioneering in the technological revolution that produced weapons with previously unimagined destructive capability, and from the continually spiraling cost of obtaining,
training, and maintaining military forces. These and other
related factors added up to an awesome increase in both the
importance and the complexity of commanding the armed
forces efficiently and economically—and, in simplest terms,
led Congress, in 1947, to give the President a "Deputy President" to aid him in handling the military facet of his office
obligations.

How does the Secretary of Defense exercise control for the
President over the military? How is the Defense Department
organized and what are the interrelationships of its key elements? How well has it performed its mission? How important
are talented people and good judgment to a supervisory
agency that often seems cold, impersonal, almost automated?
Why does the Department do what it does, and what seems to
be in its future? These are some of the questions that will be
explored in the following pages.

Someone is certain to be slighted by any attempt to thank
all those who have contributed, directly or indirectly, to this
volume; but I must give credit for good guidance to former
Defense Comptroller Wilfred McNeil and to five of the eight

past secretaries of Defense—Louis Johnson, Robert Lovett, Neil McElroy, Thomas Gates, and Robert McNamara, the only leaders of the Department still living at the time this work was undertaken.

Beyond them, if I were to list names, acknowledgments would run into the hundreds. The experts who have added freely and generously to this author's information on and understanding of Defense affairs have, in effect, been teachers, at one time or another, for a personal postgraduate course now more than a decade old—a learning program that shows no signs of stopping. The fairest thing I can think of is to thank them all as a group and hope each recalls the time or times when I asked for and he gave his help. They managed to load me up with a head full of facts. But, far more important, they have also given me a fascinating insight into Defense people— and their problems and progress in one of the most important fields of contemporary American endeavor.

Washington, D.C.   C. W. BORKLUND
October, 1967

Contents

Charts

A section of photographs follows page 86.

x

The Department of Defense

I

Why the Defense Department Was Established

The Department of Defense (DOD) is by far the largest organization in the executive branch of the federal government, requiring each year approximately half of all federal expenditures to carry out its operations. Since its primary responsibility is to ensure the security of the United States, the Defense Department is also considered by many to be the most important of federal agencies. Not a day passes that at least one of its actions or proposed projects does not receive nationwide —even worldwide—scrutiny and comment. Yet it is a latecomer to government, not having been created until after World War II, when the "National Military Establishment" was set up by the National Security Act of 1947, under the Secretary of Defense. In 1949, amended legislation gave the Department its present name.

During the debates leading up to the Defense Department's creation, and with the steps taken since then to strengthen it, the Department's merit and its proper role in government affairs have been the subject of continual conflict and controversy. Interestingly, however, the philosophy behind its design was not a new notion, but one anchored deep in American history. Since 1789, the single direction of the armed forces of the nation has been vested in one man—the President. According to Article II, Section 2, of the U.S. Constitution, he is also "Commander-in-Chief of the Army and Navy." His military responsibility is the same today as it was in the past.

What has changed from time to time is the organizational pattern of support for the President in carrying out his military functions. During the first nine years of the Republic, when the armed forces were practically nonexistent, a single deputy, the Secretary of War (who headed the War Department), was enough to assist him. Then, in 1798, as a result of the building of a fleet to combat Barbary Coast pirates, naval activities assumed new importance, and the Department of the Navy was created. For nearly 150 years afterward, the President constituted the sole court for settling disputes between the two military departments, with the War Department representing the Army. When the post of Secretary of Defense was established in 1947, the President once again acquired a single deputy for all military matters.

In the years between 1798 and 1947, the War and Navy departments coordinated their activities only when they met at the water's edge. Generally, problems of the oceans were left to the Navy and those of the land to the Army. But having two separate military departments reporting directly to him during that time did not place an unreasonable burden on the President. For one thing, except in time of war, the departments were comparatively small. The peacetime Army's size never reached 18,000 before the Civil War and was kept below 30,000 in the years before the Spanish-American War. The peacetime Navy stayed below 13,000, the Marine Corps below 4,000. Whatever friction and bickering occurred between the departments was usually not of national importance. With the country's energy focused on internal development, military policy was not a major concern. Army and Navy missions seldom overlapped. Thus, in time of peace, the Presidential job of coordinating military affairs was not heavy.

Proposals were made, however, usually following wars, to create organizations designed to achieve closer coordination and consolidation of the War and Navy departments below the Presidential level. One such suggestion reached Congress in 1869, following an analysis of mistakes made by the military during the Civil War. A similar unification philosophy was embodied in the creation of the Joint Army and Navy Board in 1903. At that time, as Harry B. Yoshpe and Stanley L. Falk have noted in *Organization for National Security,* their textbook for the Industrial College of the Armed Forces,

> The United States had embarked on a more active role in world affairs . . . and central planning and advisory organizations came into use both in the Army and the Navy. These developments, the poor organization and inefficiency of the Santiago Expedition during the Spanish-American War, and the emergence of jurisdictional conflicts over the newly acquired overseas possessions, emphasized the need for some mechanism of coordination at a level below the President. . . .
>
> Comprised of specifically named senior officers of the Army and Navy, the Board served as a forum for consideration of matters requiring inter-Service cooperation. It lacked a working staff and had little to show for its efforts at the onset of World War I. Nonetheless, the Board's existence was an early, if faint and unappreciated, appearance of the concept of "unification" in the military.

World War I pointed up some serious problems regarding the waste of time, money, and resources caused by conflicting demands on the nation for war matériel from uncoordinated Army and Navy procurement officials. In addition, the birth of the combat airplane raised for the military a touchy question (made glaringly public by Brigadier General William "Billy" Mitchell's open argument with both the Army and the Navy) over the value of air power and how it should be utilized— separately by the two services or independently by a third service, an air force. On February 12, 1925, for instance, Mitchell showed a House of Representatives investigating committee the conclusive damage aerial bombs had wreaked on battleships during joint Army-Navy tests in 1921. He wrapped up his testimony by urging Congress to frame a law establishing three branches of military service—air, sea, and land—with one individual, a Secretary of Defense, responsible for all national defense.

As a result of these questions, more than a dozen studies and in excess of fifty bills and resolutions were presented to Congress between 1921 and 1945, all calling, essentially, for a unified organization to handle military affairs. This flurry of activity reached its peak in 1932, in the middle of the Great Depression, when an out-and-out economy proposal for a single department promised to save $100 million—and was narrowly defeated on the floor of the House of Representatives. Few of the other bills ever got beyond committee investigation. None were approved. The debate over unification quieted down in the mid-1930's and stayed dormant for a decade.

Pressures for Unification

Then, in the years 1943–46, all the factors seemed to well up together that individually, at one time or another, had provoked renewed discussion of the idea of a single military department. Key pressures were the constantly increasing responsibilities of the chief executive; U.S. assumption of Free World leadership in the face of increasing Communist aggression; the technological revolution, heralded first by military aircraft and later by atomic bombs, intercontinental missiles, electronics, etc.; the success of combined Army–Navy–Air Force operations in World War II battles; and the rapidly rising costs of developing modern weaponry, as weighed against growing public demand for economy in military spending. All these long-evolving trends, taken together, suddenly made it very attractive, if not absolutely necessary, for the

President to delegate to a subordinate much of the burden for coordinating and directing military activities.

Wartime experience had driven home the lesson that the military establishment was but one element in the nation's security. Although the form that postwar organization of a military department should take was to be the subject of long and heated controversy, there was wide agreement among responsible officials and leaders on other aspects of national security. Preservation of peace would depend not only upon the armed services, but also upon the economic growth of the nation and the skill and wisdom with which the government conducted its foreign relations. Improved organizational means would have to be designed for closer linking of military, foreign, and domestic policies in setting national goals.

Moreover, it was obvious that another world conflict, involving atomic bombs and bombers, would hardly permit the United States time to prepare for war while powerful allies held back the enemy. Careful, coordinated, and thorough planning for rapid and effective counterattack would have to be done in advance. As one writer was to record, looking back on this period:

> Heretofore, the tasks of the armed forces in peacetime had been primarily to maintain cadres of trained officers and men, to engage in mobilization planning, develop prototypes of the weapons they would like to order in quantity, and try to foresee the circumstances and places in which they would be called upon to fight. Each Service had had a [fighting] capability in being, especially the Navy; but these forces were rarely expected to become involved in major military operations until after America's friends had been precipitated into a war. . . . Now all this had changed. Contingency plans might have to be executed, forces in being might have to be used without a period of grace for mobilization. And weapons in the inventory were certain to be the ones that would be fired in anger. The old

days, in which the United States could act as the second line of
Western defense, seemingly had gone forever.*

Collective Security

Foreign policy, military plans, and domestic economic programs could no longer be three relatively independent, largely
isolated fields of government endeavor. Instead, in world politics, they would have to march together, developing and executing in coordination something called "national security
policy." The significance of the new environment became clear
to the military rather quickly.

Implementing this policy meant entering into a long list of
bilateral and multilateral mutual assistance treaties and agreements. The United States, under the Truman Doctrine,
promised primarily economic and financial support to "free
peoples . . . resisting attempted subjection by armed minor-
ities or by outside pressures" and, under the Marshall Plan,
granted what became billions in financial assistance to help
war-devastated Europe rebuild. Later, it strengthened its support of the North Atlantic Treaty Organization (NATO) to
toughen European military defenses against Communist aggression and, in all, within ten years after the end of World War
II, entered into more than forty commitments to help a host of
world nations defend themselves.

Underscoring the scope and size of the challenge to military
preparedness created by these international promises was the
supporting conclusion reached by the United States at the end
of the war, but voiced by George Washington more than a
century and a half earlier, that "To be prepared for war is one
of the most effectual ways of preserving peace."

These national decisions and attitudes had a far-reaching
impact on the armed forces. From the mid-1940's on, practi-

* William W. Kaufmann, *The McNamara Strategy* (New York: Harper
& Row, 1964), p. 5.

cally every military plan and program was tempered in some way by the policy of collective security, which affected the size and deployment of forces, as well as their organization, training, and equipment. Over-all budgetary considerations assumed new significance, since it is one thing for the military services to decide privately what forces they need to support collective security agreements, and quite another to get those forces if the nation, viz., Congress, is not willing to appropriate the funds.

The Technological Revolution

Related to the drastic change in the world politico-military environment, influencing and being influenced by it, was—and is—the technological revolution. At the end of World War II, society was on the doorstep of an explosive growth in the exploitation of basic scientific knowledge to produce new materials, new products, and even new research. The first doubling of man's scientific knowledge, reported the National Education Association twenty years after the war ended, occurred in 1750, "the second in 1900, the third in 1950, and the fourth only ten years later."

Looking back, the eighth Secretary of Defense, Robert S. McNamara, in a commencement address at Chatham College (Pennsylvania), in 1966, described this explosive change as having "no precedent in the 40,000 years of Homo Sapiens."

Change took place, of course, even in the ancient and medieval world. But the rate of change, relative to man's life-span, was slow enough to guarantee that the quantum of knowledge, acquired in youth, would remain valid even into old age.

What has happened today is that the progression of technological and social change is no longer merely arithmetical or geometric with respect to man's life-span. It is explosively exponential. The engineer, for example, graduating this summer will find ten short years from now that fully half his expensively acquired engineering education is already obsolete. And the other 50 per cent, which he will then require to remain relevant in his field, has not yet even been discovered. But this galloping ratio of radical change is a problem not merely for the engineer. It is a problem for anyone—the poet, the philosopher, the pedagogue, or the parent—who wishes to remain relevant in his own society.

Air Force General Bernard A. Schriever, who played a leading role in the 1950's in both fostering and utilizing the technological revolution to produce new and newer military weapons, suggested, in his commencement address at Colorado State University, in 1964, that students

> . . . look at a graph showing the technical progress of mankind over the past 2,000 years. For most of that period the line on the graph stays practically horizontal. . . . About 1830, the line starts to slope upward, as it begins to reflect the inventions of the last half century. After 1900, with the invention of the automobile, airplane, and radio, the upward trend becomes more pronounced. But around 1945, the line suddenly takes a sharp turn upward, reflecting a completely new rate of discovery and invention. . . .

> Today, patents are issued for approximately 50,000 new inventions every year. About 80 per cent of all the scientists and engineers who ever lived are alive today. In the past eight years, our population of scientists and engineers has increased by 40 per cent—and supply still has not caught up with demand.

> To a large degree the technological explosion has been the result of demands of our national security. Our military needs during World War II gave the first big push in science and technology. Then, as the Soviet threat became increasingly clear, our research and development efforts grew in scope and urgency.

Specifically, in 1945, the military had on the drawing board, in the laboratory, on the test stand, or already in the first stages of routine use the kinds of weapons and warhead delivery systems that promised—and threatened—to make feasible brand-new kinds of wars, which had no historical precedent.

Comic strip characters with death-ray guns and spaceships were no longer considered fantasy by the military. Jet engines, for example, had been developed—boosting the speed of aircraft to three, four, and more times that of planes driven by piston engines. Radar, automatic homing devices, and other forms of engineering wizardry had raised the ability of weapons to hit targets beyond anything imagined ten years earlier. New types of explosives had increased the destructive power of a bomb 2,000 and more times. And electronics, particularly in communications and computers, was making it increasingly practical for fewer and fewer men to control larger military forces in the field from higher and higher levels with increasingly reliable accuracy. Under development were delivery vehicles that would be able, in a matter of minutes, to deliver explosives halfway around the world. A new expression, "the collapse of time," was heard among military planners.

In 1945, Army Air Forces General Carl Spaatz testified before the Senate Military Affairs Committee that

> . . . the blessing of time lag which we enjoyed in two world wars is gone. . . . As top dog, America becomes target No. 1. There will be no time lag. The airplane will possibly exceed the speed of sound. The possibilities for surprise are thus multiplied beyond measurement. That is the impact of science, which is changing the world no matter what we say or do. . . . Science, therefore, dictates a new approach to the problems of national security. . . . We can have only one goal: a national security system consistent with the new technical era. In an age dominated by speed that means a streamlined defense, constantly on the alert.

That same year, British Prime Minister Clement Attlee recalled a time when "we in Britain" were "safe behind our moat, the inviolable sea. Those days are past," he said. "Defensive frontiers, mountain barriers, the seas and even the oceans are no obstacle to attack. The old discontinuity of earth and sea has been replaced by the continuity of the air."

Only one example was really needed to make the point. The atomic bomb, housing a destructive power far in excess of anything ever known before, was conclusive evidence that the military departments dared not ignore whatever the scientist had to offer. The first atomic bomb used in warfare exploded a force equal to 22,000 tons of TNT—2,000 times more powerful than the largest high-explosive bomb, the "block-buster," used in World War II. Detonated over Hiroshima, Japan, by a U.S. bomber on August 6, 1945, it killed 66,000 persons and injured 69,000 more, destroying or damaging 67 per cent of the city's buildings. Another atomic bomb, dropped three days later on Nagasaki, Japan, killed or injured more than 36 per cent of that city's 200,000 residents and destroyed or damaged about 88 per cent of its buildings. By the time the Department of Defense was given its name four years later, scientists had already successfully tested nuclear weapons with much greater destructive power. It took only simple arithmetic by men versed in blast effects to figure out that an arsenal of atomic bombs, together with a rapid delivery system like the airplane or missile, could destroy an entire enemy nation within hours. Obviously, if two opposing countries, each armed with such power, released that kind of devastation on the other, there would be no winner.

The evolution of nuclear weapons grimly illustrated, too, that military decision-makers faced a shrinking margin for error in what they chose to exploit from technology. Although no one nation can get very far ahead of the rest of the world in scientific knowledge, what each country does with that knowledge is another matter. For example, splitting the uranium atom, the toughest obstacle to building an atomic bomb, was first done successfully in Germany in 1938, but Germany did not produce the bomb. However, using discoveries made primarily in the United States, the Germans moved faster in developing their long-range Vengeance missiles (V-1 and

V-2). They managed to launch a handful against England near the end of the war, but had started too late to build successfully what they had reportedly intended—enough weapons to force at least a stalemate in the war.

It takes, on the average, about seven years after a decision is made to complete the building of a specific, complex weapon system that research has said can be built. During that seven-year development-and-test cycle, before the first proven quantities of that system are ready for delivery to combat forces, research and engineering can be expected to produce knowledge promising an even better weapon possibility if the development in process is stopped and the new one started. Thus, one by-product of the technological revolution is the rapid obsolescence of its principal products. Yesterday's development is an outdated approach today, and today's idea, predictably, will be old thinking tomorrow. As military research and development experts were already beginning to see in the late 1940's, and would consider an inherent headache of their responsibilities in the 1950's, if a weapon works, it's obsolete.

Still, combat forces that might have to fight at any moment could not wait forever, armed only with outmoded weapons, while their scientific compatriots postponed giving them a next generation of weaponry because "the generation after that will be even better." Choices had to be made.

The challenge to pluck the best available out of the rushing stream of possibilities became, for the military, a critical test of perceptive judgment. During 1945–47, when there were two separate military departments analyzing technological developments independently, simply making these complex and extremely difficult judgments in voluntary cooperation with each other would have been hard enough; but the services aggravated their problem by choosing to compete instead of cooperate. They simply accepted the most glamorous weapons offered and argued principally over who should be given sole possession of the lot. As a result, Congress and the nation, looking for assurance that the military leadership was on top of the problem of making sound judgments for new arsenals, heard not that, but contentious debate over ownership. This public squabbling among the Army, the Navy, and the Army Air Forces (then striving to become a separate service) helped convince the country that it was, indeed, time to centralize the command and direction of the armed forces.

In a message to Congress on December 19, 1945, President Harry S. Truman said:

> We should allocate systematically our limited resources for scientific research. . . . No aspect of military preparedness is more important than scientific research. Given the limited amount of scientific talent that will be available for military purposes, we must systematically apply that talent to research in the most promising lines and on the weapons with the greatest potentiality, regardless of the Service in which these weapons will be used. We cannot afford to waste any of our scientific resources in duplication of effort.

Another key factor building up the pressure for unification of the armed forces was closely allied to the service rivalries being revealed in the competition for new weapons. Military service has never been a very popular career among Americans, and one of the black marks regularly chalked up against it as an almost inherent characteristic has been the charge of waste and inefficiency. Indeed, out of military operations during World War II—and the private American citizen-soldier's comment on them—came a new word for the dictionary: "snafu," meaning, in the bowdlerized version, "situation normal, all fouled up." Misassignment of men, overprocurement of matériel, misdirected shipment of supplies have not always been as bad as publicized, of course, taken against the hundreds of thousands of times such decisions have to be made during a war. Private companies, other government organizations, and individuals are probably wrong just as often. But, especially in war, with so much at stake for the whole nation and under the glaring scrutiny of both the press and Congress, defense errors in judgment tend to be spotlighted quickly and chastised widely.

Reasons of Economy

"Economy" had long been one of the supporting arguments for most military department unification proposals and it was again in 1945–47, this time bolstered by President Truman, who later wrote that he had

> not fully realized the extent of the waste and inefficiency existing as a result of the operation of two separate and uncoordinated military departments until I became chairman of the special Senate committee created in 1941 to check up on the national defense program. I had long believed that a coordinated defense organization was an absolute necessity. The duplications of time, material, and manpower resulting from independent Army and Navy operations which were paraded before my committee intensified this conviction.*

That was the kind of attitude the nation wanted to hear. It was in an economy frame of mind. Rushing to "bring the boys home," the United States, at the end of World War II, was not just demobilizing but dismantling what months earlier had been the strongest military power in the world. From having more than 12 million men and women in uniform in 1945, the military establishment's size fell to less than 1.6 million by 1947. Thousands of tons of supplies were given away to World War II Allies, left to rust in huge stacks overseas, or brought back to the United States to be put in storage, sold as surplus, or cannibalized for parts.

There is a persistent conviction in some government circles, generally, and the military, specifically, that when a problem becomes unbearable, the way to solve it is to reorganize.

* Harry S. Truman, *Memoirs by Harry S. Truman*, Vol. II: *Years of Trial and Hope* (New York: Doubleday, 1958), p. 46.

It is questionable if the wasting of resources can be corrected simply by reorganizing; inefficiency is primarily the result of ordinary human error. But a listening nation found attractive the promise implied by unification proponents, i.e. that continually increasing worldwide U.S. commitments could still be met without maintaining a large, costly military force, if there were just tighter control by fewer organizations at the top.

Need for Teamwork

Added to these three pressures—the policy of collective security with United States leadership, the impact of revolutionary new weapons, and the public insistence on military economy—was another: the contention that military forces of the future would work well only if they worked as a team. In his aforementioned message to Congress in 1945, urging legislation to combine the War and Navy departments into a single Department of Defense, President Harry Truman also said: "One of the lessons learned which have most clearly come from the costly and dangerous experience of this war is that there must be unified direction of land, sea and air forces at home as well as in other parts of the world where our Armed Forces are serving. We did not have that kind of direction when we were attacked four years ago and we certainly paid a high price for not having it." And, he added,

In 1941, we had two completely independent organizations with no well-established habits of collaboration and cooperation between them. If disputes arose, if there was failure to agree on a question of planning or a question of action, only the President of the United States could make a decision effective on both. Besides, in 1941, the air power of the United States was not organized on a par with the ground and sea forces.

Our expedient for meeting these defects was the creation of the Joint Chiefs of Staff. On this committee sat the President's Chief of Staff and the chiefs of the land forces, the naval forces, and the air forces. Under the Joint Chiefs were organized a number of committees bringing together personnel of the three services for joint strategic planning and for coordination of operations. This kind of coordination was better than no coordination at all, but it was in no sense a unified command.

In the theaters of operation, meanwhile, we went further in the direction of unity by establishing unified commands. We came to the conclusion, soon confirmed by experience, that any extended military effort required overall coordinated control in order to get the most out of the three armed forces. Had we not early in the war adopted this principle of a unified command for operations, our efforts, no matter how heroic, might have failed.

In testimony before the Senate Military Affairs Committee during the previous three months, most of the nation's World War II military leaders had echoed that argument. "In unity will lie military strength," said General of the Army Douglas MacArthur, adding, "We cannot win with only backs and ends. And no line, however strong, can go alone. Victory will rest with the team." General of the Army Henry H. "Hap" Arnold, who commanded the Army Air Forces in the war, agreed: "In every war theater throughout the world, the pattern I have described—an autonomous coequal air force under supreme command—has . . . emerged under entirely different conditions . . . impelled by entirely different influences and sets of circumstances."

General Dwight Eisenhower testified that, "One of the most important and least understood factors in modern war is that it is essentially a matter of perfected teamwork," and Fleet Admiral William Halsey, Jr. that, "During the periods of greatest stress and toughest going, we had utter, complete, and total unity of our forces. On one team, Army, Navy, Marine Corps, Coast Guard." There was more of the same from other highly regarded military leaders—their messages perhaps best summed up by General George Kenney's statement that

> Such an organization we can achieve only with unified control in Washington—a control capable of planning and developing new weapons, and new tactics unlimited by the restrictions of jurisdiction and outlook of a single service. . . . Only through an organization which centralizes responsibility for our entire military structure—land, sea, air, guided missiles, atomic power —can we develop the vision to use all those resources to their fullest.

Nor was this solely a U.S. military opinion. British Army Commander Sir Bernard L. Montgomery noted:

> It is a grave question whether any large organization which is not closely integrated and gripped tightly at the top can adapt itself successfully to the required speed of modern life. If this is not done, the lack of adaptability of the organization as a whole will tend continuously to promote individual Service interests over those of the nation concerned. Under such conditions, politicians have to step in to keep things going; they do this in the only way they know how, i.e., by the creation of more committees and by additional bureaucracies for coordination and arbitration above those already existing.

There was nothing new about this plea for teamwork. During the American Revolution, for example, when small groups of Minutemen fought entirely independently of one another, George Washington called for better organization, unity of command, and teamwork. From the Civil War, and in other wars that followed, the evolution of teamwork in U.S. military operations can be traced. As the size and complexity of forces increased to the joint task forces of World War II, so also did the requirement for proper control.

But general agreement about the goals of a new defense organization did not preclude heated disagreement about how to organize to achieve those goals. In his message to Congress, Truman had listed several guidelines. Among them were integrated strategic plans and a unified military program and budget; economies through unified control of supply and service functions; the best organization for coordination with the rest of government ("We cannot have the sea, land and air members of our defense team working at what may turn out to be cross purposes," said President Truman, "planning their programs on different assumptions as to the nature of the military establishment we need, and engaging in an open competition for funds."); in keeping with American tradition, the strongest means for civilian control of the military; parity for air power with the Army and the Navy; a unified training system; systematic allocation of limited scientific resources; unity of command at outlying bases; and consistent and equitable personnel policies.

ARGUMENT ERUPTS

The only real problem with the President's guidelines was that they still left plenty of room for debate on how, specifically, to do these things. Emotion-charged argument reached almost vitriolic levels in some military circles by 1946. This often studious but sometimes spurious dialectic had begun the same year the United States entered World War II. The Navy started it, surprisingly enough, since the Navy, at the end of it, would be the chief opponent to change. In June, 1941, the Navy General Board recommended unanimously that "unification" take place, proposing a single department with a Joint Chiefs of Staff.

That proposal went to the service secretaries by way of the Joint Board and the Joint War Plans Committee, whose Navy member opposed the notion, while the Army member (Brigadier General Dwight D. Eisenhower) "strongly endorsed it." Before any higher-level action could occur, the Japanese attacked Pearl Harbor. Unification plans were put in storage. "Let's win the war first" became the standard rebuttal to unification talk; President Roosevelt used it, for instance, to halt strictly internal Navy Department plans to reorganize their offices for procurement and industrial mobilization—plans that augured potential major revamping of all military organization.* Army Chief of Staff General George C. Marshall agreed with the principle of unification, "but not until after the war," and supported the request for independent service status of the Army Air Forces made by General "Hap" Arnold.

Such admonitions did not delay the move toward a unified military team very much, however. Out of wartime necessity, commanders of forces in the field were soon planning and executing combined operations and unified control of combat power, particularly in the European theater. This cohesion was not as strong in the Pacific, where the Army and the Navy (and, toward the end of the war with Japan, the Army Air Forces) often tended to fight independent, uncoordinated campaigns. In general though, unified control was attained in the field during World War II.

Mistakes in the Pacific served only to reinforce the generally accepted principle that modern warfare required unified command. In the direction of war strategy, however, the leaders in Washington, D.C., managed throughout the war to remain largely untouched by these field experiences. The civilian side of the military departments in Washington argued, sometimes bitterly, over such things as who should have top-priority claim to limited national resources of men and matériel. On the military side, the Joint Board had no real authority, and little influence; it lapsed into disuse by 1943, although it was not formally abolished until 1947.

---

* In simplest terms, the plans proposed by the Navy admirals would have taken control of mobilization functions away from civilians in the Navy Department and centralized them under the military. In a peacetime environment, however, this could have become a serious challenge to the traditional American tenet that military forces and military men are to operate under civilian control. (Take away procurement and related functions and the single, most effective tool for peacetime control, the expenditure of funds, is gone.)

BACKGROUND OF THE JOINT CHIEFS

The Joint Chiefs of Staff organization was created in Washington at the beginning of World War II. But its birth was an expedient, a hasty assembly to provide, according to protocol, American counterparts to the British Chiefs of Staff Committee, which accompanied British Prime Minister Winston Churchill to a meeting in Washington in December, 1941. The Joint Chiefs included not only the Army chief of staff and his Navy counterpart, the chief of naval operations, but also Commanding General Arnold of the Army Air Forces. Including Arnold as a member was not a military idea but the result of insistence by the powerful White House assistant Harry Hopkins that "our organization must parallel [the British] organization." (Neither the Army nor the Navy objected to this move, which amounted to a first big step toward the kind of coequal status Army airmen had been after since the Billy Mitchell era.)

These three men soon joined with the British Chiefs of Staff Committee to form the Combined Chiefs of Staff. When working together, the mission of the two groups was to give Anglo-American strategic advice to Roosevelt and Churchill. To support them in their collective deliberations, both among themselves and with the British, the Joint Chiefs built up a Joint Staff that included roughly equal numbers of Army and Navy personnel, with half of the Army's membership coming from the Army Air Forces. Because the Chiefs had this manpower at their disposal and because they were not just members of the JCS but also the heads of their separate military organizations, they were virtually assured supremacy over the already weak Joint Board. Their position also led, almost inevitably, to the acquisition of important, far-ranging powers in strategic planning and direction.

Yet, it would be misleading to exaggerate the importance of the wartime Joint Chiefs of Staff. Especially during the early war years, the Joint Chiefs were not an unqualified success in performing their role as a theoretically integrated planning unit, i.e., a team reaching agreements to be presented as a common U.S. military voice to the British on the Combined Chiefs of Staff. Worse, on the most important issues, they were unable to resolve differences at all or else settled for a comparatively weak compromise. As a result, in the planning of the Allied counterattack against Germany and Italy, the tightly integrated British military staff more strongly influenced both Churchill and Roosevelt. Consequently, in 1942, Roosevelt accepted British proposals to invade North Africa first, rather than the European continent, and bypassed the Joint Chiefs when he sent Hopkins and Joint Chiefs members General Marshall and Admiral Ernest King, but not General Arnold, directly to London to work out details. Then, after North Africa was liberated, he again followed Churchill's plan to attack Italy ("the soft underbelly of Europe"), rather than to hit the continent from the Atlantic side.

Not until planning began in 1943 for an attack across the English Channel to open up a second front in northern Europe did the Joint Chiefs begin to function, in that theater at least, as their job description said they should. Until then, although Arnold was supposedly equal to his JCS partners, King preferred negotiating with him through his organizational superior, Marshall. In 1943, however, when a large-scale strategic bombing program was decided upon as the prelude to a cross-channel invasion, the Navy was forced to deal directly with Arnold and his staff—and thus began using the Joint Chiefs of Staff organization as a mechanism for reaching common agreement with the War Department.

While there were occasional conflicts between Army forces commander General Douglas MacArthur and Navy forces commander Admiral Chester Nimitz in the Pacific, the paramount role of the Navy in that theater was generally recognized; although, as historian Paul Hammond has noted, "when, in the closing phase of the Pacific war, the Twentieth Air Force was established, it seemed that all three services were to fight their own individual war with Japan."* The Navy had dealt directly with the War (Army) Department in Washington on Pacific matters rather than working through the Joint Chiefs; and in the battle area itself two basic command arrangements—Army and Navy—had existed throughout the war. Not until the atomic bomb forced a quick Japanese surrender was it learned that no unified command arrangements had been made for what would certainly have been a hazardous and costly Army-Navy invasion of the home islands, scheduled to occur in a matter of weeks.

The JCS came out of the war with credit, deserved or not, for having had significant influence in forcing coordinated Washington war planning. Even the severest critics of its wartime performance granted that much, although these critics tried hard to refute the war record of the institution and thereby undermine the authority granted it in the postwar military establishment. In so doing, they missed two key points. First, the conceptual platform on which JCS activities were founded—teamwork—jibed with postwar thinking on what was best, militarily, for the nation. Second, had the group performed voluntarily and selflessly throughout the war, the case for further military unification in Washington would have been seriously weakened, if not undermined. As became more and more clear during the decade after 1948, each time an independent military department failed of its own volition to yield some part of a strong individual position to the common good, that service, as well as its sister services, lost some of its autonomy to a central, and higher, authority. If Army, Navy, and Army Air Forces officials in the Pentagon had demonstrated an effective ability to agree among them-

* Paul Y. Hammond, *Organizing for Defense: The American Military Establishment in the Twentieth Century* (Princeton, N.J.: Princeton University Press, 1961), p. 163.

selves, little justification would have existed for passing laws ordering them in that direction.

Thus, the Joint Chiefs' tendency to offer sometimes diluted, unproductive answers to tough problems served not to challenge the very philosophy upon which it was founded, but rather to toughen the national determination to give the institution better tools so the philosophy behind it would work better. Such thinking was inherent in Army Chief of Staff George Marshall's revival of the issue in September, 1943, when he presented a unification proposal to—significantly—the Joint Chiefs of Staff.

THE McNARNEY PLAN

Nothing much came of the Marshall idea until the following year, when a select committee of the House, chaired by Representative Clifton A. Woodrum, began hearings on postwar military policy and organization. The Army's most dramatic contribution to the Woodrum committee was a reorganization plan, presented by Army Air Forces General Joseph T. McNarney. What was soon labeled the McNarney Plan called for creation of a single military department of the armed forces headed by a civilian secretary with under secretaries for the Army, Navy, and Air Force, a director for "common supply" and, in addition, a U.S. joint chiefs of staff group.

Building its justification more on the general need for an integrated structure than on adamant support of the McNarney Plan details, the Army and its Air Forces, predictably, backed the proposal. The Navy was set against it. To avoid an open row while the war was still on, the Army, the Navy, and the committee reached a behind-the-scenes agreement that they would shelve the matter until the war's end, provided no party to the debate tried to obtain a commitment from the others on postwar organization in the meantime. The committee's public report stuck to that agreement.

But, that same year, in May, the JCS set up its own Special

Committee for Reorganization of National Defense. Manned by two officers each from the Army and Navy, it was chaired by retired Admiral J. O. Richardson (who had been a member of the Navy General Board that recommended unification in 1941). In the next ten strenuous months, the Richardson committee interviewed thoroughly some 800 officers from all the services and traveled overseas to talk to the nation's leading combat commanders. Busy fighting a war, and with no briefing on the conflicting views their superiors had presented to the Woodrum committee, the commanders answered with their own frank, personal views on unification, untempered by the politico-military contest simmering in Washington. Understandably, their attitudes in the field— admirals' and generals' alike—were based, to an important extent, on (a) the merit and even the necessity of combined land-sea-air operations in battle, and (b) their occasional frustration with the home front over priorities they got or failed to get, both in strategic planning and in supply support. The latter they could attribute, at least in part, to divided Army and Navy authority in Washington. (In fairness to the Pentagon's performance in World War II, it should be pointed out, however, that no good military field commander ever feels he has enough support in wartime—even when he has all that's available.)

THE RICHARDSON REPORT

In April, 1945, the Richardson committee submitted its report (with which Richardson, himself, disagreed) to the JCS. According to one observer, "Its recommendations for a single armed forces department went as far as any official group had gone in urging complete Service merger and integration."*

* Timothy W. Stanley, *American Defense And National Security* (Washington, D.C.: Public Affairs Press, 1956), p. 73.

The report argued, in part:

The fundamental reason that unity of command in theaters of operations has not accomplished the necessary integration is that each component of the Army and Navy under a theater commander is actually part of a separate department in the United States to which it owes its first allegiance and from which it derives different methods and techniques for accomplishing similar operational and supply purposes. Because of this, the theater commander's ability effectively and efficiently to carry out his command decisions is hampered by conditions over which he has little or no control.

Components must owe allegiance and loyalty to the same organization. This is essential to attain singleness of purpose and to avoid jealousies and misunderstandings. The Departments [in Washington] have no mission to perform nor any excuse for existence other than to direct and serve the fighting forces and to increase their efficiency. . . . History forcibly indicates that as funds grow tighter and conflicting interests and personalities make themselves felt, agreements on major issues of policy, strategy and administration become difficult, if not impossible, to reach. Teamwork disappears. Each Service withdraws into its own shell, as it has done in the past, and each concentrates on those things essential to its own profession without giving consideration to common problems.

Also recommended was creation of a single department of the armed forces headed by a civilian secretary, aided by an under secretary and some civilian assistants. Reporting to him would be a commander of the armed forces, who would also act as chief of staff to the President (much in the manner that Admiral William D. Leahy had worked, during World War II, in the White House as the President's personal military adviser). A joint chiefs of staff organization, comprising a secretary of the armed forces, commander of the armed forces, and the three commanders of the Army, the Navy, and a separate air force, would advise the President on military strategy and related budgetary matters.

In Washington's military headquarters, the Pentagon, reaction to this proposal was immediate and sharp. The Army and the Army Air Forces were in favor; the Navy was outspokenly opposed.

When the Senate Military Affairs Committee began hearings, in the summer of 1945, on bills proposing a single department of the armed forces, admirals interviewed by the Richardson group were called to reiterate their earlier views. In front of the Senate, most of them changed their minds. The variety of reasons they gave added up to saying, with some validity, that they simply had not completely understood Washington's military coordination problems when asked their opinions before. To only partially informed observers, this sudden outburst of argument looked like nothing more than additional proof that the separate military departments were incapable, under pressure, of putting cause and country before parochial service ambition. Actually, for most of the military there was more admirable motivation. Perceptive leaders among them knew, or suspected, that, perhaps for the first time in military history, their wartime experience did not provide a completely valid base upon which to build plans for the future.

The new position of the United States as a world leader, as well as the use of military force to help prevent, rather than correct, foreign-policy failures, was a challenge. The awesomely destructive force of the atomic bomb had barely been tested in war. Even the full potential of the aircraft had not been examined, let alone all the other new and untested armament ideas being offered by science. Fearing correctly that the Soviet Union would soon own a similar arsenal, the military felt that they could not risk the penalties of another— perhaps atomic—Pearl Harbor. Even the standard demand for economy in military spending at the end of a war was no longer based simply on the old criteria of not needing an army if there was no fighting. Instead, there was a demand for economic efficiency because of the high cost of modern weapons and the admission, inherent in collective security policy, that the United States could not and did not want to finance the protection of the whole Free World by itself. All this was largely uncharted ground for the military. Each responsible official had strong opinions on how to answer properly the challenges of the new military environment—answers that could neither be proved nor disproved entirely on the basis of past discoveries. Civilian and military leaders alike— men whose patriotic sincerity was beyond question—promptly took sides. Strong and convincing arguments were heard both for and against unification.

On the pro side, the reasons generally given for single civilian control were: to avoid expensive and useless duplication, especially in the logistics field; to help avoid a repetition of the Pearl Harbor disaster; to assure against military domination; and to avoid the haphazard and uncoordinated manner in which the military departments competed before Congress for appropriations.

Arguments against the move ran: the Germans had established, on paper, just such a single-staff organization and it had not worked very well for them; the plan would concentrate too much power in the hands of a single person other than the President; and such a vast military organization would be too complex for any one man to handle.

Many of these objections did not have much merit. As Eisenhower pointed out, during the Senate hearings, if the job were too big for one man to handle, so was the Presidency. The worry of concentrating too much power in a single person, to be valid, required assuming that such a person would function independent of rather than as deputy to the President. Besides being unconstitutional, such a setup had never been proposed by even the strongest advocates of unification. Finally, the contention that the Allies had beaten a single-staff organization in Germany ignored two irrefutable facts. For one, the "single German general staff" outlined on paper had operated in practice as three separate, uncoordinated Army, Navy, and Air Force staffs, each reporting direct to a dictatorial military neophyte, Adolf Hitler, through his small personal staff—whose members were picked not for their military talent but because of their political loyalty to him and the Nazi Party. Indeed, the German record in World War II suggests very strongly that if a true, high-level single staff had been at work in Berlin coordinating the efforts of all German military forces, the war's outcome might have been different. Finally, even if the German single staff had worked as its paper outline said it should, the Allies also had beaten the Japanese, who had two departments, and the Italians, who had three.

But inaccuracy did not dilute fear of the "Prussian General Staff" idea. In the aftermath of the postwar U.S. debates on unification, historian E. L. Katzenbach summarized the general reaction in a lecture to the Navy War College in 1956:

Across the pages of American legislative history there flits a curious Man on Horseback. He is a military man—usually a general and almost never an admiral, incidentally—who sits in the wings waiting to take over the government from civilians. He has, of course, never existed and yet he is quite as real as if he had. . . . At the beginning of our history, he was at times called Julius Caesar; at others, Oliver Cromwell. He lost these identities a few decades later to be reincarnated as Napoleon; in the 1860's he became Napoleon III. And finally, after 1914, the Man on Horseback became a multi-headed monster, to wit, the Prussian General Staff. But despite the fact that this Man on Horseback has always been a foreigner, and has grown up in other surroundings and circumstances, he plays and has played a very real role in the development of civil-military organization in the United States. . . . In any military reorganization which tends to bring the Services closer together, this nonexistent personality is important because he is the man whom many see in the organization chart box marked "Chairman, Joint Chiefs of Staff" or "Chief of Military Service."

There is really little opposition to a general staff organization as such. After all, congressional committees have staffs, as do businesses and nearly all organizations operated on the principle that one man cannot know everything about everything and must have others to advise and assist him. The commander of a Navy fleet at sea or the head of a major air command or comparable army unit may safely have a "general's staff," and offend no one. Nor is there any question that he should exercise absolute authority over all elements of that command. Trying to apply the same organizational principles to military functions in Washington, however, historically has produced a rash of negative reactions. Couched in scholarly language though they usually are, these objections most often hint of deeply rooted worries. Washington is where the money is. It is also where the basic decisions are made on how best to use the various elements of military force. Justifiably, each service will tend to ask for the first and propose strategies for the second in the terms it knows best—the capabilities of its own military organization.

Much of the pulling and tugging over unification was and is the product of individual values, connected with personal military service identification. Since the services traditionally have been associated with particular roles and missions, and with particular types of military hardware, a member of a service tends to consider national strategy in these established terms of reference. Thus, opposing positions on unification became closely related to long-standing arguments among the military regarding their respective roles and missions. Moreover, not only money and primacy of mission were at stake. So were promotions and career opportunities.

In the early stages of the Senate hearings, Admiral King commented that "if the Navy's welfare is one of the prerequisites to the Nation's welfare—and I sincerely believe that to be the case—any step that is not good for the Navy is not good for the Nation." Thus, the Navy, which, with the Marine Corps included, had a completely integrated and coordinated military land, sea, and air machine of its own, opposed unification because it feared loss of control of that team or some part of its hardware. Conversely, unification proponents in the Army and the Army Air Forces saw in merger potential gains for themselves—or, at least, consolidation of their control over certain high priority missions, such as strategic bombing, which they had earned during the war.

Any short account of the debates in 1945–47 runs the risk of oversimplification. As defense authority Timothy Stanley once pointed out:

> The subject is so enmeshed in personalities and controversy that historians in the various Services . . . have avoided it except to document some particular viewpoint. Besides, the matter is inherently complex. To speak of the *Army view* or the *Navy plan* is merely a necessary bit of shorthand. Within each Department there were many shades of view. Even names attached to various specific proposals merely identify the official sponsors before Congress; in some cases the officers involved had little or no part in drafting the proposals.

Under such circumstances, while individuals at high levels were sorting out what they stood to gain or lose or what they could afford to give away both militarily and personally in return for something equally good, it was not very clear what official position the Army, Navy, Marine Corps, or Army Air Forces took on unification.

THE COLLINS PLAN

As military arguments in the Senate ground along, however, and relatively minor agreements were reached among men in a particular service, the War Department—especially its already close-to-autonomous Army Air Forces—became the spearhead of the drive for unification. The Navy was opposed. The catalyst generating War Department support on Capitol Hill was the Collins Plan, named after Army Lieutenant General J. Lawton Collins. Not a great deal different in general outline from other Army suggestions, the Collins Plan called for a department of the armed forces headed by a civilian secretary, supported by an under secretary; assistant secretaries for research, for procurement and mobilization, and for legislative and public affairs; a single chief of staff of the armed forces supported by chiefs of staff for Army, Navy, and a separate Air Force, and commanding both the military forces in the field, plus a single common supply agency.

Basically, the Collins scheme amounted to giving the Commander-in-Chief a military organization much like the War Department general staff in format, modified only as necessary to include Navy and Air Force missions. Disagreement over the proposal, even in the War Department, centered primarily around just how much command authority the single chief of staff of the armed forces should have. The answers War Department spokesmen gave to questions on that point were, usually, that such details could be worked out later—establishing a single, coordinated staff to provide the President with military advice was, they said, the important first step that must be taken. The Navy protested that it was precisely those details of power and control it wanted spelled out before agreeing to anything.

The Navy's opposition was symptomatic of the real substance of the reorganization arguments. Dissertations on proper organization are frivolous "how to" exercises unless conclusions have been drawn from previously reached accord on what the organization is supposed to do. In military terms, that translated, in 1945–47—and for more than a decade afterward—into deciding: (a) what is the proper military peace-keeping role in a tense world? (b) what strategic plans

Chart 1

THE COLLINS PLAN

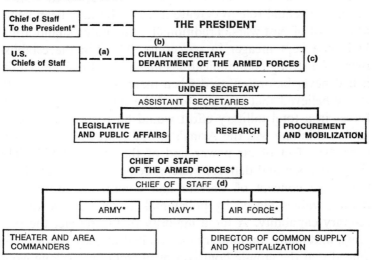

*Denotes membership in U.S. (or Joint) Chiefs of Staff

(a) To advise the President on military strategy and the budget

(b) To advise the President on politico-economic-industrial matters

(c) Can comment on, but not change, military recommendations while forwarding them to the President

(d) Has command authority over military service

need implementing to carry out that role? and (c) who has the best weapons and talents for performing those missions?

Little higher-level agreement had been reached in 1946 on the proper military peace-keeping role other than an imprecise "to keep the peace, one must be strong enough to win a war." No agreed-upon strategic plans or mission assignments existed, either. Lacking such necessary guidance, the military had considerable leeway to clash over what that guidance ought to be and which service was most essential to backing it.

To be sure, the Army wanted unification because of what it had learned about the need for combined operations in its primary war theater, Europe, and what it had learned about the price of not having a strong voice in the Pacific, where its command influence on war planning was often subordinated. But, the Army also wanted Pentagon unification to gain for itself the coequal role in defense it had habitually been denied at the end of past wars. Traditionally, the nation's land armies had been kept meager in peacetime. Through the establishment of a strong communications line to the President (a link it had never before enjoyed when there was no fighting), the Army believed that recognition of the importance of ground forces in a total military effort would be preserved. Inherent in that thinking was the Army's worry (shared by the Navy) over the effect of air power and of the atomic bomb. That single weapon and delivery system seemed destined to change the entire concept of warfare and completely reshuffle the relative values placed by policy-makers on various kinds of military capability. A large majority of the public, the Congress, and many top military experts had already become convinced that the atomic bomb dropped from an airplane would decide, all by itself, the victor in another war—if there were to be a victor.

For the Army Air Forces, that belief was the culmination of a wartime trend, which had earned the air arm its near-autonomy, separate from the rest of the Army, even before the war ended. Many observers wondered why the Army Air Forces backed unification so strongly. The fact is the Army Air Forces believed that unification was the best way to assure their gaining full-fledged military partnership with their sister services. Possession of the bomb and the best means of delivering it guaranteed them considerable influence in military circles. But pushing for complete organizational autonomy would have been flying in the face of a clear national demand for consolidation, coordination, and economy. A nation already complaining of the waste in having two military departments in Washington was not likely to favor creating another, unless the whole group were tightly held by a single organization at the top.

For the Washington-based Navy, unification clanged threat to their once strong empire. Even before the war's end, the Navy's leadership had fought a rear-guard action against the Army Air Forces, who wanted to take over the Navy's land-based, antisubmarine aircraft work in the Atlantic, at least. Footnotes to the Army reorganization concepts included proposals to merge the Marine Corps into the Army; to give Navy's aircraft to the proposed new air force; and similar "consolidation" ideas. Especially in the Pacific, with their amphibious army (the Marine Corps), carrier-based aircraft, and integrated fleet, the admirals had been functioning with self-contained unified commands almost throughout the war. But that had been "all Navy." When the admirals returned to Washington, their service's civilian leaders pointed out to them just what unification could cost in command authority at the highest levels. The message: unification, as their sister services proposed it, might cost the Navy control over key elements of its unified fleet units and take away certain "glamour" hardware, such as bomber aircraft; in short, the Navy might lose its once powerful peacetime influence in the annual budget battle over the allocation of congressional funds to the military establishment. As the Navy saw it, the Army and the Army Air Forces intended to lock the Navy into a closet through the appointment of a single chief of staff of the armed forces, these high-level unification proponents arguing that the chief of staff should be an Army man because only an "Army general had the breadth of command experience over air, land, and logistics (i.e., sea) forces required" for the job.

The Navy's traditional role as the "nation's first line of defense" between wars had already been dimmed in the public mind by the existence of the Army Air Forces' bomber. Navy people felt that an Army commander for all the services would cut them off from their previous direct contact with the President and Congress, and even drop them from coequal status in Washington military planning. "We would be a taxicab Service," grumbled one Navy spokesman, "hauling somebody else's combat team into battle."

The admirals' chagrin turned to gloom and agitation when Navy Secretary James V. Forrestal also told them that the Navy had "lost its case, and either in Congress or in a public poll the Army's point of view would prevail." Moreover, as the pressures for unification mounted, it became apparent, as the chairman of the Senate Naval Affairs Committee* pointed out to Forrestal, that the Navy must offer a "constructive alternative."

THE EBERSTADT PLAN

The Navy's "constructive alternative" was a report to Forrestal in late 1945 by his long-time business associate and friend, Ferdinand Eberstadt. It amounted not to a reorganization of the military but to a revamping of responsibilities in large sections of the entire executive branch of government. The Eberstadt Plan, as it was soon identified, argued that the need for unification was much more all-inclusive than either the Army or the Army Air Force's had implied in their reorganization proposals. Unification required, it said, not just the coordination of military forces but the coordination of all the nation's resources.

Eberstadt proposed three coordinate services, each headed by a secretary of cabinet rank, and strongly linked by coordi-

---

* To avoid confusion over this committee title, in relation to previous references to the Senate Armed Services Committee, it should be noted that the committee advice to Forrestal was given in 1945. Not until 1946 did Congress "eliminate interservice rivalry" in its own bailiwick by merging, in both the Senate and the House of Representatives, the Military Affairs and Naval Affairs committees into House and Senate "Armed Services" committees.

Chart 2

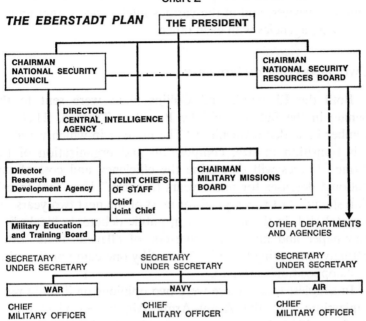

THE EBERSTADT PLAN

THE PRESIDENT

CHAIRMAN NATIONAL SECURITY COUNCIL

CHAIRMAN NATIONAL SECURITY RESOURCES BOARD

DIRECTOR CENTRAL INTELLIGENCE AGENCY

Director Research and Development Agency

JOINT CHIEFS OF STAFF

Chief Joint Chief

CHAIRMAN MILITARY MISSIONS BOARD

Military Education and Training Board

OTHER DEPARTMENTS AND AGENCIES

SECRETARY UNDER SECRETARY

SECRETARY UNDER SECRETARY

SECRETARY UNDER SECRETARY

WAR

NAVY

AIR

CHIEF MILITARY OFFICER

CHIEF MILITARY OFFICER

CHIEF MILITARY OFFICER

nating devices. He recognized a distinction between unified operational command and unified strategic planning, opposing the latter, and thus recommended that the JCS be made a statutory body. He proposed a battery of committees, a national security council, a central intelligence agency, a national security resources board for mobilization planning, a central research and development agency, and a military education and training board to deal with the larger problem of coordination. He argued that, while in the purely military field wartime performance had been relatively good, the real difficulties lay on the periphery of military concerns (and were, therefore, outside the purview of the Army proposals). All involved coordination—the coordination of military and foreign policy, of strategic planning and its logistic feasibility and implementation, of procurement and logistics as an integrated process, and of the various intelligence gathering and analyzing agencies with each other.

Two Years of Controversy

Both the Eberstadt and Collins plans were sent to the Senate in the fall of 1945 by President Truman. That December he added a warning: "The manner in which we make this transition in size, composition and organization of the Armed Forces will determine the efficiency and cost of our national defenses for many years to come." How that transition should start was argued for most of the next two years, on Capitol Hill, in the Pentagon, in public debate, in "leaks," to newspaper and magazine reporters, of alleged "facts" often actually amounting to an indictment by one camp or the other of its opposition's motives.

In simplest terms, there were two opinions on defense reorganization: (1) the Army–Army Air Forces view that a single, unified department was needed in Washington; and (2) the Navy view that a new management layer on top of the existing organization, strictly to coordinate everything better, was all that was required. Throughout the congressional hearings, heated contradictions snapped back and forth, while Congress seemed to wait, often with admirable patience, postponing legislation until the military people who would have to live with it agreed on what kind of organization all of them could accept.

In the end, Congress supported the Navy's approach—probably, in part, because of the long-standing Navy influence on Capitol Hill; in part, because of the Navy's insistence that there were certain boundaries beyond which it would not go (such as losing its seat in the President's Cabinet); and, in part, because of congressional recognition that the nation's ability to fulfill its worldwide commitments might be compromised if a too dramatic first step created a too drastic disruption of existing internal military relationships and procedures.

THE NATIONAL SECURITY ACT IS PASSED

On July 25, 1947, Congress passed the National Security Act. After its signing by President Truman, it took effect on September 17, 1947, with the swearing in of James Vincent Forrestal as first Secretary of Defense.

The Office of the Secretary of Defense was not the only important new creation in the Act. (Indeed, Congress directed that the new office be kept quite small.) As Forrestal, Eberstadt, and others with similar beliefs had urged, Congress abandoned the old concept that national defense be conceived almost entirely in military terms. They replaced that traditional attitude with a broad, new concept of "national security" requiring close, interlocking coordination among military and civilian offices in the entire government. As it noted in the "Declaration of Policy" preceding the specific terms of the Act, Congress' intent was to provide "a comprehensive program for the future security of the United States," including "integrated policies and procedures for the departments, agencies, and functions of the Government relating to the national security."

Specifically, Congress set up under the Act three agencies outside the military to play a role in "coordination for national security." A key one, went the supporting theory, was the National Security Council (NSC), to be presided over by the President. NSC permanent members were to include the Secretary of State, Secretary of Defense, secretaries of the Army, Navy, and Air Force and the chairman of the new National Security Resources Board. In addition, with the consent of the Senate, the President could add to the Council membership any secretaries he chose from other executive departments or the chairman of the Munitions Board and Research and Development Board, the latter also newly created parts of the "Military Establishment."

Working at the pinnacle of government decision-making, the NSC was to "advise the President with respect to the integration of domestic, foreign, and military policies relating to the national security so as to enable the military services and the other departments and agencies of the Government to cooperate more effectively in matters involving the national security." The Act specified Council duties to be:

(1) to assess and appraise the objectives, commitments, and risks of the United States in relation to our actual and potential military power . . . for the purpose of making recommendations to the President in connection therewith; and

(2) to consider policies on matters of common interest to the departments and agencies of the Government concerned with the national security, and to make recommendations to the President in connection therewith.

To support Council deliberations and "insure a sound and adequate intelligence base for the formulation and execution of national security policies," the Central Intelligence Agency (CIA) was to be organized under NSC direction. The CIA was to:

(1) advise the National Security Council in matters concerning such intelligence activities of the Government departments and agencies as relate to national security;

(2) make recommendations to the National Security Council for the coordination of such intelligence activities . . .

(3) correlate and evaluate intelligence relating to the national security, and provide for the appropriate dissemination of such intelligence* . . .

* The immediate objective here was to avoid such incidents as the mishandling of advance warning information, which many believed had been the major reason for the success of the Japanese surprise attack on Pearl Harbor in 1941. As a justification for creating the CIA, this thinking is symptomatic of what has been called the "reorganization syndrome" or

(4) perform, for the benefit of existing intelligence agencies, such additional services of common concern as the National Security Council determines can be more effectively accomplished centrally.

The third key agency established under the Act was the National Security Resources Board (NSRB). Composed of a chairman and such representatives of departments and agencies as the President might designate, the Board was to "advise the President concerning the coordination of military, industrial, and civilian mobilization." The Board's advisory role was to encompass:

(1) policies concerning industrial and civilian mobilization in order to assure the most effective mobilization and maximum utilization of the Nation's manpower in the event of war;

(2) programs for the effective use in time of war of the Nation's natural and industrial resources for military and civilian needs, for the maintenance and stabilization of the civilian economy in time of war, and for the adjustment of such economy to war needs and conditions;

(3) policies for unifying, in time of war, the activities of Federal agencies and departments engaged in or concerned with production, procurement, distribution, or transportation of military or civilian supplies, materials, and products;*

(4) the relationship between potential supplies of, and potential requirements for, manpower, resources, and productive facilities in time of war;

(5) policies for establishing adequate reserves of strategic and critical material, and for the conservation of these reserves;

(6) the strategic relocation of industries, services, government, and economic activities, the continuous operation of which is essential to the Nation's security.

"when in doubt about the right answer, reorganize." That the single factor, lack of intelligence, had caused the disaster in 1941 was highly questionable; and, even if it had, a new organization was no guarantee, in itself, that the same errors in human judgment would not occur again.

* If the military departments were to be as truly coordinated as the rest of the Act instructed, this function of the NSRB would seem to be unnecessary.

Although the Board was given a staff to help carry out its functions, the Act directed that it "utilize to the maximum extent the facilities and resources of the [other] departments and agencies of Government."

In creating these agencies, Congress gave formal recognition to the fact that the guardianship of the nation's safety was now to be the collective responsibility of the entire government. In the future, military defense, although playing a vital, even central, role, would function within this larger framework of national security. Besides the coordination of the armed services, there would have to be coordination of domestic, foreign, and military policies relating to national security. Conceptually at least, these new institutional arrangements seemed to hold out hopes for a logical and orderly approach to the security problems of the postwar period.

"The theory," according to one account, "was that NSC, composed of the highest civilian officials responsible for diplomatic, military and industrial planning, and informed by CIA, would generate the basic policy recommendations in all matters affecting the national security."*

But logical and attractive as that theory might have been, putting it to work was another matter. The chief flaw to practical implementation was that one team member—the military —was not "one," but a collection, and, at that, a collection of too many independent chiefs and not enough Indians. The product of compromise and concession to adamant Navy opposition, the Act's remolding of internal military organizations was something less than a decisive step toward unification. Obviously, Congress had accepted here, as in the broader scope of the legislation, the Navy's thesis that "there's nothing wrong with the present military arrangements—the services just need to work together more," and, as a result, had cre-

* Walter Millis, Harvey C. Mansfield, and Harold Stein, *Arms and the State: Civil-Military Elements in National Policy* (New York: Twentieth Century Fund, 1958), p. 179.

ated a department that was not an entity and that was headed by a Secretary of Defense whose powers were stringently confined and authority questionable.

Instead, Congress had set up three executive departments—Army, Navy, and Air Force—gingerly joined together under the amorphous title of "National Military Establishment." Each department secretary was a full member of the President's Cabinet as well as of the National Security Council. The "Establishment" was headed by the Secretary of Defense, whose mission was to coordinate the three separate executive depart-

Chart 3

THE NATIONAL SECURITY STRUCTURE
(as established by the National Security Act of 1947)

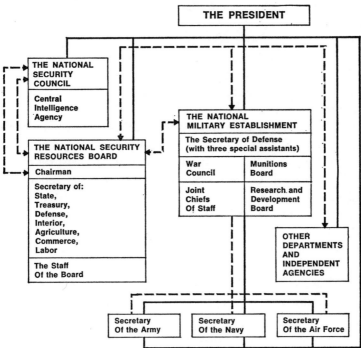

Note: solid line indicates direction, authority and control; broken line indicates coordination

ments. The Act said he was to be "the principal (but not necessarily the only) assistant to the President in all matters relating to the national security." He could set "general policies and programs" for and exercise "general direction, authority, and control" over the departments.*

The Secretary of Defense was to take "appropriate steps to eliminate unnecessary duplication or overlapping in the fields of procurement, supply, transportation, storage, health, and research"; and to "supervise and coordinate the preparation of the budget estimates of the departments and agencies comprising the National Military Establishment; formulate and determine the budget estimates for submittal to the Bureau of the Budget; and supervise the budget programs of such departments and agencies under the applicable appropriation Act."

Impressive as those administrative weapons might appear, the Defense Secretary's authority was, nonetheless, tightly limited. For one thing, the three individual services were to be run as "individual executive departments by their respective Secretaries" who retained all powers and duties related to those departments that were not specifically granted to the Secretary of Defense. Since the Defense Secretary's authority was only "general," the services could and did insist on retaining a great deal. On matters, such as the crucial request for budget funds, the service secretaries were permitted, "after first informing the Secretary of Defense," to present directly to the President, the Bureau of the Budget, and the Congress, any reports, recommendations, or appeals they felt necessary regarding their individual departments. Thus, they could bypass their Secretary of Defense. Moreover, the Defense Secretary was expressly forbidden to build a military staff of his

* In U.S. Government vernacular, "direction" means "the act of governing, management"; "authority" means "the legal power; a right to command, the right and power of a public officer to require obedience to his order"; and "control" means the "power or authority to manage, to direct, to superintend, regulate, direct, govern, administer, or oversee."

own, and he could appoint no more than three special assistants from civilian life to aid him. In short, the Defense management structure for running the military forces began as a confederacy.

His office size purposely limited "to avoid creating another Government bureaucracy," the Secretary was to perform his coordinating and supervisory work partly through drawing on the staffs of the three military departments and partly through the use of joint agencies also set up by the Act. One, the War Council (renamed the Armed Forces Policy Council in 1949) was to be chaired by the Secretary of Defense and manned by the secretaries and chiefs of staff of the military departments, and was to advise the Secretary on "matters of broad policy relating to the Armed Forces."

Another, the Munitions Board, was to be chaired by a civilian and manned by under or assistant secretaries from each of the three departments; it was to "coordinate the appropriate activities within . . . the Establishment with regard to industrial matters including the procurement, production and distribution plans of the departments and agencies comprising the Establishment" and a host of related chores falling under the general title of promoting economy, efficiency, standardization, and assignment of priorities in drawing on the nation's industrial base to support the armed forces.

A third agency, the Research and Development Board, composed of a civilian chairman and two representatives from each of the departments, was to perform much the same advisory and coordinating functions for the Secretary of Defense in research and development, among other things, to:

(1) prepare a complete and integrated program of research and development for military purposes;

(2) advise with regard to trends in scientific research relating to national security and the measures necessary to assure continued and increasing progress;

(3) recommend measures of coordination of research and de-

velopment among the military Departments, and the allocation among them of responsibilities for specific programs of joint interest.

Finally, the Congress gave statutory recognition to the existing Joint Chiefs of Staff (JCS); provided them with a 100-officer Joint Staff to do the staff work involved in their joint deliberations; and named the JCS principal military advisers to the President, the Secretary of Defense, and the National Security Council. Among other things, Congress said, the JCS would (1) prepare strategic plans and provide for the strategic direction of the military forces; (2) prepare joint logistic plans and assign to the military services logistic responsibilities in accordance with such plans; (3) establish unified commands in strategic areas when such unified commands are in the interest of national security; and (4) formulate policies for joint training, coordinating education, and review of major matériel and personnel requirements of the military forces.

In sum, the first congressional version of unification called for coordination at the top while retaining separate service autonomies below. The Defense Secretary would be responsible for broad policy formulation and over-all coordination, while the separate services would handle operations and the internal administration of their own departments. Out of this structure, it was hoped, would come an end to unnecessary duplication, uncoordinated planning, and interservice rivalries. Yet, there was considerable skepticism about its possible success.

After Eighteen Months

At the end of his "Establishment's" first year and a half of operation, Forrestal could point to some progress. Most was in the easiest-to-do areas where there was already some sort of basis for service compromise. All kinds of study committees were set up, some temporary, some that soon began to have a status comparable to the statutory boards created by the National Security Act itself.

They made a host of analyses. Included were (1) military pay levels and compensation discrepancies among the separate services; (2) consolidation of the separate service medical departments; (3) writing a uniform code of military justice; (4) the strengths and weaknesses of all Reserve forces; (5) proposals for single-manager agencies to perform a series of common functions for all the services—tasks such as purchase of common supplies, intelligence gathering and analysis, communications, transportation, procurement. Numerous joint officer advanced training courses and maneuvers were set up to start the long, arduous process of developing teamwork through better understanding of the other services' perspective and doctrine on how to fight battles. "It was amazing," noted one Forrestal special assistant at the time, "how little the services really knew about each other."

One of the biggest steps forward was the setting up of the Military Air Transport Service (MATS)—since renamed Military Airlift Command—by merging the old Air Transport Command of the Air Force and the Naval Air Transport Service into one. Run by the Air Force, MATS was the single manager to provide air transportation to all the services. In management approach, it became the forerunner for many such single-manager organizations that, in the future, would perform for the services a function needed in common by all. (The Navy's anger at losing its own transport arm was calmed by giving it command of a similar "executive agent" for sea transportation, the Military Sea Transportation Service.)

A Weapons Systems Evaluation Group, manned by military experts from the services, was organized—to give the Secretary what, it was hoped, would be nonparochial military opinion on the relative merits of separate service weapons as they related to or duplicated each other. The first steps toward setting up unified commands in overseas theaters were taken—although they had a lot of the characteristics of a "horse trade." ("The Air Force can have command of the Alaskan theater if the Navy gets the Pacific if the Army will settle for the Caribbean.") The first steps were taken toward defining the interrelated service roles and missions—tenuous and sensitive as those definitions were—and toward allocating a fair share of total budgeted defense funds to carry out those functions. Unfortunately, the exercise was largely frustrating since there wasn't enough money appropriated to go around.

Mainly, however, during that first eighteen months, the services battled—over roles and missions, over the funds each deemed necessary to perform its "absolutely essential" functions, over a standardization in uniform, over consolidation of bases and installations, over anything that sounded like a chipping away at individual service autonomy. Still stinging from the barbs they had thrown at each other during the long unification debates, and lacking any real government policy guidance from the NSC, each made the most of its authority. Their chief target, when they weren't shooting at one another, was the Secretary of Defense.

As already pointed out, they interpreted the word "general" in the Secretary's power of "general direction, authority, and control" to be a stringent limitation on the specific fields in which he could roam. Also, each of the Joint Chiefs, in practice, used his own service staffs, not the Joint Staff, to prepare his individual positions in joint deliberations on important questions. The JCS managed mainly to agree just to let each keep what it already had in weapons and combat capability (plus any new or related developments it might bring along later); and, in case of a war threat flaring up, to appoint one of the JCS members as an executive agent to run the unified command. (Predictably, under such circumstances, he would tend to rely on his own service to handle a conflict instead of utilizing a truly unified force in which approximately two-thirds of the manpower could owe primary allegiance to someone else.)

Forrestal worked almost inhuman hours for nearly two years trying to make this organizational structure, and the people in it, work together. He finally decided that it did not and could not function as it should. Then, he recommended to President Truman that the pace of unification be stepped up, and he moved closer to the approach suggested by the school of thought he had originally opposed. He indicated that his experience as the first Secretary of Defense had shown that, to make theory work, the man in that job had to be something more than coordinator of a loosely knit confederation. For all its weaknesses, the 1947 Act had achieved its basic purpose in that it had established the organizational nucleus for coordination of the various government agencies involved in national security. But, by 1949, the need to strengthen the original Act had become all too apparent.

II

Evolution and Reorganization
1949–58

During his eighteen-month tenure as Secretary of Defense, Forrestal had to cope with far more than the standard variety of procedural growing pains inherent in the evolution of any new organization. He was hit daily by interservice rivalries for possession of limited resources and by inadequate communication among "Establishment" members on mutual problems of strategic, logistical, or industrial mobilization planning. Each service worked hard to enlarge its share of the domain. Twice in 1948—to Key West, Florida, in March and to Newport, Rhode Island, in August—he dragged the JCS, hoping these out-of-town meetings "away from the telephone" would produce a resolution of their conflicts over roles and missions. Their agreement to meet at all was his only significant achievement. The roles-and-missions papers they signed at the end of those meetings were little more than a compromise restatement of what each service considered to be its previous status. The papers did next to nothing to soothe interservice abrasions.

How far apart they were, not only from each other but in relation to over-all national policy, was evident in their contribution to the fiscal year 1950 federal budget. A Presidential directive of July 26, 1948, placed a $15 billion ceiling on the National Military Establishment budget for fiscal 1950. It was a limit based primarily on what the Truman Administration thought the nation could afford, a decision reached seemingly without benefit of any counterbalancing advice from the National Security Council on what foreign and military policies such as the Truman Doctrine should cost. The $15 billion was well below the "absolute minimum" ($23.5 billion) budget request for carrying out their missions that the services had been able to agree upon among themselves. Nor did Forrestal have the statutory power to order a more meaningful rationalization.

Even if all the other, often petty, debates had not been occuring regularly, the gross irrelevance between the Pentagon and White House figures on "necessary" military funding was enough to show Forrestal that the Military Establishment was not functioning as it should. Another important government advisory group reached the same conclusion at about the same time. In 1947, the eightieth Congress had established a Commission on Organization of the Executive Branch of Government. Its objective was to seek ways of improving executive branch efficiency and eliminating wasteful methods of operation. Popularly known as the Hoover Commission, after its chairman, former President Herbert Hoover, it counted among its task forces one on national security organization, headed by the same Ferdinand Eberstadt who had drawn up for Forrestal the Navy's "constructive alternative on national security organization."

Eberstadt's task force reported in November, 1948, on what it considered the inadequacies of the national security establishment. Highlighted in the report was the indictment that,

> Presently, national policy is not emanating, clearly and firmly, from above and descending effectively through the chain of agencies for translation into an efficient and economical military establishment measured against our national needs. As a result, the military have picked up the ball of national policy and are starting down the field with it. Justly concerned about our national security—but at the same time with an eye to individual

Service ambitions—they have sometimes made their own assessments and appraisals of our "objectives, commitments, and risks" and have translated them into their own ideas of our proper military strength.

In addition, because the separate agencies concerned with national security

are not performing their respective functions adequately, either individually or in sound relation to each other . . . instead of policy determining strategy, and strategy in turn determining its military implementation in terms of the size and nature of the military establishment, the tendency is in the reverse direction. To far too great an extent the unilateral aims and policies of the military services are combining to make the strategy they are supposed to serve, and the strategy is tending to make the national policy.

Although the Eberstadt study had probed beyond just the National Military Establishment into other national security agency areas, the task force recommendations for improvement conformed closely to Forrestal's own, published at about the same time in his "First Report of the Secretary of Defense." Forrestal advised that provision should be made for an under secretary of Defense to serve as the Secretary's alter ego in his absence; the statutory authority of the Secretary should be materially strengthened by, among other things, eliminating the word "general" from "general policies and programs" and "general direction, authority, and control" in the 1947 statute; the chief of staff to the Commander-in-Chief (if there be one) should not be a member of the JCS; a chairman of the JCS should be designated instead, either from among the three present chiefs or by picking a fourth; limitation on the size of the Joint Staff "should be either removed or raised"; the Secretary's authority over personnel, particularly civilians and especially within the services, should be clarified; and, finally, but probably most important in Forrestal's mind, the secretaries of the Army, the Navy, and the Air Force should be removed from membership in the National Security Council, and the Secretary of Defense be the only representative of the National Military Establishment on the Council.

Forrestal wrapped up his report with a pair of short, pointed observations. They read simply as a summary of the nation's over-all military security needs—which they were. But, with a little reading between the lines, they emerged also as a sharp appeal for cooperation among the services and a call for ending the internal squabble over relative service mission importance and over the atomic bomb. The Secretary said:

> In conclusion I should like to re-emphasize two thoughts implicit in this report. The first is that this nation has endeavored constantly to maintain peace. The United States came out of the war with the atomic bomb, the most deadly and devastating weapon that man ever devised. As proof of our good faith and peaceful intentions, we have offered voluntarily to deny ourselves the use of this lethal instrument. We have proposed that it be placed under international control and have offered to surrender our proprietary rights, including the right of visitation and inspection of atomic energy plants, to an international commission. This proposal, still pending before the United Nations, has been continuously blocked by the exercise of the veto power in that organization.
>
> Our ownership of the atomic bomb undoubtedly engendered to a wide extent the mistaken sense of security and complacency which pervaded the public mind immediately after the war and which was in some measure responsible for demobilization. The atomic bomb does not give us automatic immunity from attack, as some people would like to believe, nor does its mere possession guarantee victory if war should come. With or without the atomic bomb, there can be no absolute security for the United States or for any other nation in the world until all nations agree to the regulation of the armed forces and the substitution therefor of peaceful methods in the settlement of international disputes.
>
> The second thought I should like to re-emphasize is that true

unification of the armed might of the United States cannot spring from legislation alone. The spark generated by the Unification Act must be fanned into flame by the thoughts and actions of generals and admirals, ensigns and lieutenants, soldiers, sailors, and airmen, and civilians. We must all learn that we are working together for a common cause—the security of our country—and that the good of all transcends that of the few.

AMENDMENTS TO THE NATIONAL SECURITY ACT, 1949

Neither Congress nor the public nor the more outspoken military department leaders accepted much of Forrestal's warning that the atomic bomb, all by itself, did not guarantee winning, or preventing, wars. The Congress did, however, accept his views on what should be done about the military organization in Washington. Congress passed, and on August 10, 1949, President Truman signed into law amendments to the National Security Act, "thus," Truman wrote later, in his *Memoirs,* "moving a step nearer true unification of the armed forces." Among the significant 1949 amendments:

(1) The "Establishment" was converted into an executive department and renamed the Department of Defense, giving it and its Secretary far greater status and prestige in the government family. The departments of the Army, Navy, and Air Force lost their rating as executive branch departments separate from Defense, lost their Presidential cabinet rank, and lost their seats on the National Security Council.

(2) The word "general" was removed from the Defense Secretary's job description, to end the semantics debate over the Secretary's powers, putting him clearly in direct authority and control of the military departments. The services also lost their "right" to bypass the Defense Secretary to appeal their problems directly to the President or Director of the Budget Bureau—although they could still appeal directly to the Congress.

(3) Although no longer "individual Executive departments," the military services would continue to be "separately administered" by their respective secretaries. Also, the Secretary of Defense could not transfer, reassign, abolish, or consolidate any of the "combatant functions" already assigned to the separate services; nor could he assign military personnel so as to "impair such combatant functions."

(4) The Secretary of Defense was given a deputy to assist him. The two boards under his control were elevated from discussion committees to boards that could make decisions for the Secretary binding on the services. His three special assistants were elevated to the rank of assistant secretaries, which in government organizational parlance gave them less challengeable authority to dig into problems among the services in his behalf. One assistant was specifically named "Comptroller" and was given caretaker power over probably the most important addition to the Defense Secretary's management weapons, the budget. By the 1949 addition of a "Title IV" to the National Security Act, uniform budgetary and accounting procedures were established for all the military departments, and firm budget controls over the whole money-handling process were set in the Office of the Secretary of Defense. (The implications of this rearrangement, particularly in peacetime, were recognized in a Pentagon adage that "Power flows where the money goes.") The only qualification on this budget control was that the Secretary could not direct the expenditure of Defense funds in a way that would circumvent the limitations on his power to reassign service combatant functions, i.e., starve a service unit into impotence simply by denying it money.

(5) Finally, although saying explicitly that it did not intend to "establish a single Chief of Staff over the armed forces nor an armed forces general staff," Congress raised its ceiling on Joint Staff size to 210 officers. It also gave the JCS a chairman to be senior in rank to all other military officers, preside

over JCS meetings, expedite its business, and bring to the Secretary of Defense and the President matters on which the JCS had divided opinions. The JCS chairman was not to have "a vote" in JCS debates, however.

That limitation on the chairman was meaningless. The JCS have never acted by majority vote, anyway. As Louis Johnson, who replaced Forrestal as Secretary of Defense on March 28, 1949, said: "Whether the JCS vote two-to-one or unanimously, they are only advisers to the Secretary of Defense and the President who do the deciding." The provision, in the opinion of veteran Pentagon employee Timothy Stanley, was inserted "to pacify those who did not want the office of the Chairman in the first place, just as the word 'general' had been inserted in the 1947 Act before the phrase 'direction, authority, and control,'" in delineating the Defense Secretary's power. On the whole, the institution of the position of chairman of the JCS has affected the way in which the Joint Chiefs work more than almost any other development. He has come to be the spokesman having the most personal contact with the Secretary of Defense, the National Security Council, the President, and Congress. This arrangement frees the other chiefs to run their own services, but it reduces their influence.

Theorists can argue convincingly that none of these 1949 changes should have been necessary—with the possible exceptions of boosting the Department of Defense to executive status and giving the Secretary more authoritative people just to help handle his workload. Most of the other alterations amounted simply to a stronger statement, with fewer legalistic loopholes, of the goals that Congress clearly had sought from military reorganization in 1947. The 1949 refinements represented, largely, a conviction on the part of many government decision-makers that the separate military departments could not or would not work within the spirit, as well as the letter, of the law unless they got a stronger dose of medicine.

INTERSERVICE CONFLICTS CONTINUE

Much casuistic analysis has gone into why the services continued to fight each other. Most often listed among the reasons were (a) sincere, patriotic concern for the nation's security, coupled with a conviction within each service that it should play the major role in assuring that security; (b) standard human reluctance to accept a change of "tried and true" old organizations; (c) specious efforts by one service or another to gain or retain preemptive national prominence and prestige and, thus, a lion's share of scarce budget funds to carry out their prized individual programs. The "true" reason was probably all of these together, and several shadings in between; there had been a similar kaleidoscope of individual Army, Navy, and Air Force reactions to the idea of unification in the first place.

The 1949 amendments did little to end these service conflicts. The crux of the coordination problem was not so much in organizational weakness as in fundamental disagreement over the best strategy and proper composition of forces to carry out national security policy. And, in their defense, the military could rightly claim that no formal policy for their guidance existed.

By 1949, the essential elements for such a policy had become apparent. Since the end of World War II, in the face of successive crises at explosive points around the world, the United States had undertaken to "contain" the Russians by bolstering the non-Communist nations on the periphery of the Soviet bloc. At the same time, the United States was bent on economy in defense expenditures and on the invigoration of its domestic productivity, its social health, and its public and private institutions.

President Truman believed that what he allocated to the military was enough to enable maintaining adequate preparedness. The assumption was that, while an element of risk was ever present, war was neither imminent nor inevitable, and, as long as essentials were assured, it was reasonable to prepare gradually. There was sufficient flexibility in existing and planned strength, Truman believed, to permit rapid expansion should developments in technology or international conditions make it necessary. The maintenance of America's superior long-range bomber force with atomic weapons, the relative readiness of its conventional forces, its expanding economic potential, its foreign economic aid, its support of the United Nations, and its regional defense pacts and military assistance program—all of these, Truman held, combined to provide effective deterrents to Soviet aggression.

The President's second Secretary of Defense, Louis Johnson, concluded, "I don't think it is necessary for this country to do everything to be in a readiness for full, all-out war on a moment's notice. It will bankrupt us." But one perceptive Congressman questioned that principle's validity in a tense world: "The real question is just how much is enough? If there is peace, a $13 billion budget is entirely too much, and if there is war, this is entirely too little."

One basic source of conflict among the services was that the military tended to believe war was imminent, and unable to convince the President, or even the Secretary of Defense, of how imminent, they received insufficient funds to fulfill what they conceived of as their basic preparedness needs. Through an honest "sharing of shortages," they doubtless could have done more than they did with what they did receive. But, unwilling to accept the central authority of the Secretary of Defense, who could have served as catalyst for coordination, they contested bitterly with each other, each service attempting to see that it got its "minimum essential" share of the budget— although, if it had, little or nothing would have been left for the other two.

At this period, still judging on the basis of its European

experience, the Army felt justified in wanting to take from the Marine Corps the major responsibility for amphibious operations, particularly where an amphibious landing would lead to sustained combat beyond the beachheads. The Air Force wanted Navy air efforts confined to carrier decks. On their side, Navy aviators were alarmed lest they lose their air arm as the British naval arm had been integrated with the newly created Royal Air Force following World War I, and all this just when the large aircraft carrier with its complement of combat aircraft had replaced the battleship as the Navy's major attack unit. Moreover, while Air Force representatives argued that all land-based air operations belonged under their purview, the Navy insisted it needed land-based aircraft to support its operations, especially in the areas of antisubmarine warfare, protection of shipping, and long-range reconnaissance. Another big argument was over delivery of the atomic bomb. The Air Force believed that strategic nuclear bombing was the main function of the Air Force and should be confined to it. The Navy countered that some duplication was justified because strategic bombing from large carriers was feasible and, under the right circumstances, justifiable.

All these views had some merit in them. When a budget that could not begin to accommodate them all was presented, the result, said one participant in the contest, Stuart Symington, was "like throwing a piece of meat into an arena and letting 300 hungry tigers go in after it."

Military worries about the threats to national security inherent in the low Defense budget were not unfounded. In late 1947, when the Truman Doctrine promised help to Greece, Turkey, and Near East nations fighting against the spread of Communism, Defense privately warned the White House that then available combat-ready forces were inadequate to back up that promise if it were strongly enough challenged to require force. Fortunately it was not.

In 1948, the Russians blockaded West Berlin, attempting

to force the French, British, and American occupation powers out of the city. Russian pressure on the city was neutralized by the prompt, effective, and now famous Berlin airlift, in which a coordinated Army–Navy–Air Force–British Royal Air Force team hauled essential supplies over the land blockade into the city by cargo plane to keep the city fed and its economy working. This move was complemented by rapid deployment of two atomic-bomb-carrying Air Force bomber groups to Britain. The clear if unannounced threat was that, if the Russians let their blockade escalate into a shooting war, the United States would answer with an atomic attack on the U.S.S.R. The combination of the airlift's success and the bombers' presence led to lifting of the blockade the following spring. But, again, military strategists in Washington privately warned that, if Russia had started firing, not the best, but the only, counter the United States could have relied on would have been strategic atomic bombing.

To many in the military, it did not seem sensible for the United States to place so much faith in the ability of nuclear force to keep the peace. That apprehension grew by leaps and bounds when the Russians exploded an atomic device in 1949, promising that they, too, would soon have nuclear weapons. But atomic advocates still argued that the United States could ensure a stalemate merely by maintaining the ability to deliver its atomic bombs on target. Surely, they pointed out, any sane leader in either of the two countries could see clearly that neither would win in a nuclear exchange. Reasonable as that argument may have been, it left unanswered the question of how much military capability was needed to prevent or, failing that, to win a less-than-nuclear contest. On Capitol Hill, the military argued bitterly first, the relative merits of bombers versus aircraft carriers and, later, the entire status of the nation's defense. At the same time, the National Security Council used the Soviet atomic explosion as reason for a detailed review of the entire U.S.

foreign and military policy. The Soviet nuclear challenge helped produce both a Truman decision to proceed with development of the hydrogen bomb, and an NSC conclusion that a sizable expansion of other-than-atomic U.S. military strength was needed.

The Defense Department was deep in study of the budgetary and force level implications of the NSC analysis when, at 4 A.M. on June 25, 1950, Korean time, Communist North Koreans attacked South Korea at several points along the 38th Parallel. As they swept down the Korean peninsula, the Communist troops showed, among other things, that whatever nonatomic military strength the United States theoretically should have, what it did have was not enough.

The last American combat team had been withdrawn from the 38th Parallel twelve months earlier, partly as a result of over-all reduction in U.S. conventional war forces. And, just five months before the invasion, the U.S. Secretary of State, Dean Acheson, had declared Korea outside the U.S. defensive perimeter. Whether an American presence there would have deterred the attack or not was a moot question, although hotly argued at the time. The fact remains that it was not there, and the South Korean force that was proved no match for the Russian-equipped North Koreans.

The United Nations Security Council received an appeal from South Korea for military aid to prevent its almost certain fall to the Communist bloc. Through a series of three resolutions, on June 25, June 27, and July 7, the United Nations first appealed to the North Koreans to cease fire and return to the 38th Parallel; then, when that was ignored, asked all U.N. members who were making their military forces available to place them under the command of a unified commander to be designated by the United States. Truman selected General of the Army Douglas MacArthur, who at the time was commander of Allied occupation forces in Japan.

The first thought in the United States was to provide military assistance to South Korea, but a MacArthur trip to the battlefield convinced him that this was not enough. U.S. forces would be needed as well.

EFFECTS OF THE KOREAN WAR

With the Korean War, U.S. Defense Department expenditures went from $12 billion in fiscal 1950 to a high of $43.6 billion in fiscal 1953, the year a truce agreement was finally reached. U.S. military personnel strength climbed during the same time from 1,460,000 persons to 3,355,067 persons. The United States alone spent about $5 billion a year on the war, and contributed almost half the U.N. troops that were fighting the war at its peak. And from this war the United States learned another series of hard lessons. The experience altered a great deal of thinking about national security policy, military planning, and Defense Department organization.

In January, 1953, General Dwight Eisenhower took office as the thirty-fourth President of the United States. He brought with him to the job strong feelings about the proper relationships of the military services to foreign policy, to the economy, and to each other. Some time later, he wrote:

> With some oversimplification, it seemed to me, as I took over the office, that five basic considerations provided logical guidelines for designing and employing a security establishment.
>
> I had long been convinced that the composition and structure of our military establishment should be based on the assumption that the United States on its own initiative would never start a major war. This meant that the nation had to maintain forces of greater strength and effectiveness than would be necessary if our purposes had been aggressive. So long as we were to allow an enemy the initiative, we would have to be capable of defeating him even after having sustained the first blow. . . . [That did not, however,] presuppose that America's response to attack . . . had to be limited to force of the same kind. . . .

As will be explained more fully in subsequent pages, formal job descriptions of the various organizational elements in the present-day Defense Department structure, as in the past, and in most agencies most of the time, tend to obscure the practical, working reality. Usually left out, for instance, is the human interplay among the offices described, such as the influence a powerful personality may have on officials in other offices, even though the organization chart may label him co-equal to many other staff advisers. This interplay, informal or formal, of communications among people can be of over-riding importance to getting things done.

For instance, the organization chart and formalized procedures say that the proper way for a newspaperman to obtain an interview with the Secretary of Defense is to file a written request with his assistant secretary for public affairs. Yet, experienced Pentagon reporters know that a much better way is to ask for the interview through a career civil servant in the public affairs office, who sits about three levels down on the organization chart. If he thinks the reporter's request is worth fulfilling, he will arrange an appointment time with the Defense Secretary's administrative assistant, who happens to be a close personal friend. For the reporter, taking the informal, personal approach rather than the formal one (which he can always do later "for the record") can mean the difference between waiting two or three days and waiting a month for his interview.

Or, by way of illustration in a more substantive area, key Pentagon employees are well aware that if they want to learn something about a career development program, they should not call the assistant secretary for manpower, but the assistant secretary for installations and logistics—who initiated the program when he held the manpower post. When this man was transferred to head the installations office, the Defense Secretary had such a high regard for his abilities, and considered the program so important, that he asked the assistant secretary to continue running his old job from his new position. Yet, nowhere does that essential fact appear on the organization chart.

The office job title states only the *primary* specialty of the people inside; but these people do not carry out their functional specialties in a vacuum. Each individual and each group must have or quickly acquire some understanding of how other specialists view a problem, since, without continual liaison, any one group's proposed solution tends to be too narrow and unrealistic.

For example, if the support organization, i.e., the military departments and similar agencies, do not maintain unbroken liaison with the unified commands (which the organization chart puts in a different set of boxes under the Secretary of Defense), they will lose the intimate awareness of the problems they really face and the tasks they must do. Carried to its outer limits, this loss of close communication could result in the Defense Department's developing and supplying hardware and troops inappropriate to the environment in which the combat commands may have to fight. Conversely, if the combat commands are unaware of what the support departments expect to deliver, they could arbitrarily and inadvertently put themselves in the position of planning and executing theater operations with something less than the best possible combat capability.

THE JOB DESCRIPTIONS

With the caution in mind that the organizational job descriptions are not a "be all and end all" but only a starting point to understanding how the Defense Department works, the organizational structure at present sorts out this way:

The "Secretary of Defense" is actually more than 4,400 persons, including some 2,700 in the Office of the Secretary of Defense and another 1,700 in the Joint Chiefs of Staff organ-

Chart 4

DEPARTMENT OF DEFENSE ORGANIZATION*

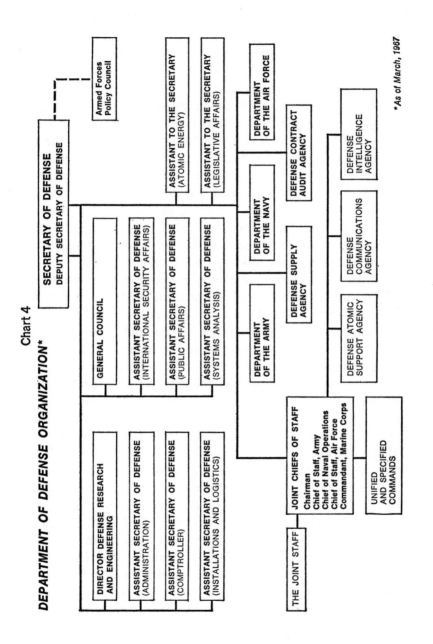

*As of March, 1967

ization. Although, in the strictest legal sense, all decisions are the Secretary's, these people have considerable delegated authority from him to act on and influence the actions of the rest of the Department world wide.

Secretary of Defense. Principal assistant to the President in all matters relating to the Department of Defense, the Secretary is appointed from civil life by the President with the advice and consent of the Senate; exercises direction, authority, and control over the Department; and serves as a member of the National Security Council, the National Aeronautics and Space Council, and the North Atlantic Council of defense secretaries and ministers from the North Atlantic Treaty Organization member nations. In his immediate office are seven assistants, four military and three civilian.*

Deputy Secretary of Defense. Responsible for the supervision and coordination of Department activities as directed by the Secretary, the deputy secretary is appointed from civil life by the President with the advice and consent of the Senate; exercises the powers of the Secretary during the latter's absence or disability; and, for all practical purposes, has come to be, unquestionably, the alter ego to the Secretary whose instructions to the Department or commitments to other government or international groups carry the same weight as if they had been made by the Secretary himself. He also has seven assistants, five military and two civilian.

Armed Forces Policy Council. Composed of the Secretary of Defense as chairman, the deputy secretary, the secretaries of the services, the director of Defense Research and Engineering, the chairman of the Joint Chiefs of Staff, the chiefs of staff of the services (and, by standing invitation, the commandant of the Marine Corps), regularly, and by officials from elsewhere in the executive branch invited for appropriate meetings, this committee advises the Secretary on matters of broad policy relating to the armed forces (especially,

* These and the following manpower statistics are as of June 30, 1966.

in the broadest sense, logistics matters) and considers and reports to him on other subjects as he may direct.

Director of Defense Research and Engineering. Another Presidential appointive post, the director is, as noted earlier, principal adviser and staff assistant to the Secretary on scientific and technical matters. His 558-man staff includes 177 military and 381 civilian personnel. His functions include consultation with the JCS on interaction of research and development with strategy; coordination as appropriate with other Defense agencies; and liaison with appropriate research and development groups outside the Department of Defense. He is authorized to approve, modify, or disapprove programs and projects of the military departments and of other Defense agencies to eliminate unpromising or unnecessarily duplicative programs; and he can start or support promising ones.

He also runs the Advanced Research Projects Agency (ARPA), which is responsible for basic and applied research and development of such advanced projects as he assigns, utilizing some or all of the following: the services of the military departments, other government agencies, private industrial and public entities, individuals, and educational or research institutions.

Finally, he operates the Weapons Systems Evaluation Group, which handles "comprehensive, objective, and independent" operations analysis studies for both his office and the Joint Chiefs of Staff. The evaluations under projected war conditions by this officer group include but are not necessarily confined to: present and future weapon systems; the influence of those systems on strategy, organization, and tactics; and the comparative effectiveness and cost of the weapons and systems. The purpose of their work, in total, is to aid Defense top management in deciding the proper allocation of resources for development of the most effective combination of weapon systems. Actually set up by name in the Forrestal era of Defense organization, their contribution in the military has been diluted and counterbalanced somewhat lately by the work of the Systems Analysis secretariat (noted below).

Assistant Secretary of Defense (Administration). Like all the assistant secretaries and the Defense general counsel, this man is appointed from civil life by the President with the advice and consent of the Senate. The assistant secretary (Administration) is principal staff assistant to the Secretary in the fields of administration, management, and organization. He also serves as the Secretary's principal adviser for the National Communications System and has certain inspection, investigation, and audit functions to perform. His 420-man staff (252 civilian, 168 military) ranges by title over some twenty-two fields related to those functions. Among the more significant: research into and timely, effective solutions for both short- and long-range Defense management and organizational problems; improvement in Defense management practices; provision of criminal or counterintelligence capability as needed to conduct investigations within the Office of the Secretary of Defense, the organization of the JCS, and other Defense components; a capability to conduct inspections or studies of operational or administrative effectiveness within the Defense agencies as well as in the unified and specified commands; handling of a host of administrative details within the Office of the Secretary; coordination in the area of command, control, and communications; supervision of, and recommendations for, improvement in the management, economy, efficiency, and effectiveness of the National Communications System; and policy guidance for, and (especially in Washington, D.C.) coordination and supervision of, a veritable "dog's dinner" of Department-wide administrative services, such as maintenance of historical records, provision and maintenance of office space, parking facilities, and executive transportation, overseeing of employee hours of duty, mail delivery, building protection, and office supplies.

Assistant Secretary of Defense (Comptroller). As chief budgetary and fiscal assistant to the Secretary, the comptroller directs the preparation of Defense budget estimates; supervises the dispensing of funds once allocated by Congress; establishes and supervises the execution of principles, policies, and procedures on fiscal, cost, operating, and capital property accounting, progress and statistical reporting, internal audit, and the expenditure and collection of funds administered by the Department; and establishes uniform terminologies, classification, and procedures in all such matters. His 314-man staff has only eight military members.

Assistant Secretary of Defense (Installations and Logistics). Product of a merger, in 1961, of the assistant secretariats of Supply and Logistics and of Properties and Installations, this position covers the range of responsibility described in the two former titles. I&L, as the Pentagon commonly calls it, has a 286-man staff (264 civilian, 22 military). The assistant secretary recommends policies and provides guidance to the Secretary—and can issue orders to the military departments on the basis of Secretary-approved policy—in the fields of establishing combat command matériel requirements, production planning and scheduling; acquisition, inventory management, storage, maintenance, distribution, movement and disposal of matériel, supplies, tools, and equipment; the encouragement of small business to bid on Defense contracts; transportation, telecommunications, petroleum, and other logistical services; supply cataloguing, standardization, and matériel quality control; use, consolidation, and abolition of military, commercial, and industrial bases and activities; military construction, including family housing; and purchase, use, and retention of real estate and real property.

He also develops plans and programs to carry out policy in these areas,* sets up systems and standards for the administra-

* To clarify what Defense Department people mean by their vernacular use of "policy," "plan," and "program": roughly, a policy is a statement of

tion and management of approved plans and programs, and evaluates how well the military and other defense agencies live up to those standards.

Probably the two best-known examples of what this office does are: (a) its recommendations to the Secretary on military bases, camps, and installations that should be consolidated or closed; and (b) its work in writing, revising, and continually updating the Armed Services Procurement Regulations, the "bible" on how the military is to deal with industry in buying goods and services.

Assistant Secretary of Defense (International Security Affairs). Sometimes called the Pentagon's "little State Department," this office is the Secretary's principal staff liaison with foreign policy; developing, coordinating, and recommending to the Secretary the Defense Department's position on politico-military affairs: The office also manages the Military Assistance Program and handles the planning, organizing, and monitoring of work by the Military Assistance Advisory Groups to foreign allies. The 289-man staff includes 210 civilians.

Assistant Secretary of Defense (Manpower). As the title suggests, he is the principal staff assistant to the Secretary on policy, plans, programs, and the military level of success in managing its manpower, personnel, and reserve forces affairs. These include recruitment, training, and retention of personnel (both military and civilian); health and medical care of Defense Department personnel and their dependents; armed forces internal information and education programs; veterans benefit programs; recommendations on general levels of Defense Department personnel pay and fringe benefits. The 172-man office includes sixty military personnel.

Assistant Secretary of Defense (Public Affairs). As principal assistant to the Secretary on all public information

---

objective or pattern of operating that the Defense Department management seeks; a plan is the scheme by which it hopes to achieve the policy it wants; and the programs are the steps it decides to take to carry out the plan to achieve the policy.

The Pentagon, or National Defense Building. Five-sided, five-storied head-quarters of the Department of Defense, the U.S. Army, Navy, and Air Force.

Interior of the office of the Secretary of Defense. Every Secretary since the founding of the Department, in 1947, has worked at this desk.

Within the Pentagon, countless services and functions are performed. This military affiliate radio system contacts servicemen around the world.

Press conferences enhance the effectiveness of the Department and inform the public of important decisions. Here, in 1963, Secretary of Defense McNamara announces the assignment of a new program for the development of a Manned Orbiting Laboratory to the U.S. Air Force.

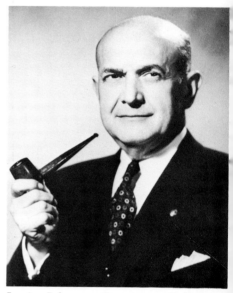

James Forrestal, first Secretary of Defense, 1947–49.

Louis Johnson, Secretary of Defense, 1949–50.

George C. Marshall, Secretary of Defense, 1950–51.

Robert A. Lovett, Secretary of Defense, 1951–53.

Charles E. Wilson, Secretary of Defense, 1953–57.

Neil H. McElroy, Secretary of Defense, 1957–59.

Thomas S. Gates, Jr., Secretary of Defense, 1959–61.

Robert S. McNamara, Secretary of Defense, 1961–68.

British Admiral of the Fleet Earl Mountbatten (right) receives full military honors on his arrival at the Pentagon, in 1965. He is accompanied by General Earle G. Wheeler, USA, Chairman of the Joint Chiefs of Staff (center), and Colonel Joseph B. Conmy, Jr., Commander of Troops.

activities and community relations of the military, this office functions as an operating agency as well as in an advisory capacity to the Secretary of Defense. It deals directly and daily with the nation's newspaper, magazine, radio, and television representatives, providing news releases and press conferences and arranging interviews for the press with Defense officials, wherever they are located.

In addition to recommending public information and public relations policies to the Secretary, the office is also responsible for review and approval for release, from a security and classified information standpoint, of all information originating within the Department, including planned public testimony before congressional committees, information on defense contracts, proposed public speeches by Defense Department officials, and similar documents. (The people in this section of public affairs carry out policy rather than set it. They receive their guidance on how and what to release from the operating agencies and other Defense secretariats, with primary direction funneled to them from the Administration secretariat.) The office includes ninety civilians and ninety-nine military personnel.*

Assistant Secretary of Defense (Systems Analysis). Newest of the assistant secretariats, this office was elevated to the assistant secretary level in October, 1965, from a subordinate location in the comptroller's office. It is manned by thirty-four military and 119 civilians. While the other assistant secretariat tend to stick to their functional specialties, Systems Analysis cuts horizontally across all functional fields. In simplest terms, the Systems Analysis office performs studies to provide Defense decision-makers (mainly the Secretary of Defense), with a "menu of choices" from which the decision-maker can select one most likely to achieve a given objective, primarily in combat effectiveness. In judging the advisability of any proposed program, the responsible leader must con-

* For a fuller account of this secretariat's role, see Chapter VIII.

sider the alternate methods of using his limited resources to achieve his goals. The task of the systems analysis people is to provide him with an appraisal, as statistically detailed, realistic, and unbiased as possible, of the probable effectiveness of possible alternative problem solutions and what each will cost. Cost-effectiveness analysis amounts to the application of economic principles to military planning, and it is intended, of course, to provide the military planner with an additional tool, other than intuitive judgment based on experience, to use in making decisions.

General Counsel. As noted earlier, this is the chief legal office of the Department of Defense, responsible for all legal services to be performed within and involving the Department. Of its fifty-three personnel, fifty-two are civilians. The function includes giving legal opinions or interpretations to the Secretary and deputy secretary as required; monitoring the development of the Defense Department legislative program; and the development of the Defense Department's position on other items of proposed legislation that may affect the Department.

In addition to the foregoing, there are two offices of assistants to the Secretary of Defense:

Assistant to the Secretary for Atomic Energy. This staff adviser recommends policies on, coordinates, and evaluates atomic energy planning and program development activities for the entire Department.

Assistant to the Secretary for Legislative Affairs. Principal Pentagon staff liaison with Congress, he advises and assists the Secretary and other officials of the Defense Department on congressional aspects of departmental policies, plans, and programs; coordinates Defense Department actions relating to congressional consideration of the defense legislative program; arranges for Defense Department witnesses before committees of Congress; furnishes defense information to members of

Congress who request it; and maintains direct contact with Congress, the Office of the President, and other government agencies on legislative investigations affecting defense.

These special staff assistants to the Secretary have a total of 151 personnel in their offices, ninety-one civilian, sixty military.

Joint Chiefs of Staff. As principal military advisers to the President, the National Security Council, and the Secretary of Defense, the JCS's primary duties are (1) to prepare strategic plans and provide for the strategic direction of the armed forces, including the direction of operations conducted by commanders of unified and specified commands; (2) to prepare integrated plans for military mobilization and integrated logistic plans; (3) to recommend to the Secretary the establishment and force structure of unified and specified commands and the assignment to the military departments of responsibility for providing support to such commands; (4) to review the plans of commanders of unified and specified commands; (5) to establish doctrines for unified operations and training and for coordination of the military education of members of the armed forces; and (6) to provide the Secretary with military requirements and strategic plans guidance for use in developing budgets, foreign military air programs, industrial mobilization plans, and programs of scientific research and development; and other functions already noted earlier.

The chairman of the JCS is appointed by the President with the advice and consent of the Senate, and while holding office, he outranks all other officers of the armed services. Besides participating as a member, the chairman is presiding officer of the JCS, provides the agenda for meetings, and informs the Secretary of those issues upon which JCS agreement has not been reached. The chairman also manages the Joint Staff and its director.

The Joint Staff, headed by a director, is composed of not more than 400 officers selected in approximately equal numbers from the Army, the Navy (including the Marine Corps),

Chart 5

JOINT STAFF ORGANIZATION

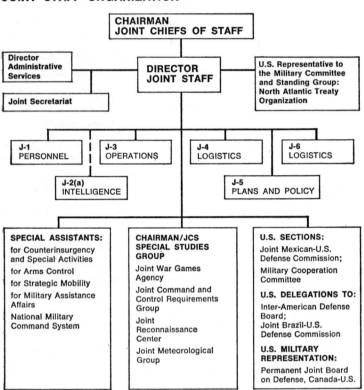

(a) J-2 or Intelligence, function is handled by the Defense Intelligence Agency

and the Air Force. Besides the J-1, J-3, etc., directorates (noted earlier) into which it is organized, it also includes offices for special assistants—one for counterinsurgency and special activities, and one each for military assistance affairs, arms control, and strategic mobility. The over-all organization also includes a number of groups, committees, commissions, and agencies such as the Joint Command and Control Requirements Group, the Joint War Games Agency, a Special Studies Group, the U.S. Delegation to the Inter-American Defense Board, the National Military Command System Office, and some others. All told, including the office of the chairman, the Joint Staff, and these other JCS activities (which are not considered part of the 400-officer ceiling imposed by Congress), approximately 1,700 persons work in this organization, some 1,200 of them military.

At the direction of the Secretary of Defense, seven unified (two or more services) commands and one specified (a single service) command report through the JCS organization to the Secretary. The specified command is the Strategic Air Command, made up of Air Force units, headquartered at Offutt Air Force Base, Nebraska. The seven unified commands, which below the headquarters level are built up typically of two or more Army, Navy, and Air Force units, are: the European Command headquartered in Germany; the Pacific Command headquartered in Hawaii; the Atlantic Command headquartered in Norfolk, Virginia; the Southern Command headquartered in the Canal Zone; the Alaskan Command headquartered at Elmendorf Air Force Base, Alaska; the Continental Air Defense Command at Ent Air Force Base, Colorado; and the Strike Command (sometimes called a "fire fighting brigade" because it is geared to fly anywhere in the world to fight on a few hours notice) headquartered at MacDill Air Force Base, Florida.

In addition to all its other activities, the JCS has under its direction a trio of Joint Service schools. They include the National War College, which conducts a course of study of those agencies of government and those military, economic, scientific, political, psychological, and social factors of potential power that are essential considerations in national security. The course is designed to help prepare selected personnel of the armed forces and State Department for joint and combined high-level policy, command, and staff functions, and for the planning of national strategy. The College was established in 1946. Its standard course runs ten months.

Another, the Industrial College of the Armed Forces, also has a course of ten months duration for selected senior officers and civilian executives of government. It is designed to provide broad educational preparation for higher policy-making, command, and staff assignments within the national security structure, and gives particular attention to management policies, systems, and techniques.

The third postgraduate school is the Armed Forces Staff College. Its course of study in joint and combined organization, planning, and operations—and related aspects of national and international security—helps prepare selected military officers for duty in all echelons of joint and combined commands.

The Defense Agencies

On the producer side of the house, there are, of course, what have sometimes been called the Defense Secretary's "executive vice presidents," the secretaries of the Army, the Navy (including the Marine Corps), and the Air Force.*

In addition, five agencies, which have been set up from time to time to perform a single function, or group of functions, for the entire Department of Defense, are essential to the over-all organizational picture.

The Defense Atomic Support Agency (DASA). A renaming (in 1959) of what had been called the Armed Forces Special Weapons Project, which was activated in 1947 when the Manhattan Engineer District (developer of the atomic

---

* Other volumes in this series—the Praeger Library of Government Departments and Agencies—are devoted to the separate services. They give full details on mission, organization, and function. See *The United States Army,* by Vernon Pizer; *The United States Air Force,* by Monro MacCloskey; *The United States Navy,* by Daniel J. Carrison; and *The United States Marine Corps,* by James A. Donovan, Jr.

bomb) was dissolved, DASA is responsible for consolidated management and direction of nuclear weapons, weapons effects, and nuclear weapons test programs. The work of its 6,621 personnel (4,547 of them military) includes acting as the central Defense Department coordinating agency with the Atomic Energy Commission on matters pertaining to the research, development, production, stockpiling, and testing of nuclear weapons; advising and assisting the JCS in the development of recommendations concerning the stockpile composition, allocation, and dispersal of nuclear weapons; planning for and supervising the conduct of defense weapons effects tests; conducting inspections of units that assemble, maintain, or store nuclear weapons, their components, and auxiliary equipment; and operating a variety of training and orientation courses in nuclear weapons.

The Defense Contract Audit Agency. Created in 1965 to function as a separate and independent audit agency within the Department, it provides uniform handling of procurement and contract administration audits; independent, objective, and consistent cost and related audit advice to military departmental procurement personnel; and a single Defense Department audit agency with which contractors can deal—rather than the three with which industry once had to negotiate in the separate military departments. The agency employs 3,668 persons, six of them military.

The Defense Communications Agency (DCA). Set up in 1960, this agency does not handle tactical battlefield and unified command theater communications, but, rather, is responsible for seeing that the Defense Communications System is so established, improved, and operated as to meet the long-haul, point-to-point, telecommunications requirements of the Department of Defense—and other government agencies as directed. The 2,541-man (1,464 military) DCA also gives technical support to the JCS National Military Command System and is the focal point for continuing integration of the space and ground elements of national communications satellite systems to see that they meet defense requirements. Like DASA, DCA reports to the Secretary through the JCS organization rather than direct to the Secretary as the Contract Audit Agency does.

The Defense Intelligence Agency (DIA). Set up in 1961, DIA also reports to the Secretary through the Joint Staff director and the JCS. With its creation, the Joint Staff abolished as no longer necessary the J-2 (Intelligence) directorate it once had in its own structure. Under its director, the 6,009-man (3,219 civilians included) agency organizes, directs, manages, and controls Defense Department intelligence resources assigned to or included in DIA; reviews and coordinates those defense intelligence functions retained by or assigned to the military departments; satisfies the intelligence requirements of the major components of the Department; supervises the execution of all approved plans, programs, policies for intelligence functions not assigned to DIA; and is responsible for obtaining maximum economy and efficiency in the allocation and management of all Defense Department intelligence resources.

The Defense Supply Agency (DSA). Established in 1961, DSA was spurred into existence by the Reorganization Act of 1958, but the functional principle on which it is based goes back several years to early Defense use of single managers appointed from the military departments to provide a common supply or service, e.g., food (Army), clothing and textiles (Army), petroleum, medical, and industrial supplies (Navy), automotive and construction supplies (Army).

Reporting directly to the Secretary, its 56,980 personnel (including 1,129 military) operate some eighteen major field activities. At present, DSA is responsible for (1) the provision of the most effective economical support of assigned common supplies and services to the military departments and other Defense components; (2) a wholesale distribution system for assigned supplies; (3) contract administration services for the military departments in their dealings with industry; and (4) a series of procurement coordination, matériel utilization, equipment reutilization, and surplus property disposal programs for all the military; as well as (5) the design and implementation of uniform, standard data handling procedures in specified areas of research and development (scientific and technical documents) and supply (including, but not exclusively, the requisition and issue forms). They are also responsible for the Defense portion of the Federal Catalog Program, whereby the U.S. Government identifies in one catalog under standard, correlated nomenclature all the items it buys or stores in its whole inventory of products and parts.

One other agency, different from the five above, is worth noting.

The National Security Agency (NSA). Formed by Presidential directive in 1952, NSA does not perform department-wide functions, but is responsible for certain highly specialized national intelligence functions for the Department of Defense and other government departments as well, including the Office of the President and the National Security Council. The Secretary of Defense is the National Security Council's executive agent for the administration of NSA.

A MATTER OF IMMENSITY

The Defense Department's size and complexity today overwhelm the imagination. Measured in dollars, it has spent an average of about $55 billion per year to date in the 1960's—more than half the total yearly budget of the federal government, or approximately 10 per cent of the annual gross national product. (To visualize the amount, imagine a tightly packed stack of $1,000 bills more than 4 miles high!) Measured in property, the Defense Department is the second largest real estate operator in the country. (Only the Department of the Interior controls more land.) Its real property and equipment are valued at more than $180 billion—twice the combined worth of the nation's 100 largest manufacturers.

Most major defense installations—some 600 in the United States alone—are actually small cities with all the attendant utility, transportation, housing, maintenance, policing, school, shopping, and hospital facilities. The Department's Washington, D.C., headquarters, the Pentagon, is one of the largest office buildings in the world, covering, under one roof, 17½ miles of corridors running into and around 83 acres of offices, drafting rooms, tabulating sections, storerooms, laboratories, libraries, restaurants, auditoriums, dispensaries, banks, a shopping center, a printing plant, and even its own fire department.

The organization employs nearly 4 million persons, about two-thirds of them in uniform, the rest civilians. Its policies directly affect not only these but another 5 million families, including National Guard and other reservists, military personnel on retirement pay, and foreign nationals hired by one of the Department's myriad installations around the world. Scarcely a single known occupation is not represented in the armed forces, and the Department or one of its components performs just about every conceivable function. To do its work, it must operate its own communications network (which rivals any in the world for size and use of modern equipment), its own airline, shipping lines, procurement, warehousing, maintenance, and supply systems. Primarily through the military departments, the Defense Department handles the recruiting, training, equipping, and transporting of personnel. It also feeds, clothes, houses, pays, hospitalizes, insures, and buries most of them. The scope and complexity of its business once prompted a Pentagon executive to remark, "With headaches like these, is it any wonder that the military services each year procure $120,000 worth of aspirin and $1 million worth of tranquilizers?"

Besides medicine, the Department buys annually more than 4 million different items of equipment and supplies. Some of them any consumer in the nation also buys at the store nearly every day, but many are Defense Department products of unique design. Its arsenal of weaponry is fully capable, given the order, of obliterating all the world's major cities in something less than half a day. What the Department's leaders do, or want to do, affects directly at least the peace of mind if not the lives of several million persons on the globe. Its activities consume the largest portion of the attention of the U.S. Congress. The Department's decisions can create or depress whole industries and economic areas not only in the United States but elsewhere, help weaken or cement relations with foreign countries, prevent or propagate wars.

Any one of these functions—and many similar ones performed within the Department—is a major management task in its own right. Added together, they make the Secretary of Defense probably both the most burdened and the most powerful nonelected official in the Free World. When first exposed to the full sum of the job in late 1961, Secretary of Defense Robert S. McNamara found, as he later wrote in the *Civil Service Journal,* "The sheer magnitude of the task as it unfolded made me question . . . whether I or anyone could really manage the Department."

Actually, a large part of the Department manages itself. Literally thousands of decisions are made each day, mostly of an administrative nature, at various lower management levels of the Department. They are decisions the Secretary never hears of and rarely cares to know about. His main concern is, or should be, the setting of broad policy and program goals for the Department to pursue, and then having and operating the necessary controls to be sure the Department does, in fact, achieve—or at least head toward—those objectives.

What the Secretary Cannot Do

In that regard, as far as the law goes, it is easier to recite what he is *not* permitted to do in running the Department than to tell what he can do. The list of limitations is very short. For one, the military departments have to be separately organized; i.e., he cannot merge them. He is not permitted to appoint a single chief of staff to command all the armed forces. He may have no single military staff other than the Joint Staff.

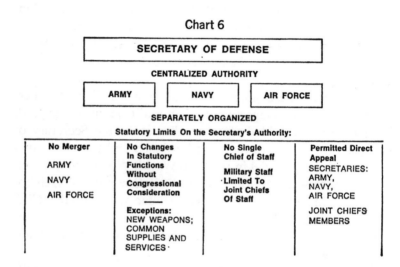

Chart 6

SECRETARY OF DEFENSE			
CENTRALIZED AUTHORITY			

ARMY	NAVY	AIR FORCE

SEPARATELY ORGANIZED

Statutory Limits On the Secretary's Authority:

No Merger	No Changes In Statutory Functions Without Congressional Consideration	No Single Chief of Staff	Permitted Direct Appeal
ARMY NAVY AIR FORCE		Military Staff ·Limited To Joint Chiefs Of Staff	SECRETARIES: ARMY, NAVY, AIR FORCE
	Exceptions: NEW WEAPONS; COMMON SUPPLIES AND SERVICES·		JOINT CHIEFS MEMBERS

He may not prevent the secretary of one of the military departments or any member of the Joint Chiefs of Staff from appealing directly to Congress for relief from one of his decisions. In practice, this rule is not much of an infringement on the Secretary's authority. As his subordinates in the Department know very well, any move by one of them direct to Congress without his approval would probably provoke in the Secretary the same reaction President Ulysses S. Grant once expressed when he said, "I cannot make the Comptroller General change his mind, but I can get a new Comptroller General." The clause remains in the law, however, mainly to reiterate the strong protective attitude Congress has toward its constitutionally granted powers to "raise and support Armies," and, to a lesser extent, because it does provide a kind of safety valve for frustrated individuals at lower military levels (if they feel strongly enough about an issue and believe they cannot get a fair hearing from superiors in the Department itself).

Finally, the Secretary of Defense may not transfer, reassign, abolish, or consolidate any of the statutory functions of the military departments without first permitting the Armed Services committees of the Senate and House thirty days in continuous session to evaluate any such proposal. (If either committee objects, the proposal is put before the whole Congress. If it fails to endorse the committee's objection within forty days, the proposal is considered to have tacit approval.) Except for the President, no other Cabinet officer is permitted this power to change the legislated structure of an executive department. What is more, Congress grants to the Secretary of Defense exceptions even to this rule.

Exceptions Congress Grants

For one, he may transfer from the military departments and consolidate under a single, separate organization, the procurement, storage, maintenance, and issuance to the armed forces of any items previously being bought in common by all the services, without first asking Congress for permission to make this transfer. (The Defense Supply Agency, among others, was created as a result of this exception to the law. It has been estimated that conceivably upwards of 60 per cent of the annual military budget plus the real personal property holdings of the departments themselves are embraced by this one agency.)

The other transfer the Secretary can make without first asking Congress is in equipment. Specifically, he may assign or reassign the development and support in operational use of any weapon or weapon system to a military department in the first place, or, in the second place, from the department that developed it to another department to support it. These kinds of activity—development of weapons, procurement, and supply—amount to a major portion of the military department's total responsibility. Thus, Congress' two exceptions to the things the Secretary cannot do give him a great deal of command over military department activities, particularly in addition to all the things the law expressly says he can do.

WHAT THE SECRETARY CAN DO

What he can do, and has been doing, in management terms for twenty years, is summed up as follows by Yoshpe and Falk:

One basic theme has highlighted the development of the Defense organization since its creation in 1947: the clarification and strengthening of the authority of the Secretary of Defense over the entire structure. The process has been evolutionary, and has sought to combine centralization of authority in the Secretary of Defense with the substantial retention of traditional Service structures in support of the combatant forces. Through the course of this development [however], critics have pointed to the Service departmental and JCS structures as impediments to fully effective management. They would completely functionalize the Defense Establishment [that is, abolish the military services as separate entities] so as to leave no doubt concerning the authority and control of the Secretary of Defense over all elements at all levels of the Department.

No President since 1947 has been inclined to go that far, nor have most proponents of unification in Congress—nor, for that matter, has any Secretary of Defense. Any dramatic reorganization almost certainly would have disrupted internal Defense Department communications and caused a breakdown in control channels that the nation could not have afforded in the perilous times it faced. But, gradual though the march to unification has been, the need for unification itself has been clear. Soon after taking office, Secretary McNamara said:

As I saw it, the [organizational] changes which had been made since 1947 had recognized two highly significant facts. First, it is clear that our international political problems and our military problems are now indivisible. On the one hand we have global commitments growing out of our position of world leadership. On the other, the vast strides made in communications and means of transportation have shrunk both the time and distance factors which influence our relationships throughout the world. The need is for a capability to react quickly with both strength and restraint. The importance of any action which the United States may take anywhere in the world is so great that it must be carefully considered and decided upon at the highest levels of our Government.

Second, it is equally clear that the role of the Joint Chiefs of Staff has significantly changed. No longer is their influence greatest as chiefs of their respective Services. Rather, as members of the Joint Chiefs of Staff in the command channel from the President to the Unified and Specified Commanders, their greatest influence is in the strategic dispositions and employment of our combined forces deployed throughout the world.

IV

How the Secretary of Defense
Exercises Functional Control

Changes to the National Security Act after 1949 notwithstanding, as early as 1953 the Committee on Defense Organization, headed by Nelson Rockefeller, reported to Congress:

> The Secretary of Defense has by statute full and complete au-
> thority over the Department of Defense, all its agencies, sub-
> divisions and personnel subject only to the President. . . .
> There are no separately administered preserves in the Depart-
> ment of Defense. . . . The Secretaries of the Military Depart-
> ments, the Joint Chiefs of Staff, all officers and other personnel
> are *under* the Secretary of Defense. . . . His power extends to
> all affairs and activities of the Department.

Counsel for the Rockefeller Committee, comparing the law
with the way that the organization was actually working at the
time, added, "It remains only to sweep away the annoying
challenges to that authority from time to time." Thus, there
have been many all along who contended that the organization was not as tightly controlled at the top in the 1950's as
it might have been, not because the Secretary had not had
the authority, but rather that much of the latent command
power that he had was largely unused.

Problems in control in the 1950's arose mostly from the

continuing emotional reaction to enforced change in past service concepts and traditional ways of doing things.

In November, 1952, Secretary of Defense Lovett alluded to this climate of resistance in a memorandum he sent President Truman, suggesting solutions to some of the Department's administrative problems. His actual experience in these matters, he said, had not been particularly onerous, primarily because of the attitude taken by the President and also by the Joint Chiefs themselves. He contended, however, "that the position of the Secretary of Defense, in relationship to the President and the Joint Chiefs of Staff, could, with benefit, be clarified" either by legislation or "a simple directive" from the President. For instance, he wrote:

> The question is occasionally raised by legal beavers as to whether or not, in view of vagueness in the language of the Act, the Joint Chiefs of Staff are directly under the Secretary of Defense. . . . Another problem . . . arises out of possible confusion in the Act which provides that the three Military Departments shall be "separately administered" while at the same time providing that the Secretary of Defense shall be head of the Department of Defense, which shall have within it the three Military Departments over which the Secretary of Defense shall have "direction, authority, and control." No great difficulties have been encountered because of this straddle, except in the field of supply, warehousing and issue, where certain ardent separatists occasionally pop up with the suggestion that the Secretary of Defense play in his own backyard and not trespass on their separately administered preserves. . . . To avoid a waste of time in arguments, it would be well, I think, to have this clarified definitely.

But that "Let's-quit-debating-and-get-on-with-it" feeling did not jell in Defense until it became the official attitude of the Kennedy Administration. In January, 1961, the running of government took on a strongly personalized flavor in high places. Where a rather formalized distinction had been drawn during the previous eight years between those department heads who developed policy and those in operations who carried it out, the new leadership wanted, as McGeorge Bundy wrote, in a letter to Senator Henry M. Jackson, "men who can serve equally well in the process of planning and in that of operational follow-up." In other words, top executive branch officials would not only help make policy but also get down in the trenches to carry it out—and be willing to accept the blame personally if execution of policy did not give the results policy said it should. This management philosophy was a sharp change from an earlier, growing government tendency to smother action and bury blame under amorphous committee study.

McNamara accepted that "project manager" kind of responsibility when he accepted office. Merely selecting a man willing to assume the whole workload—planning and doing—is not enough, however. The Department of Defense, like any other organization, is still primarily an organization of people, not things. And the Secretary has to establish his authority in a veritable jungle of potential opposition to what he wants done. In this regard, his problems are very like those that the President faces. Richard E. Neustadt, in his book *Presidential Power: The Policies of Leadership*, vividly describes the situation:

> In the early summer of 1952, before the heat of the campaign, President Truman used to contemplate the problems of the General-become-President should Eisenhower win the forthcoming election. "He'll sit here," Truman would remark (tapping his desk for emphasis), "and he'll say, 'Do this! Do that!' *And nothing will happen*. Poor Ike—it won't be a bit like the Army. He'll find it very frustrating."
>
> Eisenhower evidently found it so. "In the face of the continuing dissidence and disunity, the President sometimes simply exploded with exasperation," wrote Robert Donovan in comment on the early months of Eisenhower's first term. "What

was the use, he demanded to know, of his trying to lead . . ."
And this reaction was not limited to early months alone, or to
his party alone. "The President still feels," an Eisenhower aide
remarked to me in 1958, "that when he's decided something,
that *ought* to be the end of it . . . and when it bounces back
undone or done wrong, he tends to react with shocked surprise.". . .

Long before he came to talk of Eisenhower, [Truman] had
put his own experience in other words: "I sit here all day trying
to persuade people to do the things they ought to have sense
enough to do without my persuading them. . . . That's all the
powers of the President amount to."

The President's "Deputy Commander-in-Chief," the Secretary of Defense, heads a department of government populated
by several different collections of specialists who require persuading. (Even generals are specialists in a particular branch
of military service.) Their functions are to advise the Secretary on what proper policy (and within that framework,
proper programs and projects) ought to be. Then, once the
Secretary has made a decision, they carry it out, presumably
to the best of their ability even if they disagree with it.
Whether it develops by design or default, opposition to or
faulty execution of what the Secretary wants done can come
from any one or some or all of these specialists. They compete with each other for the Secretary's approval—and for the
men, money, and material resources that must accompany
that approval. Abrasions and controversy develop, of course.

Persuading the Specialists

The Secretary of Defense, who sits at the top of the management pyramid, is the one man who can best see where each
national security need fits in proper priority relationship to the
others. McNamara had this in mind when he said:

Once you [the Secretary of Defense] decide you intend to do
what you think best for total national security, the rest is rela-

tively easy. . . . The great interest of our total public is never focused on you in this position; only the pressures of the group immediately affected. There is a great temptation to yield to that pressure . . . [but] if we act in the national interest, the dedicated people [in the Pentagon] eventually will fall in behind. Any group will always respond to the common good if it can be convinced this is the common good.

The problem for the Secretary, in motivating these groups, is complicated by the fact that there are a lot of them. His task is further complicated by the fact that a Defense employee may belong to several at the same time.

Their Many Identities

Certain of these human clusters are easily identifiable and generally well known. The individuals in them have both professionally expert and personal (career-oriented) views about how the Department should work. Two generic factions are, of course, the military personnel, officer and enlisted, and the civilian Civil Service employees. Logically, in terms of job function, the fighting forces are almost entirely military, with only some 2 to 3 per cent civilian technicians—most of them in categories where years of specialized training and education are essential to efficient handling of a highly complex, sophisticated machine. At the other extreme, in what Defense usually calls the "industrial establishment," i.e., the shipyards, arsenals, storage, supply, and maintenance depots, the support forces or logistics organization is made up about 95–98 per cent of civilian employees directed by a small military cadre. In between is a whole range of gray areas. Here, when the unit's task is to evaluate the worth of combat hardware requirements or planning military operations or the like, the tendency is to weight the agency's makeup heavily toward military personnel and, when the work is research and development or contracting negotiations with industry or similar functions of a classic business-management nature, to fill the operation more with civilians.

In terms of judging job proficiency and, thus, eligibility for promotions and pay raises, the scheme for rating job performance of military individuals is much more elaborate and sophisticated than the civilian. It is drawn up in almost excruciating detail to minimize the impact of subjective opinion by superiors in judging the worth of an individual for promotion. The system is designed so that, in general terms, a person in one rank must compete for advancement with all other persons of that rank in the entire military. This contest does not become heated competition until an individual has advanced to the higher latitudes where the numbers of open slots are fewest, especially in the officer corps. (As of July 31, 1966, out of a total 3,136,305 military personnel on active duty, 349,130 were officers from the lowest ranks of warrant officer, second lieutenant, and ensign up to the highest of general of the Army and fleet admiral. Of that officer total, 104,329 were captains or Navy lieutenants. Another 129,782 held ranks below that level. Only 58,374 were in the major–lieutenant commander category, one rank above captain–Navy lieutenant. Thus, even if all the majors and lieutenant commanders were promoted, and many of them would not be, that still left approximately two captain–Navy lieutenant ranks fighting for every vacated post.)

Although not many organizations could use the system because it is so costly to operate, the Department's military career growth routine has been called one of the best executive development setups in the world. Inherent in the procedure, in the officer group, is a policy of rotating the men (usually every three years or so) from one specialized function to another, giving them experience in a full range of military affairs from supply and logistics to combat unit command. That is to say, the system theoretically gives everyone a full chance to make general or admiral. But, an officer who tends to specialize in one field, especially on the logistics side of the house, has less chance of climbing to the pinnacle of the rank structure. Moreover, even when he sticks to the approved pattern of diversifying his experience, he can be retired involuntarily after he reaches a certain age-in-rank if for one reason or another he is unable to break through the promotion barrier to the next higher level.

In contrast, Civil Service civilians, who comprise about one-third the total Department personnel, tend to stay in one specialty, developing their careers. In simplified terms, a man may begin at the lowest rating in the Civil Service General Schedule, GS-1, and climb to the highest, GS-18 (roughly the equivalent to a two- or three-star general officer in management importance and prerogatives). On the way up, he will acquire more responsibility and authority over more persons and activities. But they will tend to remain in one discipline, supply, for instance, or procurement or research or budgeting.

The method of evaluating a civil servant's performance is very simple. His immediate superior fills out a form, saying he is satisfactory or otherwise. Only if the rating is "otherwise," i.e. either "unsatisfactory" or "more than" satisfactory, does the boss have to document his judgment. And a GS-15, for instance, doesn't have to compete against all other GS-15's in government to be promoted to GS-16. Strict limitations exist on the total number of civil servants by grade that a given organization may employ, just as there are limits on total by rank of the military personnel it's permitted. But when, say, a GS-16 position opens up, either through another man's retirement or expansion in the size and importance of the organization itself, GS-15 candidate for the promotion is usually considered only against a relative handful of other GS15's whom his superiors happen to know. Thus, compared to the uniformed personnel, the civil servant enjoys (except when a base is closed or an office abolished or transferred) a good deal of job security and long tenure in one location. This longevity, or "continuity" as it is called, is considered by many one of the chief assets of the civil servant to the organization. That is, with the purposeful turnover of military leadership at a given installation and the continual need for the incoming element to spend a certain amount of time "learning the ropes," the civilian executives who remain throughout the transition can do a great deal to prevent military rotations from disrupting the smooth handling of an organization's work load.

What this all adds up to is that the military and the civilians lead two different ways of career life. Their pay is different; their eligibility for fringe benefits—and even the benefits themselves—are different. Along with their criteria for promotion and their job security, many of their rules of behavior are not the same. Yet, particularly in the "gray" functions of procurement, etc., noted earlier, they frequently sit almost side by side doing nearly the same kinds of work. The personal rub comes because a civil servant can be outstanding in his work on a weapon development program for five years, and his career will probably be in wonderful shape. A colonel or a Navy captain can do the same job for the same length of time with the same success (as many have because of their high value to a particular project) and his career will face a major crisis. A Pentagon personnel administration expert once noted, "Under the circumstances, it's amazing that we get along as well as we do."

Subdivided under these two broad job-function categories of military and civilian are other conclaves, which nurture and promote additional differing attitudes and opinions. There are seven main ones, and military and civilians alike in all ranks work in all of them. They are: the Office of the Secretary of Defense, the unified-specified commands, the Army, the Navy, the Air Force, the Marine Corps, and the Defense Supply Agency. Their already complex interrelationships are

Chart 7

BI-LINEAL ORGANIZATION

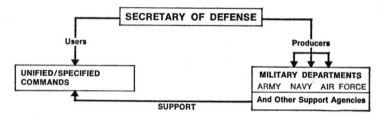

Functional view of the Defense Department bi-lineal, i.e. (1) operations and (2) support, organization.

cluttered by overlap. For instance, the Army is responsible for buying and supplying an air force (primarily of helicopters) as well as providing ground forces; the Navy supports a carrier-based air force as well as ships and its own small army, the Marine Corps—which, incidentally, does not consider itself solely the Navy's army. The Marine Corps also has an air force. Other than bombers and missiles, much of what the Air Force buys is closely related in function and design to the Army's helicopters or the Navy's aircraft. And wherever there is overlap a natural breeding ground exists for individual conflict and controversy on who should handle the larger share of the operation.

In the military, there is an even further subdivision, one more closely attuned to specialized combat duty. Zeal varies from man to man, naturally, but fighter pilots, for instance, tend to consider that their special capability is most essential in certain circumstances. Missile men and bomber pilots will disagree on who is more important to strategic warfare. Sea-launched missiles, say those who work them, are more reliable weapons than land-launched; those who work on the ground will say the same thing in reverse about their weapons. Submariners believe their important function should not suffer at the hands of those who operate carriers; carrier advocates will insist submarines are mostly sitting-duck targets for their kind of weaponry. Special Forces and paratroops can be provoked into arguing that the regular Army is too slow and cumbersome to carry out a mission effectively. Regular Army advocates will insist that no little group of specialists is ever going to win a war. And there are some chemical warfare experts who will plot for the Secretary of Defense an "irrefutable" argument that the nation could retire all the rest of its military forces if their branch were put in charge.

These seemingly contradictory views are by no means pushed entirely out of spurious self-interest. Quite the contrary, as one Navy admiral stated in 1959, in an unpublished study. Particularly in the battle theater, he wrote:

Esprit de corps is an essential prerequisite to military success, and where it is absent, it is the first duty of responsible leaders to build it. It would be utter nonsense to attempt to convince a man that he should risk his life in a submarine, a jet aircraft, or as a member of a landing force, and to train for years to become proficient at his tasks, and at the same time tell him that, after all, what he is doing is not really important; that others in other branches could accomplish the goals just as well; that there is no real necessity to perpetuate the skills.

The dedicated submariner *must* believe in the importance of submarines—and a submarine service cannot be built without dedicated men who possess a deep conviction of the importance of their tasks and a loyalty to their organization. Thus, even within the Navy itself, there are competing loyalties. This is clearly recognized as a healthy situation, however, and the divisive effect is controlled, moderated, and kept within proper bounds by a loyalty to the Navy as a whole. The same is true of the other Services.

Outside Washington, this essential allegiance factor has rarely erupted beyond the "controlled, moderated" bounds the admiral described. But (especially in the early years of the Defense Department's history), the closer a man, particularly a military one, has come to the Pentagon and Capitol Hill, the more insistent and unrelenting he has tended to be about having the needs of his branch of service or his job specialty cared for first. With a touch of sympathy, Lovett once commented regarding the human emotions involved:

> It is difficult for them to detach themselves from the hopes and ambitions of their own Service. . . . The maintenance of an impartial, nonpartisan position becomes increasingly difficult in times of shortage of either men, money, or material. In fact, it is remarkable that the form of organization currently in being has worked so well and it is, I think, a tribute to the quality of the individual involved.

Interestingly enough, as the trend toward unification has accelerated from theory to fact, notably in the last half dozen years or so, military men assigned to unified and specified commands or one of the joint agencies have shifted their loyalties with more alacrity to these unified forces—and with less and less apprehension about whether this was going to hurt their careers in their own services.

One of the byproducts of an increased maturity in the unified Defense organization has been a growth in services teamwork and a dilution of the venomous arguments once sponsored, and challenged, on an individual service basis. (Not that officers advising the Secretary don't still, and often heatedly, propose solutions to Defense problems based on what they learned while in their own services.)

There is still another set of groups which vie with the Secretary and with each other for program approvals. Again made up of military and civilians both, these specialists are in all the major military subordinate organizations, including the Office of the Secretary himself. Put together (as listed in

Chapter III), they look a lot like the organization chart of any business firm. Some are plans and requirements experts; some are operations planners; some are in research and development, in procurement, in transportation, in supply, in training, and so on. Each of these concentrations of experts would always like more resources from the Secretary for research, or for procurement, or for personnel—depending on where the advocate of "more" works.

Over this whole churning milieu is spread a small, powerful layer of temporary appointees, usually selected because they have drawn attention from or have good connections with the political party in power at the moment. These appointees, including the Secretary of Defense, sit at the top, not only in the Office of the Secretary of Defense but also in the military departments. Some stay throughout an entire Presidential term, though they may be moved around within the Department from one key assistant secretariat to another during that time. Many, however, come and go in much less than that four-year cycle. Some resign just as they have begun to learn how to function effectively. Since all are important aides to the Secretary, turnover here can hurt his ability to control the rest of the Department. Holding onto these key people has always been one of the Secretary's toughest problems. (Prior to McNamara, these men, mostly the assistant secretaries of Defense, the secretaries of the military departments and their assistant secretaries, taken together averaged about two years' tenure. McNamara's team of top civilians has held together better, having averaged out by the end of 1966 to almost four years per man in office.)

USING THE POWER TOOLS

To direct all these human forces, the Secretary of Defense has several power tools at his disposal. Some, like the National Security Act, are spelled out in writing, but many of the most effective are not. He may use his reorganization powers granted by Congress to change the "who-does-what-to-whom" relationships within the Department. He may issue Department of Defense directives and similar managerial devices. When signed by him, they have the effect of law within the Department. (The directives and instructions ordering creation of the Defense single-manager agencies are one good example. So are the Armed Services Procurement regulations, which govern military contracting personnel behavior in dealing with industry.)

Probably the most effective of the Secretary's formalized weapons is his command over development of the annual budget request to Congress and subsequent power to apportion Congress-appropriated funds to the various Defense subordinate organizations. How much the Secretary agrees to spend on what reflects his judgment on the relative merit of all the programs and projects that lower Defense levels have insisted need doing. And his subordinates can do little to nurture pet programs and ambitions without those funds. Secretary Gates once said of the whole budget business, "My powers here are plenary."

But there is a good deal more to controlling and directing the organization effectively than simply exercising these officially recognized tools of authority. It might easily be assumed, particularly in a military environment, that the right to command would be enough. Actually, it is not. The higher one climbs in the Defense management pyramid, the more decisive is the ability to persuade in determining if not what, at least how well, Defense fulfills the Secretary's demand.

Two fundamental types of decision are made in Defense. Assistant Secretary of Defense (Administration) Solis Horwitz wrote, in a study paper, in 1965:

> First of all, there are a host of minor decisions. The important part about these is that they must be made. It really does not make much difference whether most of these decisions are "yes" or "no." They are administrative type decisions. They arise from

the type of problems where you should decide that either you are going to do something or not do something and get it over with.

On the other hand, there are important problems . . . they must be thoroughly studied. They must be thoroughly analyzed. They must be subjected to review and every fact brought out—but most importantly, they must be brought to a head. They must be resolved. A decision must be made, and appropriate action must be taken.

In arriving at a decision [on these significant issues], Mr. McNamara does not want to be presented with a single staff study that says: Do it this way. He wants a problem analyzed. He wants to know: what are the alternative solutions? . . . including the status quo? . . . He wants to see the advantages and the disadvantages of each alternative. . . . He wants the various alternatives weighed in terms of their advantages and disadvantages. . . . Unless he is given the choice of [weighed] alternatives, he soon ceases to be the decision maker, because his staff is really making the decisions.

As already noted, proposed solutions to problems may reach the Secretary from any one of a variety of sources: from Congress, from the President, from any interested or informed observers of defense affairs in the public, from defense industry contractors, from other agencies of government or foreign allies, and from among the several specialized groups that make up the Defense organization itself. And, certainly, the Secretary may propose his own solutions to the staff. Whatever the source, the subject must run the gauntlet of a staff advocacy process. By law, the Secretary is responsible for running the Department, and, as a result, he must make the ultimate decisions. But, if he uses his staff properly, his choices will be based on the best advice those specialized experts, in combat operations, research, logistics, etc.—military and civilian—can provide. In developing that advice, these experts will compare notes, exchange opinions in staff meetings, sometimes argue informally among themselves, sometimes with the Secretary present.

For example, suppose that intelligence experts revealed Russia was deploying a new antimissile defense system around its major cities and military installations, and indicated that such a move could pose a serious threat to the presently persuasive U.S. balance of nuclear-war deterrent power. Suppose, further, that plans and strategy experts in the Department of the Air Force convinced their secretary and chief of staff, who in turn advocated the program to the Secretary of Defense, that the best counter move to assure continued deterrence was to develop a new, advanced, supersonic bomber—thus complicating the potential enemy's defense problem.

The Navy Department might advocate, instead, simply building more long-range attack missiles to guarantee enough destructive force penetrating the antimissile defense—their assumption being that the United States could build just as effective a defense as the Russians and, therefore, the threat to one another's offensive missile weapons would remain on a par.

Each department would approach the other members of the Joint Chiefs and the Joint Staff and the Defense Secretary's civilian assistants seeking for the answer it advocates—known, in Pentagon parlance, as "a concurrency." (In clearer language, that means going around from one Defense Secretarial staff office to another collecting votes.) In the process, the Joint Staff, for instance, would evaluate how seriously this Russian move threatened the Department's strategic strength, as well as the relative effectiveness of the proposed answers— plus possibly a solution of their own. The comptroller's office would put a price tag on each solution. The research and development people would judge the technical feasibility of producing whatever new hardware might be involved in both the Communist action and the different possible U.S. reactions. Installations and Logistics would consider each in terms of the impact on procurement, supply problems, and increased need for facilities. Manpower would study the implications on people and training requirements. Systems Analysis would evaluate all these inputs on the basis of total cost related to effectiveness, scoring each solution alone and compared to the others or possibly a "mix" of two of them together (the merits of partly building more missiles and partly deploying a limited antimissile defense, for example). They might even comment on whether anything be needed at all beyond the forces Defense already had in being.

From the Defense Secretary's viewpoint, this pulling and tugging of pros and cons is the preliminary negotiation over what, eventually, will be his decision. How well he directs and encourages the idea exchange will have a lot to do with the quality and the general understanding and acceptance of the result.

Most people looking at the Defense Department talk about the sheer size of it. What isn't talked about enough is that the huge complexity creates a built-in time problem. The struggle for a question and its possible answers to move up through the formal paperwork and tangled layers of offices before it reaches the Secretary can take months. Not bothering to wait that long can cost the Secretary the kind of important senior analysis he needs to have thoroughly applied to a major problem.

Taking the time can delay formulation of the decision until what started out as a small headache has become a big crisis. Moving too fast increases the chance of making a wrong or bad decision. Speed also can cause otherwise unnecessary, action-delaying obstacles to crop up after the Secretary's decision has been made. Moreover, if a question is not thoroughly aired in advance of the decision, some of that aerating will persist afterwards. If the decision goes against them, highly motivated staff elements with strong convictions will charge, "Insufficient study." They will appeal. A new round of discussion will start. The result can be that, while one part of Defense is trying to do what the Secretary wants, another group, which has a role in its execution, is still arguing. Emotion gets wrapped up in the fact of the matter. So does morale. Handling it is tricky business. Too much problem review and analysis will strangle in paperwork an organization's ability to act. Too brusque a cutoff of that analysis will tend to discourage creativity and the volunteering of new ideas to the Secretary.

Secretary Gates, who had a reputation while in office for being as well attuned as any Defense Secretary to these human pressures, said one time, "I saw to it that everyone, particularly the Chiefs [of Staff], had their innings. They have leadership problems of their own. They can't afford to lose face with their own people. It's worth taking the time to listen before you do something, even when you know at the outset what you're going to do." Teamwork cannot be ordered into existence. It is an allegiance offered, willingly or unwillingly. As Gates also noted, "The Pentagon runs a high percentage on emotion. Families are uprooted. Assignments changed. There is rumor, gossip. It is so important to pay attention to morale."

The Secretary of Defense needs from his organization both creativity and administrative harmony, doled out in proper proportions at the right time. How well he tends to the chore of getting these sometimes contradictory qualities from his people can determine to a large extent how effective he is in his work. The challenge is doubly difficult because, to much of the organization, he is an impersonal symbol that they rarely see and hardly ever hear from directly. The image he creates, or fails to create, in public, in directives, and in other communications, of interest in and understanding about their problems produces confidence or the lack of it in their evaluation of him as a leader. That in turn can have much to do with how anxious they are to act or argue when he gives an order. It is not a question, however, of how "nice a guy" he must be. Carried too far, a soft approach only encourages the organization to run him. The question is how much of a tyrant he must be, and how blunt in dictating orders without raising hackles within the operation and thus cutting down his own effectiveness.

THE INDIVIDUAL'S APPROACH

Obviously, it is somewhat unrealistic to talk about how the Secretary exercises control over the Defense Department and its functions without talking a little about the men who have held the post. In each case, what has happened in the Department's short history to bring it to what it is and how it operates today, has had a good deal of the human element in it. And, after Forrestal, each man benefited from knowing of the pitfalls his predecessors had experienced. In sum, how well each Secretary has exercised control has been, in part, a product of his own preference in management methods, and, in part, a product of the time and circumstances when he served. (Predictably, changes in the Department will occur in the future with each new Secretary, to some extent anyway, for the same reasons.)

Forrestal

The first Secretary of Defense had been well trained for the job, having held high-level civilian posts in the Navy during the war and immediate postwar years, first as a Navy assistant secretary and eventually as secretary of the Navy. James Vincent Forrestal had led the Navy's fight to get, in legislation, what the National Military Establishment ended up being in 1947 and, on appointment as head of the Establishment, he saw his proper role primarily as one of coordination among the military departments on those matters in which they had a common interest.

During his period in office, however, instead of cooperating, the services fought often bitter battles among themselves, each seeking funds to fulfill what each judged individually to be the most critical defense programs. The battleground was a budget too small to accommodate most, let alone all of them. Forrestal's first year as Secretary was filled with frustration; it was spent trying, largely without success, to convince the services that their best, possibly only, way to achieve most of what they wanted in total was to work together.

Although he was admired, personally, for his ability and integrity, he became, officially, the services' image of opposition to what they believed were their justifiable and necessary requirements in military strength. They refused to follow his expressed desires, began to circumvent his office, took their appeals direct to Congress and, through newspapers and magazines, to the public, and when they were turned down by an economy-minded nation, blamed him for their defeats. Even the Air Force, which might have been his ally because it got most of what limited Defense funds there were, was angered because he questioned "putting all the national security eggs in one basket."

More significantly, Forrestal began to lose the support of the President about halfway through his tour as Secretary of Defense. There were many reasons, probably the most important being his constant objections that the President's Defense budget was too small. By the spring of 1949, Forrestal had lost White House backing entirely and was asked to resign. Two months later on May 22, 1949, apparently recuperating at Bethesda Naval Medical Center after a mental breakdown, he committed suicide. His death was caused partly by his conviction that he had been a failure as Secretary of Defense—although even his opposition in the Pentagon conceded that nearly all the plans, policies, and programs he pioneered should be pursued.

Johnson

Forrestal's replacement, Louis Johnson, was a long-time friend of the President and had headed the President's campaign fund-raising committee during the 1948 elections. Serving from March 28, 1949, to September 19, 1950, Johnson insisted even before the 1949 National Security Act amendments were passed that he was in complete charge of the Defense organization. He also believed that, if the Commander-in-Chief wanted to spend no more than $11 billion on defense (as he did at the time), then that was all the Department should spend and "with no internal quibbling." He made tough, sweeping decisions, slashing expenses particularly in regard to how much of what kind of weapons the services could buy.

Unfortunately, in his rush to carry out the President's wishes, he often neglected giving the services "their innings" (as Gates later put it). On top of the services' conviction that the Defense budget was too low to provide properly for security, this hard-headed Johnson approach shattered Department morale. In addition, because he lacked Forrestal's background, the organization believed he was not suitably equipped to make these decisions. "A West Virginia lawyer! What does he know about warships?" was the angry, and typical, military comment. When the Korean War erupted in June, 1950, much of Washington blamed him for its having happened—although, in fairness, the facts make that charge highly questionable.

Marshall

Johnson was replaced by General George C. Marshall. (With only one day of debate, Congress passed an exception to their own law, which expressly forbade a former general officer from serving as Defense Secretary.) World War II Army Chief of Staff, former Secretary of State and sponsor of the Marshall Plan for economic aid to help rebuild Europe's war-wrecked economy, and long-time friend and associate of the Pentagon officers whom Johnson had embittered, Marshall was already a veritable man of history when he agreed to serve. In office from September 21, 1950, to September 12, 1951, he took as one of his primary missions the boosting of Pentagon morale. He did what he set out to do—helped to a large extent because the Korean War had broken the conflict-provoking budget ceiling.

Lovett

With morale rebuilt and the Korean military operation on a firm footing, Marshall left. He was replaced by his deputy secretary of Defense, Robert Lovett, who stayed until January 20, 1953, when the incoming Republican administration took over the government. Like Forrestal and Marshall, Lovett had a strong background in defense affairs, having been a combat pilot in World War I, an assistant secretary of the Army in World War II, and Marshall's under secretary of State following the war—in addition to having worked a year in Defense as Marshall's deputy. His talents were highly respected in the organization, and he was well-liked, generally.There were still no particularly tight reins on the budget, and the services had put aside, by unwritten agreement, most of their more far-reaching differences to concentrate on the war. Moreover, like Marshall, Lovett had the almost totally unquestioning approval of President Truman—and possible insurrectionists in the Department knew it. His control of the organization remained firm.

Wilson, McElroy, and Gates

Lovett's successors in the Eisenhower Administration, Charles E. Wilson (in office from January 28, 1953, to October 8, 1957), Neil McElroy (October 9, 1957, to December 1, 1959), and Thomas Gates (December 2, 1959, to January

20, 1961), all enjoyed strong White House endorsement while in office. Support from within their own organization, however, varied from man to man. Wilson and McElroy rode into the Pentagon on proven abilities to run large, complex business operations—Wilson as former head of General Motors, McElroy as the top man at Proctor & Gamble. Both injected a strong sense of sound business-management planning, procedures, and practice into Defense activities, notably those involving research, development, procurement, supply, and maintenance.

Although it was difficult for either man to gauge how successful he had been in his management effort, both felt they had left much undone. (Their evaluation of performance was hampered because, unlike private businesses, the Department of Defense can have no true profit-and-loss statement—other than war—to use as an unequivocating report card on whether income is exceeding costs and on the quality of its work.) Partly, the problem was that both men tended to leave the handling of strictly military affairs to the military, and the military was reluctant to accept any "strange new notion" that the use of efficient business management techniques and effective combat command are inseparable parts of the same organizational asset, leadership.

A McElroy aide later recalled:

He [McElroy] went down there with the idea his major job would be to develop in these military leaders a sense of being good businessmen in these times as well as good combat commanders. He had the feeling when he left that he was never able to get it across.

He was accustomed to dealing with business operations where you have vice presidents for various departments. If the vice president for sales doesn't like a proposal, a discussion is held. He presents his case and the problem is hassled out. Then the President says, "OK, we'll do this." From then on the vice president of sales breaks his back to make it work. He's a management man.

Not so in the military. In the Joint Chiefs, when a Service takes a view, from that point on, that Service does everything it can to continue to sell its views. State Department does the same thing. All his life, a private citizen is shifting allegiances, but in the military they instill in the man the opinion "This is the greatest Service there is, and you can't *really* be sure unless, for instance, you are in the Army and have your own fighter aircraft."

The Services really have a lot of very effective ways to get their way. Publicity programs, reserve organizations, companies that benefit from the contracts, all can put on pressure, particularly with Congressmen. So can the Service friends who are columnists, the Services' own Congress liaison officers, their military associations. You do resist, but you can't resist everything.

Gates did a good deal better, even though he was Defense Secretary only thirteen months. For one thing, he had, besides White House support, the 1958 Reorganization Act, which shifted to his office and away from the separate services the last important remnants of their heretofore autonomous "rights." Moreover, Gates was one of the Pentagon's own. Like Forrestal, Marshall, and Lovett, he knew the organization and what made it tick, having been a World War II Navy officer, under secretary and later secretary of the Navy and then deputy secretary of Defense prior to being appointed Defense Secretary. Gates accomplished a great deal, considering his short term in office, and, because of his attention to morale, succeeded without stirring up unmanageable animosity toward himself. He also did a good deal to lay the groundwork for his successor's arrival.

McNamara (and His Team)

When Ford Motor Company President Robert S. McNamara became the eighth Secretary of Defense, he reflected that, either of two broad philosophies of management could be followed by a Secretary of Defense. He could play an essentially passive role—a judicial role. In this role the Secretary would make the decisions required of him by law by approving recommendations made to him.

On the other hand, the Secretary of Defense could play an active role providing aggressive leadership—questioning, suggesting alternatives, proposing objectives, and stimulating progress. This active role represents my own philosophy of management. In talking with Mr. Gates and thinking about his experiences, I became convinced that there was room for and need of this kind of management philosophy in the Department of Defense.

Led by this philosophy, McNamara announced to the organization his determined intent to be in action what the law said he was supposed to be, chief executive officer of the Department. He assembled as his politically appointed deputies and assistant secretaries an exceptionally strong team, most of them already experienced in some defense field. (As obviously logical as such an approach to manning a staff looks, previous secretaries had not been particularly successful at it, and what experts were collected often didn't stay long.)

His deputy secretary was Roswell Gilpatric, a former Air Force under secretary who helped prepare the Rockefeller report of 1958 on Defense reorganization and, at one time, had been seriously considered by President Kennedy for McNamara's post. General counsel was Cyrus Vance, an able New York lawyer and one-time legal counsel to then Senator Lyndon B. Johnson's Senate Space Committee. Director of Defense Research and Engineering was Dr. Harold Brown, a top-rated physicist from the University of California's Livermore Laboratory. The comptroller, Charles Hitch, was one of the nation's foremost students of national defense budgeting and economics. The head of International Security Affairs, Paul Nitze, had had extensive State Department experience and was a respected authority on military strategy as it related to foreign policy, Assistant Secretary for Installations and Logistics Tom Morris was an expert in theories of business management with extensive practical Defense supply experience. To avoid as much as possible the crippling effect that turnover had had in the past among these deputy offices, McNamara asked all to stay for at least the full four-year Presidential term. (All agreed except Gilpatric, who apologized that personal finances wouldn't permit him to stay more than two years. He was accepted anyway —and ended up staying for three years.)

In retrospect, five years later, McNamara gave much of the credit for the Department's impressive progress to lengthy service by talented key executives. Each of his civilian deputies assembled his own team of talented specialists, who, like their superiors, came to stay. The Secretary has said that this "extraordinary tenure" has enabled the Department to maintain a stability of policy and a continuity in plans and procedures.

ELIMINATING RED TAPE

In any appraisal of the U.S. military posture one salient factor stands out above the rest—the threefold significance of reaction time at this stage in history.

First is the unprecedented strategic value of time—the ability to react instantly against aggression in this nuclear-space age. During World War I and World War II, the nation had at least eighteen months in which to build and mobilize its defenses. If there should ever be a World War III, the Defense Department would be fortunate to have eighteen minutes in which to react. In addition, experience has indicated that the best way to avoid the escalation of a small conflict into a holocaust is to get the military fire department to the scene in a hurry and put out the fire quickly.

Second is the crucial time element in the U.S.–Soviet arms race—the need for early selection among alternative weapon systems and for shorter lead times between conception and useful deployment. As Lovett once said, the troops can't be armed with paper promises; or, in McNamara's terms, decisions to act can't be made on the basis of accounts receivable.

Third is the effect of time on defense cost. In the rushing stream of new technology, with new and newer possible weapon developments, people tend to forget the costly effect —in relative military strength, not just in dollars—of building weapons that have already become obsolete as a result of delay.

Only by giving full recognition to these all-important time factors, can the defense establishment husband its strength. A major drag on the decision process in the Pentagon, McNamara believed, was the penchant for doing things by committee that had grown during the 1950's. Allowing that some coordination is always necessary, he still insisted that too many Defense Department executives, not wanting to take responsibility for decisions, were attempting to coordinate those decisions with everyone who might possibly object, thereby delaying action for weeks or even months.

"A consensus of opinion," he said in one interview, "is usually almost no opinion at all"; and "committees are of value only for the purpose of exchanging ideas . . . the individual in the position of responsibility must make the decision and take the responsibility for it." In addition, "committee coordination" tends to compound the size of another decision-making roadblock: complexity. "Size," McNamara argued, "can be managed if simplified; complexity is the biggest threat to an effective and efficient organization."

To combat these obstacles, he told his new team of civilian assistants, and the Joint Chiefs, and the heads of the military departments and whoever else he assigned a job, "I look to a particular individual in a position of responsibility rather than to an office." Translated into working routine, such a doctrine meant that those willing to accept liability for their own actions, and those of their staffs, got more and more to do and more delegated authority from the Secretary to do it. Those who sidestepped the duty, blaming mistakes on ineffective subordinates or inappropriate help from other coequal agencies, generally were not fired. They just no longer received very much important work. It went, instead, to someone else.

To back up this "individual-assignment" approach to controlling the Department, McNamara made what seemed, particularly during his first three years in office, like a flurry of organizational changes. Predictably, this sudden reshuffling of long-established power centers angered many and aggravated many more, although the object was to simplify, streamline, and standardize like organizational elements so they were geared more precisely and uniformly to the functions they were supposed to perform. (At the time, for example, though field commands of the military services were responsible for doing the same kinds of work within their respective departments, each had a different management structure for doing it.)

Bolstered by the information from scores of task force studies and reports that he had commissioned during his first several months in office, McNamara, among other changes, made the following alterations designed to speed up essential decisions: merged a pair of assistant secretaries at his level into one because the separate responsibilities were closely interrelated parts of the same function, logistics; formed the Defense Supply, Intelligence, and Contract Audit agencies to do for all the military common tasks each service had been performing, with considerable duplication, for itself; reorganized the Army Technical Services of Ordnance, Transportation, Signal, etc., which had each been responsible for only one part of a total weapon system design and procurement, into the Army Matériel Command with subordinate commands, each one responsible for all aspects of one kind of system, e.g., Missile Command, Aviation Command, Tank-Automotive Command, Electronics Command, etc. The Navy later set up a Material Command along the same lines; and as a result, all three departments now have very similarly organized weapons development and supply support commands, specialized generally by commodity, i.e., electronics, aviation, missiles, etc.

McNamara also put the Army's strategic combat troops (STRAC) and some of the Tactical Air Command's combat-ready Tactical Air Force into the same unified (STRIKE) command because they were responsible for related parts of the same function, i.e., to be a fire-fighting brigade able to fly on short notice anywhere in the world to put out a brushfire war; ended squabbling among the three military departments over who could make military investigation of outer space by assigning responsibility to the Air Force; and closed bases and installations of marginal value that did not fit the pattern of functional need. Most of these and similar changes had one basic motive, related to the philosophies noted above. McNamara said:

I am fully aware that the application of my management philosophy—that of active management at the top—has caused some wrenching strains in the Department as new thought-patterns have been substituted for old. I am convinced, nevertheless, that the strains have been worth it and that the Department has taken on the vital outlook which I believed it should in the interest of the best defense for the Nation.

It has been suggested in some quarters that I am unwilling to decentralize decision-making authority. Nothing could be farther from the truth. I strongly believe the pyramid nature of decision-making should be pushed to the lowest level in the organization that has the ability and information available to apply approved policy. The defense effort is entirely too big, too complex and geographically dispersed for its operations to be managed from a single control point. Our effort has been to create a framework of policy within which meaningful decentralization of operations can be accomplished. However, before we can effectively decentralize we must develop an organizational structure which will permit us to proceed to true decentralized decision-making rather than to management anarchy.

CENTRALIZING FUNCTION

Interestingly enough, what Secretary McNamara has often considered decentralization, some within the organization have considered centralization—mainly because the Secretary's decision has taken a function, or part of it, away from them and assigned it to another agency. Assistant Secretary (Administration) Horwitz has observed, in a 1965 study paper:

> One of the problems [McNamara] discovered when discussing centralization is that people sometimes don't stop to think what they are talking about. Actually, when we discuss the problem of centralization, there are three different connotations in which we use that word. The first is the centralization of responsibility. [The National Security Act, as amended, left] little question about this. Responsibility is centralized in the Secretary of Defense. However, the other two connotations are more important. We sometimes confuse them. One is the centralization of function, and the other is the centralization of authority.
>
> These two bear a very interesting relationship to each other. I think we can state it almost as a geometrical theorem. The more a function is decentralized or fragmented, the higher the organizational level on which the authority to make a decision in that functional field must be centralized. Conversely, the more a function is consolidated or centralized, the more the authority to deal with that function can be delegated to a lower level within an organization.

By way of illustration, Horwitz recalls that shortly after McNamara took office representatives of the supply corps from the separate services requested a meeting with him. They brought along a bewildering array of belt buckles and butcher's smocks. They asked the Secretary if he would decide for them which belt buckle and which smock they all should buy. Their reason—the buying authority was fragmented among the services and they could not agree. Horwitz concludes:

> I think this, more than anything else, convinced Mr. McNamara of the necessity of setting up the Defense Supply Agency [to which he could delegate] authority to make this type of standardization decision. . . . Where a function of this nature is fragmented and the fragmentation is such that it causes problems which require resolution at his level, then it is imperative that that function be consolidated so that this type of decision may be removed from his bailiwick and he can be left with those basic decisions that only the Secretary of Defense can make.

Importance of Communications

Possessing the powers of command and persuasion, having one's authority generally accepted, cutting decision time, and centralizing function are still not all of it. A related, essential tool, perhaps the most difficult to use, is communications within the organization. In all his efforts, but nowhere more pointedly than in his attempts to coordinate and centralize functions, the Secretary must see that effective communications inside the Pentagon are consistently maintained. Without the unbroken use of effective communications, there is no effective final control. Technological advances in electronics and computers have helped in recent years in seeing that essential information is reported up and that decisions are communicated down. Still, the installation of McNamara's management theories in the Defense Department did not happen overnight. It took nearly two years at the top Pentagon level itself to build a broad base of understanding about how the Department was to be run; and yet today some persons involved in or concerned with defense criticize and complain, partly from a lack of understanding that is the result of faulty communications.

THE PLANNING-PROGRAMING-BUDGET APPROACH

The control mechanism that history will probably regard as McNamara's most significant contribution to the long-range evolution of the Department is a set of tools known, in Pentagonese, as the Five-Year Force Structure Analysis and Planning-Programming-Budgeting System (PPBS).

McNamara began at the beginning, with a study of what experience could teach, "a thorough reexamination and analysis of the contingencies we might face worldwide." "The difficult question," he said, "is 'What is required?' It is far more difficult to build a defense program on this kind of foundation than it is to set a budget ceiling and then squeeze into it whatever programs you can . . . [but] this is exactly what we set out to do. We . . . took a major step forward in the development of our planning, programing and budget process."

The score card in this activity is the budget. In theory, any budget, if logically assembled and appropriately used, is supposed to be a fiscal statement of an organization's goals, programs, and priorities. It is also an important device for review and control of activities. The concept is not a new creation. As early as 1912, President Taft's Commission on Economy and Efficiency called for an executive budget with expenditures classified by function. That was the opening bell for a series of similar proposals that rang down through the years and slowly, in bits and pieces, were adopted in different areas of the federal government.

The first Hoover Commission on Organization of the Executive Branch of Government, appointed by President Truman in 1947, repeated the urging for a "performance budget," based on what work was to be done. The Title IV amendments to the National Security Act in 1949 reflected these recommendations. Broad classifications, such as Personnel, Operation and Maintenance, Procurement, and Research and Development, replaced more than 100 antiquated appropriation categories. The new arrangement permitted some comparisons of performance among the military services and considerable improvement in financial accounting. But the results fell short of being a true performance budget. In 1958, the Rockefeller defense study committee recommended that the budgetary system correspond "more closely to a coherent strategic doctrine. It should not be too difficult, for example, to restate the presentation of the Service budgets, so that instead of the present categories of 'procurement,' 'operation and maintenance,' 'military personnel,' etc., there would be a much better indication of how much goes, for example, to strategic air, to air defense, to antisubmarine warfare, etc."

The absence of that kind of budgetary analysis in his department left the Secretary without one of the essential tools to managing the over-all defense effort on a truly unified basis. In effect, military planning did not jibe with budgeting, and vice versa, as General Maxwell Taylor explained in 1960 to an interviewer:

> In spite of the fact that modern war is no longer fought in terms of a separate Army, Navy, and Air Force, nonetheless we still budget vertically in these Service terms. Yet, if we are called upon to fight, we will not be interested in the Services as such. We will be interested rather in task forces, these combinations of Army, Navy, and Air Force which are functional in nature, such as the atomic retalliatory forces, overseas deployments, continental air defense forces, limited war expeditionary forces, and the like. But the point is that we do not keep our budget in these terms. Hence it is not an exaggeration to say that we do not know what kind and how much defense we are buying with any specific budget.

Charles Hitch, the management expert called in by McNamara to head the study then under way, added, to the same interviewer:

> The revolution in military technology since the end of World War II, or even since the end of the Korean War, has a profound effect on the character of the military program. The great technical complexity of modern-day weapons, their lengthy period of development, their tremendous combat power, and their enormous cost have placed an extraordinary premium on the sound choice of major weapon systems in relation to tasks and missions and our national security objectives. These choices have become, for the top management of the Defense Department, the key decisions around which much of the Defense program revolves.
>
> Yet, it is precisely in this area that the financial management system showed its greatest weakness. It did not facilitate the relating of costs to weapon systems, tasks, and missions. Its [one-year] time horizon was too limited. It did not disclose the full time-phased [expected life-span of the weapon] costs of proposed programs. And it did not provide the data needed to assess properly the cost and effectiveness of alternative programs.

Prior to 1961, as Navy Captain David O. Cooke explained in a speech to a chapter of the Institute of Management Sciences, in 1965, the budgetary process worked, in simplified form, approximately this way:

> The President would indicate the general level of Defense expenditures which he felt was appropriate to the international situation and his over-all economic and fiscal policies. The Secretary of Defense, by one means or another, would allocate this figure among the three military departments. Each military department would in turn prepare its basic budget submission, allocating its ceiling among its own functions, units and activities, and present additional requests, which could not be accommodated within the ceiling, in what was variously called an "addendum" budget, "B" list, etc. Then all the budget sub-

missions were reviewed together by the Office of the Secretary of Defense in an attempt to achieve balance.

. . . Each service tended to exercise its own priorities, favoring its own unique missions to the detriment of joint missions, striving to lay the groundwork for an increased share of the budget in future years by concentrating on alluring new weapon systems, and protecting the over-all size of its own forces even at the cost of [combat] readiness [within those forces]. These decisions were made [generally] by patriotic generals and admirals and by dedicated civilian leaders as well, who were convinced that they were acting in the best interests of the nation as well as their own service—but the end result was not balanced effective military forces. . . .

As a consequence, the Secretary each year found himself in a position where he had, at least implicitly, to make major decisions on forces and programs without adequate information and all within the few weeks each year allocated to his budget review. Moreover, every year the plans and programs of each of the Services had to be cut back severely to fit the budget ceiling, by program cancellations, stretch-outs, or postponements—but only for that year. Beyond the budget year, unrealistic plans continued to burgeon—[because] "perhaps next year the ceiling would be higher?"

What McNamara wanted was not this but a system that would bridge the gap between planning and budgeting, and at the same time include enough flexibility to change agreed-upon priorities and requirements—which are always upset in unanticipated ways even in the course of a single year as a result of international developments, technological breakthroughs (or disappointments) and all sorts of other events. This "swingable bridge" became known as programing.

To trace the decision process, in somewhat sterilized fashion, from planning to programing to budgeting and back to planning again:

The first phase, planning, begins with the Joint Strategic Objectives Plan prepared by the Joint Chiefs of Staff, backed by the Joint Staff and planners in the military services. This is a series of recommended programs for handling a variety of possible international situations. They are developed for roughly five years into the future on estimated costs and eight years on estimated amounts of needed equipment. (There is, understandably, less and less firmness the farther out the projection is in point of time.) They include a range of variable assumptions about enemy capability, etc., from optimistic to pessimistic so that, according to McNamara, "our forces . . . would be effective even if the pessimistic factors included in that range of estimate turn out to be correct."

These programs include recommended numbers of military forces, according to function. The programing problem involves sorting out all the myriad projects, activities, and combat combinations of men, equipment, and installations of the services in being or under development designed to support the plans. (Grouped according to the missions these combinations can perform, they are called program elements. Like elements are identified together either because they support one another or because they are complementary substitutes for one another in carrying out any one of eight major defense programs.) The nine major defense programs, still much like the five that Eisenhower announced in 1953, are:

1. *Strategic Offensive and Defensive Forces,* including, in the offensive forces, manned bombers, certain land-based and sea-based missile forces, and their related headquarters and command support activities, and, in the defensive forces, the North American surveillance, warning, and control network, land-based and sea-based and airborne radars and control centers, manned interceptors, surface-to-air missiles, ballistic-missile-warning systems, antisatellite defense systems, and the civil defense program;

2. *General Purpose Forces,* the largest major program, consisting of a host of Army, Navy, and Air Force units, and including all their support costs and "overhead" allocations, de-

signed to fight local or limited wars and to engage in theater operations in general war;

3. *Intelligence and Communications,* consisting of missions and activities directly related to combat forces, but not a part of forces listed in programs 1 and 2;

4. *Airlift and Sealift Forces,* with the troop carrier wings of the Air Force, including combat theater airlift, and the singly managed military air and sea transportation services, making up the essential components of this group;

5. *Reserve and National Guard Forces,* with the program elements arranged here by the separate military department that operates each, since most of these are service-assigned components in the United States, identified within this category according to whatever other major mission-program (Air Defense, General Purpose, etc.) each element or unit can back up;

6. *Research and Development,* which includes all of the research and development projects not directly associated with program elements in other major programs, i.e. those investigative efforts that show technological promise but may not be clearly assignable as weapons or systems to one of the other forces;

7. *Central Supply and Maintenance,* which consists of supply and maintenance activities that are not organic to other program elements. Examples are non-deployable supply depots and maintenance depots;

8. *Training, Medical, and Other General Personnel Activities,* which include costs of personnel activities, such as training, medical, recreational, and subsistence, not organic to another program element; and

9. *Administration and Associated Activities,* which include resources for the administrative support of departmental and major administrative headquarters, field commands, and miscellaneous activities not otherwise accounted for.

In addition, "Military Assistance" is carried as a separate

entity under Program 3 and includes the equipment and training provided to foreign nations. For administrative purposes, primarily because Congress insists on considering this separately from U.S. defense force costs, the Pentagon has found it best to keep this as it has always been since the 1950 Military Assistance Act was passed in Congress—a separate program entity and budgeted item.

Finally, recognizing that the defense program is extremely dynamic and that changes would be required at various times during the year, a formal program change system was established. Except that it can be utilized at any time during the year (and hundreds of program change proposals are submitted each year), changes work into the system almost exactly like the evolution of the basic force structure itself. A change request may come from any major Defense Department component. It is reviewed, it receives a Secretarial decision, and the Secretary assigns responsibility for carrying out the decision.

In the fall of each year, these accumulated changes are translated into detailed dollar requests for the next annual fiscal year increment of the approved five-year program. This, in turn, is submitted to Congress the following spring.

Thus, the planning-programing-budget review serves as a continually current basis for preparation of the annual budget as well as being subordinate level guidance, when approved by the Secretary and accepted by Congress, for future planning. The heartbeat of the whole operation is that analysis, decisions, and the allocation of funds are all made on the basis of who is going to spend the money. Thus, it is a functional approach to evaluating the total military force structure. The nation now buys Strategic Offensive and Defensive Forces and General Purpose Forces, etc., not through one military department, but rather by taking the best capability a service has in each force category and putting them all together. One effect, among others, has been a dilution of interservice arguments over funds, since the roles and missions on which those budget debates were based are now handled by custom-tailored unified commands, populated by subordinate elements from the Army, the Navy, and the Air Force, all funded and supported on a unified basis.

Obviously, even if there were no law in existence to order it, these decisions on the proper formulation of interrelated combat elements can best be made at the Defense Secretary's level. Here exists the best overview of total national security requirements as they relate to the military. It is also the best place from which to pick and choose among the various possible ways to fill those needs. The object of the mission-oriented planning and programing process is to assist the decision-maker in defining and balancing the total effort.

Cost-Effectiveness or Systems Analysis

McNamara notes that "the judgment inherent in . . . balancing of programs and systems can no longer be intuitive or rely on past experience alone. The range of choice is too broad; the number and type of alternatives too great." To select specific weapon systems and courses of action from among several potentially desirable alternatives, McNamara's office (and, these days, the military leadership, generally) uses a technique called "systems analysis" or "cost-effectiveness analysis." It is relatively new as military management tools go, and an acceptable description from experts in it or those who know of it is a little hard to come by. McNamara himself says that it is best described as "quantitative common sense."

Whatever the general definition, if there is any separation between systems analysis and cost-effectiveness, systems analysis seems to be the label more often written over studies of how best to solve broad-based policy and program questions; cost-effectiveness covers more specific evaluations of particular program elements and weapon systems. But, in general military conversation, the terms are used almost interchangeably.

Cost-effectiveness analysis is more difficult in the Defense Department than in private business, and even more important because, as the Secretary has testified:

> Neither cost nor effectiveness alone is a sufficient basis upon which to choose a weapon system. Both must be considered simultaneously and in relation to each other. . . . It should always be our policy to spend whatever is necessary for defense but to spend whatever *is* spent in such a way as to achieve the greatest possible military capability—not to buy quality, necessarily, just for quality's sake when the same amount spent on quantity will purchase greater effectiveness, and *vice versa*.

He has also gone on to explain that, in adding to defense programs, the law of diminishing returns operates, since

> each additional increment of resources used produces a proportionately smaller increment of over-all defense capability. While the benefits to be gained from each additional increment cannot be measured with precision, careful cost-effectiveness analyses can greatly assist in eliminating those program proposals which clearly contribute little to our military strength in terms of the costs involved. This principle is just as applicable to qualitative improvements in weapon systems as it is to quantitative increases in our forces. The relevant question is not only "Do we want the very best for our military force?" but also, "Is the additional capability truly required and, if so, is this the least costly way of attaining it?"
>
> Let me give you one hypothetical example to illustrate the point. Suppose we have two tactical fighter aircraft which are identical in every important measure of performance, except one—aircraft A can fly 10 miles an hour faster than aircraft B. However, aircraft A costs $10,000 more per unit than aircraft B. . . .
>
> The basic question first, is, should we have either one of them; and [if so] whether you should have 100 or 200 or 1,000 of

them. [This] requires a rather sophisticated analysis of the potential threat and our potential responses to it under a variety of circumstances. [If the result of that analysis is] we need about 1,000 aircraft, [then] the total additional cost would be $10 million [if aircraft A is bought instead of aircraft B].

If the problem is approached assuming a limited amount of available resources . . . the additional combat effectiveness represented by the greater speed of aircraft A would have to be weighed against the additional combat effectiveness which the $10 million could produce if applied to other defense purposes—more aircraft B, more or better aircraft munitions, or more ships, or even more military family housing. And if we approach the problem [assuming no limit on resources and clear need for a greater] given amount of combat capability, we would have to determine whether that [capability] could be achieved at less cost by buying, for example, more of aircraft B or more aircraft munitions or better munitions, or perhaps surface-to-surface missiles. Thus, the fact that aircraft A flies 10 miles per hour faster than aircraft B is not conclusive. We still have to determine whether the greater speed is worth the greater cost.

The total effort is aimed at saving money (or at least avoiding the excessive spending of it) and improving combat capability at the same time.

Unfortunately, many who have observed these tools in implementation and use have gotten the distinct impression, and complained about it, that the end result will be the elimination of the experienced human element, that arithmetic at its present mushrooming rate of usage will replace judgment. McNamara insists not.

I am sure that no significant military problem will ever be *wholly* susceptible to purely quantitative analysis. But every piece of the total problem that can be quantitatively analyzed removes one more piece of uncertainty from our process of making a choice. There are many factors which cannot be adequately quantified and which therefore must be supplemented with judgment seasoned by experience. Furthermore, experience is necessary to determine the relevant questions with which to proceed with any analysis. . . . The very development and use of [these] techniques have placed an even greater premium on that experience and judgment, as issues have been clarified and basic problems exposed to dispassionate examination. . . . I would not, if I could, attempt to substitute analytical techniques for judgment based upon experience; [but] the better the factual basis for reflective judgment, the better the judgment is likely to be.*

The final truth is that there are no magic tools to guarantee that the Defense Department will move as directed. It is safe to say that the management techniques of today, which may look magical at the moment, will be replaced by improved control mechanisms tomorrow. But Secretary McNamara, who would be more likely than anyone else to become enamored with his own techniques as ends in themselves, has pointed to the more fundamental considerations:

Before I finish my tour of duty in the Department of Defense, I hope we will have established an approach to the job—a philosophy of management and a foundation of military security—that my successors will be able to build upon and strengthen. I think each large organization goes through a period of evaluation when the patterns of the future are formed, when the intellectual framework for decisions is established, when the administrative techniques are sharpened, when the organization structure takes shape. I believe that the Department of Defense is in such a period today.†

* Quoted in *A Modern Design for Defense Decision: A McNamara-Hitch-Enthoven Anthology*, ed. Samuel A. Tucker (Washington, D.C.: The Industrial College of the Armed Forces, 1966), pp. 15–16.
† *Ibid.,* p. 19.

V

Growth and Change in Defense Functions

The creation of new and the realignment of old government organizations since 1947 has been only one means used to improve the performance of providing national security. The nation has also spent unprecedented billions of dollars maintaining a large military operation, has made a very heavy investment in new technology to develop superior offensive and defensive weapon systems, and has acceded in military support of a permanent and powerful arms industry, again unprecedented in the peacetime economy of the United States. It has also backed the Defense Department's intimate involvement in foreign policy deliberations, once solely the State Department's purview.

In earlier years, American military forces were brought in at the last moment to settle—presumably once and for all— with victory in war, what promised to be disaster otherwise. Today, the Defense Department works continually at implementing national and foreign policy. Its component parts are no longer an emergency reserve power, but rather an active, endlessly exercised force brought to bear in operations ranging from combat to consultation with underprivileged peoples.

Precisely identifying the need for an active Defense involvement in long-range planning for national security, and convincing others of that need, has plagued the Department and affected its ability to perform its proper role from the start. And acquiring a workable understanding of the Defense role has been no less difficult for the foreign-policy experts who provide Defense with political guidance on what it must be prepared to do; for Congress, which grants the military its resources; and for the public, which, in the final analysis, must approve or disapprove all policy decisions. In the midst of the Korean War, then Secretary of State Dean Acheson analyzed the emerging nuances of national security in these words: "Our name for problems is significant. We call them headaches. You take a powder and they are gone. These . . . pains are not like that. They . . . will stay with us until death. We have got to understand that all our lives danger, the uncertainty, the need for alertness, for efforts, for discipline will be upon us. This is new for us. It will be hard for us."

Others before and after Mr. Acheson have spelled out the basic nature of national security problems, but Secretary of Defense Robert S. McNamara has provided the most detailed summary to date. In 1966, he said:

> There is still among us an almost ineradicable tendency to think of our *security* problem as being exclusively a *military* problem—and to think of the *military* problem as being exclusively a *weapon-system* or hardware problem. . . .
>
> In the United States, over the past five years, we have . . . been able to create a strengthened force structure of land, sea, and air components, with a vast increase in mobility and matériel, and with a massive superiority in nuclear retaliatory power over any combination of potential adversaries. . . . From the point of view of combat readiness, the United States has never been militarily stronger. We intend to maintain that readiness.
>
> But if we think profoundly about the matter, it is clear that this purely military posture is not the central element in our security. A nation can reach the point at which it does not buy more security for itself simply by buying more military hardware—we are at that point. The decisive factor for a powerful

nation, already adequately armed, is the *character of its relationships with the world.*

MILITARY POWER ONLY ONE FACTOR

Many civilian and military Defense Department experts have contended that military power is not the only—and often not the best—answer to potential present and future threats against the national security and that properly used military power should be only part of an economic, diplomatic, and cultural effort intended, as Forrestal had said twenty years before McNamara, to "create the conditions under which a Free World society can live."

The United States has been hard pressed, since 1947, however, in trying to turn this generally accepted philosophy into cogent, comprehensive practice. The military itself has found it hard to shed traditional shibboleths and adjust to its comparatively new role as a preventer rather than, primarily, a winner of wars. In 1951, for instance, General of the Army Douglas MacArthur complained to the Senate Committee on Armed Services and on Foreign Relations:

> The general definition which for many decades has been accepted was that war was the ultimate process of politics; that when all other political means failed, you then go to force; and when you do that, the balance of control, the balance of concept, the main interest involved, the minute you reach the killing stage, is the control of the military. A theater commander, in any campaign, is not merely limited to the handling of his troops; he commands that whole area politically, economically, and militarily.

Again, during the Korean War, MacArthur wrote in bitterness to the House Republican Party leader, Joseph Martin:

> It seems strangely difficult for some to realize that here in Asia the Communist conspirators have elected to make their

play for global conquest, and that we have joined the issue thus raised on the battlefield; that here we fight Europe's war with arms which the diplomats there still fight with words; that if we lose the war to Communism in Asia the fall of Europe is inevitable, win it and Europe most probably would avoid war and yet preserve freedom. As you pointed out, we must win. There is no substitute for victory.

To most Americans, just beginning at that time to learn the full import of the new ground rules that the world had imposed on their nation, those MacArthur pronouncements on the importance of military victory made a great deal of sense. The nation's leaders had concluded, however, that, in the mid-twentieth century, it mattered more to attack threats of war at their roots. But even all-out campaigns against the causes of war would, they felt, gain momentum only with the help of time. To buy the time, and create the environment in which this offensive could best develop, the armed forces were given the job of restoring military order in a disordered world. They were also told to contain Communist aggression in ways that would minimize the risk of provoking another world war. Neither task was familiar.

That the military did not adjust easily to these new restrictions is evidenced by the MacArthur objections. Nor did the rest of the over-all plan fall neatly and immediately into place from a military viewpoint. It is one thing to spell out, and even obtain majority agreement on, a philosophy or a general plan of operation; it is quite another to make that plan work the way it was intended to work. The many parts of a huge, complex organization like the Department of Defense cannot be turned around and moved in another direction simply by issuing an administrative order.

For one thing, there is the problem, already mentioned in Chapter IV, of the time it takes to communicate the word from the top management echelon (which decides on the action) to the middle management echelon in the organization (which decides in detail how the action is to be effected and what resources are needed for it) and on down to the supervisory level (which sees that the necessary work is done). Time is needed, also, to communicate from the bottom back up to the top confirmation that the order has been understood and is being carried out in the way top management intended.

Another major difficulty, also discussed earlier, is understandable human reluctance to abandon the "tried and true" for whatever new idea top management has ordered into operation—whether it be new military weapon systems or new ways in which the services are to function. For instance, in large measure, the legislative changes, in 1949, 1953, and 1958, of the National Security Act of 1947 did not result from shifts in the intent of the original Act, but constituted, rather, a re-emphasis of that intent, made necessary by continued internal military resistance to the new order. (It was this human—and often emotional rather than logical—hurdle to which Forrestal referred when he told the Senate Committee on Armed Services, in commenting on the substance of the original Act, that "good will can make any organization work; conversely, the best organization chart in the world is unsound if the men who have to make it work don't believe in it.")

Another obvious problem in efficient running of the Department—one that aggravates the difficulties of the first two and adds to the awesome burdens on Defense Department top management—is that what is wanted changes all the time. As already noted, there are no pat answers. Deciding the proper course to take in a fluid—indeed, volatile—world environment has presented the toughest set of choices Defense Department leadership has had to make, according to the men who have held position of Secretary. For example, the fourth Secretary, Robert Lovett, discussing only one field of his responsibility—new weapon development—said,

The amazing advances in science during recent years have created a revolutionary ferment in both machines and methods of
war. . . . In general, a steady stream of innovations is little
by little revolutionizing the fighting equipment of our armed
forces. . . . This upheaval presents enormous difficulties in
establishing an orderly and economical program. Every time a
purchase is made, we must consider when the end item is going to
be made obsolescent, or even obsolete, by newer weapons or
devices currently coming off experimental lines and undergoing
Service or firing tests. . . . At the same time, we cannot fight
today's battles with tomorrow's weapons. We have to strike a
balance between the two. We cannot count on the bold new developments always working out, and we cannot afford to arm
our troops with paper promises. We must, therefore, bring the
most careful judgment to bear on the selection of weapons for
production. We must try to have on hand enough modern weapons for our immediate protection while providing a military
production system which will easily absorb new developments
and enable us to maintain our protective strength in the years
ahead. This is a difficult and expensive undertaking, but there is
still no easy, quick, cheap, or magic way to fight or win a war—
or to prevent one.

Good judgment is the key to the matter, particularly at the
Secretary's level, where the issues are most serious and the
consequences of failure can be most costly and even tragic.
As the seventh Secretary of Defense Thomas S. Gates, who
served from December 2, 1959, to January 20, 1961, once
remarked, "The only thing I know for sure is that you don't
have any 'for sure' answers. Only history will record how well
any of us [Secretaries of Defense] did because we deal entirely
in futures."

Complex as the Defense Department environment is by its
very nature, it is, like any organization, further afflicted by the
normal pattern of lower-level failure always to understand
right away what is ordered and middle- and top-management
failure always to see clearly and early what is needed. Lovett

once said, succinctly, "Good judgment is usually the result of experience, and experience is frequently the result of bad judgment."

The military has no monopoly on mistakes, but it makes its share. And, especially in the early years of its existence, the Department of Defense was the victim of a series of bad experiences that compounded the already formidable task its elements faced in learning to function together smoothly. Crises, threats, and even attacks on allied forces at spots scattered all over the globe forced the Department to run before it had really learned how to walk—and, as might have been predicted, it stumbled a few times.

EFFECTS OF COMMUNIST AGGRESSION

Demobilization had left the National Military Establishment without the force it needed in a newly troubled world, and catching up to the requirements of a changed international situation proved frighteningly expensive. In 1952, Secretary Lovett noted that between 1945 and 1948, defense expenditures of the United States and Great Britain had been cut by over 85 per cent, while Soviet defense expenditures, including only those admitted in their published budget, were reduced from their peak wartime expense by only 48 per cent. During this period, the Soviet Union gained more than three years of intensive military production of new equipment. Consequently, the United States had to include in its rearmament effort after June, 1950, expenditures that might have been spread over many more years.

Since a good deal of the increase was the unanticipated result of having to counter unforeseen aggression, the Defense spending jumps were a major factor in forcing the federal government to pay out more than it was taking back in taxes. This spending, in turn, gave an inflationary prod to the economy—one effect of which was to force the military to ask for even more funds one year than it had the year before to buy the same item. It has been estimated that between 15 and 20 per cent of the $31 billion increase in Defense spending from fiscal 1950–52 was due to inflation.

Spending on direct U.S. military functions jumped from $11 billion in fiscal year 1948 to nearly twice that amount in fiscal 1951, reached a peak of $43.6 billion at the height of the Korean conflict in fiscal 1953, and never dropped below $35.5 billion in any year after that fighting ended. It hovered at an average of slightly more than $40 billion a year through the remainder of the decade.

By the time the Republican Administration of Dwight D. Eisenhower had replaced the Truman Administration, the list of collective security agreements, including both economic and military aid promises between the United States and other nations, was a long one. Enactment of the Truman Doctrine had been followed by the signing of a cluster of treaties and agreements within a few short years. Some were bilateral defense assistance agreements with a total of nearly eighty nations. Each individual treaty agreed to one or more of several different kinds of specific relationships with the country involved. These ranged from the United States providing mutual defense under certain circumstances if either nation were attacked to military assistance by the United States to the partner nation in the meantime. Some agreed only to U.S. use of foreign lands and facilities for military installations or to the United States's furnishing or selling military equipment and services to the agreement partner. Other treaties were multinational, covering large sections of the globe, with the treaty signers agreeing to help each other develop and maintain a capacity to resist armed attack, and to consider an armed attack on one as aggression against them all—except in the ANZUS and SEATO treaties (see below) in which it is still a matter of individual choice even after one member-nation is under fire whether each of the others comes to its aid or not.

Among the major multilateral treaties were the North Atlantic Treaty, which included economic and political as well as military mutual aid agreements, signed in 1949 by Belgium, Canada, Denmark, France, Iceland, Italy, Luxembourg, the Netherlands, Norway, Portugal, the United Kingdom, and the United States. Later, Greece, Turkey, and the Federal Republic of Germany signed the agreement, which has since been modified in spirit as well as fact by France's announced intention to withdraw from her military obligations to the North Atlantic Treaty Organization, a move certain to inspire a major rewriting of the treaty when it comes up for renewal in 1969; the Inter-American Treaty of Reciprocal Assistance (the Rio Pact), signed in 1947–48 by the United States, Argentina, Bolivia, Brazil, Chile, Colombia, Costa Rica, Cuba (which has since fallen to Communism and is now one of the Pact's primary targets), the Dominican Republic, Ecuador, El Salvador, Guatemala, Haiti, Honduras, Mexico, Nicaragua, Panama, Paraguay, Peru, Uruguay, and Venezuela; the Security (ANZUS) Treaty, signed in 1951 by the United States, Australia, and New Zealand; and the Southeast Asia Collective Defense Treaty and Protocol (SEATO), signed in 1954 by the United States, Australia, New Zealand, Pakistan, the Philippines, and Thailand. There was also a multilateral agreement of mutual defense against aggression between the United States and the governments of France, Cambodia, Laos, and Viet-Nam.

The Eisenhower Administration reviewed and re-evaluated all these commitments, as well as the lessons learned from six years of Cold War, i.e., that Communist offensives could take any form ranging from economic and political revolts to armed conflict including guerrilla insurrection or the use of conventional military forces. Most important, Russia's ownership of atomic weapons was also considered in shaping a new U.S. policy.

The new President told the nation: "This policy of ours . . . will be based on the . . . theory that a very real danger not only exists this year but may continue to exist for years to come; that our strength, which is already very real, must now be made stronger, not by inefficient stops and starts, but by steady continuous improvement." Again, in his budget message to Congress on January 21, 1954, Eisenhower noted:

> This budget is based on a new concept for planning and financing our national security program, which was partially applied in the budget revision recommended last Spring for Fiscal Year 1954. Our military planning in previous years has been based on several successive assumed fixed dates of maximum danger, which were extended from time to time, with procurement and personnel plans focused to achieve maximum readiness by each such date. This budget is aimed instead at providing a strong military position which can be maintained over the extended period of uneasy peace.

In general, few people argued then or afterward with the basic policy or even with the programs set up to carry out various parts of that policy. The public debate, internal government controversy, and often fractious disagreement among the military in the Pentagon has been—nearly all of it—over which programs rated the highest funding priority and how effectively each project within those programs was being handled.

PRIORITY CHANGES IN THE 1950's

On taking office, Eisenhower had said that the military forces would receive budget support in the following order of priority: (1) nuclear retaliatory or strike forces; (2) forces deployed overseas; (3) forces to keep the sea lanes open in the event of emergency; (4) forces to protect the United

States from air attack; and (5) reserve forces located primarily in the United States. His first year in office saw these priorities translated, for the military, in terms of men, into a post–Korean War reduction from 1.5 million to 1 million men by June, 1955, in the Army, and from 1 million down to 870,000 men in the Navy/Marine Corps; and an increase in the Air Force from 950,000 to 970,000 men. In terms of money, the fiscal year budgets of the first two services in the same period were reduced from $12.9 billion to $8.8 billion for the Army, and from $11.2 billion to $9.7 billion for the Navy; the Air Force dollar allocation jumped from $15.6 billion to $16.4 billion.

Eight years later, a new incoming Democratic Administration would chastise the Pentagon's past "neglect" of forces other than nuclear, although at the time it was put into effect the Eisenhower program had much in its favor. Regardless of strenuous Army and Navy complaints that their conventional, "limited war" forces had once again been thrown on the refuse heap, both services actually had stockpiled excesses of equipment originally headed for Korea from which they could operate for a few years at least without serious degeneration of their combat capability. Moreover, although there continued to be insurrection, political upheaval, and even armed aggression (including occasions when U.S. troops were deployed to cool down the area), nothing like a Korean threat developed elsewhere from 1953 to 1961.

But in these years, to a marked extent, the main battlefield moved from the front lines to the laboratory. Maintaining and re-equipping the same size military force with more modern weapons, despite Eisenhower's goal of making the federal government live within its income, was getting more expensive. Even in 1952, Lovett had noted, in a semiannual Department of Defense report:

> The amazing advances in science during recent years have created a revolutionary ferment in both machines and methods of

war. We are progressing from piston engines to jets, from visual operations to radar, from certain types of artillery to rockets, from piloted aircraft to guided missiles, from World War II explosives to atomic warheads . . . . In general, a steady stream of innovations is little by little revolutionizing the fighting equipment of our armed forces . . . . The complexity of modern weapons accounts for an additional significant portion of the high cost of rearmament. Constant improvements in design and performance have made meaningless a comparison between many of the World War II weapons and their modern counterparts. A contemporary fighter, for example, is no more like the World War II fighter than a modern automobile is like a buggy. The modern fighter flies so far, so fast, and so high that effective control is beyond the capacity of human faculties, which must be supplemented with electronic calculators, artificial pressure, and other gadgets.

The direct engineering manhours that went into the design of a World War II fighter amounted to nearly 42,000 while the present fighter requires 27 times more or 1,132,000 hours. The number of hours devoted to aerodynamics in the two planes increased 120 times, or from 600 to 72,000. With more manhours to be paid at the higher wage rates of the postwar years, it is inevitable that the end product is going to cost more whether it is a modern airplane, ship, tank, or any other major weapon.

The over-all military research and development effort, given its first great impetus during World War II, had, by the mid-1950's, become a major national undertaking. It involved not only major scientific breakthroughs in earth-bound equipment, but also military developments in space. Along with that jump went almost astronomical cost increases in the unit price of producing weapons and maintaining them. Adding further to those costs were increased peacetime military commitments and the push of inflation.

To be sure, the Defense Department had eased the upward cost pressures somewhat by not trying to replace old equipment on a one-for-one basis, opting instead to sacrifice quantity in favor of quality. As the Eisenhower years in Washington developed, however, a budget ceiling was created, in effect much like that in Truman's era, although higher.

Still, Eisenhower could contend that no international crisis had proven him seriously wrong in what was allocated for other-than-nuclear forces. And on that basis he could add, as he once did, that he had no intention of turning the nation into "an armed camp" if he could avoid it. What is more, in the one critical area, research and development, where answers were needed swiftly and effectively, as they had been needed in Korea, there was no budget ceiling—with the result that the Eisenhower years included several fiscal years of deficit spending, no matter how much he had wished to prevent this.

The Space Race

The Soviet Union's rapid technological progress was appreciated intimately in the Pentagon. Long before October 4, 1957, when Russia launched the first man-made earth satellite, Sputnik I, Defense was well aware it was in a race to produce the power plant, guidance system, and warhead for the first operational intercontinental ballistic missile. If the United States did not arrive at the race's finish at least in a tie, the presumed nuclear stalemate would be broken; the U.S. strategic bomber fleet would be an exposed, virtually defenseless target sitting on open runways with at best no more than about fifteen minutes' warning before a missile attack; and the world balance of nuclear strength would have swung in the Communists' favor. Unfortunately for the Pentagon's prestige, this race, on which the U.S. had spent literally billions of dollars and thousands of manhours, was already nearly won before the rest of nation outside the Department witnessed Sputnik and realized that it was even being run. Thus, throughout the first half of the decade, the Defense Department was beleaguered by critics demanding that it build more bombers when it knew the Russians were building missiles; in the second half, by critics demanding it build missiles when it knew the Russians were developing space vehicles.

It was a new kind of war for the nation. In some cases, the Defense Department purposely financed duplicate, paralleled missile development programs just to ensure that mistakes on one project would not jeopardize building in time the necessary operational missile force. In other cases, the waste of funds was not so purposeful. "Industry was really wasting money on overtime," complained one Pentagon official. "So were labor unions, going on wildcat strikes to get their way. They put a gun to our heads, but what could we do? It didn't seem to make any difference to them that this was a race for national survival we were in."

But, instead of accolades for its success, the Pentagon received technological pressures from within to push a wide spectrum of new hardware developments, military combat-readiness pressures to buy large quantities of what was already proven, and political pressures to buy more of what was already obsolete. "It's remarkable," said one observer, "that we haven't compromised the security of the country in all these things." (The charge of an actually nonexistent "missile gap" was one of the most telling points in a successful Democratic Presidential campaign in 1960.)

All this concentration on missile development (a program on which the military services worked just as enthusiastically as Pentagon top management, with or without the latter's approval) had given some renewed validity in the late 1950's to the argument that modernization of conventional forces was suffering. Just how true this contention might be only actual performance in combat could have proven one way or another, and no such test had occurred. But to the extent that it might be true, the incoming Democratic Administration of President John F. Kennedy, and the new management of the Defense Department, took immediate steps to begin correcting these possible weaknesses.

THE 1960's—AND VIET-NAM

Stating that the nation "could afford whatever is necessary" for its security, Kennedy told his Secretary of Defense, Robert S. McNamara, to determine "the military force structure necessary to support our foreign policy without regard to arbitrary budget ceilings," and "having done that, to procure and operate it at the lowest possible cost." For the military, that became the building and buying of forces to give the President a "strategy of flexible response." Not unlike Eisenhower's five categories of forces, except more detailed, the object of this spread of combat capabilities was to provide a variety of possible answers to a variety of possible military challenges. These forces were to be able to go into action effectively within the estimated allowable time frame and to fight successfully at any likely level of intensity from espionage and counterinsurgency, through large conventional wars, to nuclear retaliation.

In hardware and size of combat forces, after four years at work on the problem and spending, on the average, about $7–8 billion per year more than the previous Administration had permitted, the Pentagon reported, among other statistics: a 150 per cent increase in the number of nuclear warheads and a 200 per cent increase in the total megatonnage in the strategic alert forces; a 45 per cent increase in combat-ready Army divisions; a 44 per cent increase in number of tactical fighter squadrons; a 75 per cent increase in airlift capacity; a 100 per cent increase in general ship construction to modernize the fleet; an 800 per cent increase in Special Forces organized for counterinsurgency operations.

Again, however, the real test is performance in combat. And, in the mid-1960's, the Defense Department began to be embroiled in just such a test in Southeast Asia.

As South Viet-Nam began to crumble under North Vietnamese and Viet Cong pressure, the U.S. military force commitment to South Viet-Nam was increased to turn the tide of battle. On the battlefield, U.S. troops were soon performing with efficient and sometimes spectacular success—in spite of the fact that few of the men or their more important tactics and little of their equipment had ever before been tested in battle. The supply lines were badgered by no more than the normal amount of errors predictable for a complex operation—an amazing record considering that never before had so many men been deployed so fast to a spot halfway around the globe. And, just as important, although nearly half a million men had been committed to the area by the end of 1966, that deployment was achieved with no more than a moderate depletion of forces stationed elsewhere; and without having to impose on the economy at home any of the usual wartime controls that would normally be required from an action of this size.

There were, of course, many critics questioning the U.S. involvement itself, the way American military forces were performing, and the way they were—or were not—being backed up. In answer, Secretary McNamara said, in 1965, what the Defense Department, the State Department, and the President had said under similar circumstances in earlier years when the flare-up was over Berlin, or Korea, or some other place. He pointed out that failure to meet the attack in Southeast Asia would inevitably mean that the United States would have to confront similar challenges later under "even more disadvantageous conditions," and that "to the extent that the Communist states are convinced that war is no longer a feasible method to extend the sway of their ideology, our safety is enhanced. To the extent that they are convinced that we will resist with force, if necessary, any encroachment on our vital interests around the world, the chances of war are diminished."

The Southeast Asia crisis remains at this writing a local conflict in the larger scheme of things—though, obviously, one that does and should occupy most of the Defense Department's and the nation's personal and immediate thoughts. To call it a local conflict is not to belittle it. As McNamara has testified before the House Armed Services Committee, "It is quite possible that in the decade of the Sixties the decisive struggle between Communism and Freedom will take place in this arena." But each year has brought new crises, which have developed, been stalled by Free World determination, and subsided, leaving the basic military situation probably no better nor worse than at any time during the past fifteen years.

Aid Programs

An analysis of the continuity struggle and of the proper Department of Defense role in it was outlined by McNamara when he said, in Montreal, in mid-1966:

> there are three broad groups of nations: first, those that are struggling to develop; secondly, those free nations that have reached a level of strength and prosperity that enables them to contribute to the peace of the world; and finally, those nations who might be tempted to make themselves our adversaries. For each of these groups, the United States—to preserve its own intrinsic security—has to have distinctive sets of relationships.
>
> First, we have to help protect those developing countries which genuinely need and request our help, and which—as an essential precondition—are willing and able to help themselves. Second, we have to encourage and achieve a more effective partnership with those nations who can and should share international peace-keeping responsibilities. Third, we must do all we realistically can to reduce the risk of conflict with those who might be tempted to take up arms against us.
>
> . . . .
>
> The United States has no mandate from on high to police the world, and no inclination to do so. There have been classic cases in which our deliberate non-action was the wisest action of all. Where our help is not sought, it is seldom prudent to volunteer. Certainly we have no charter to rescue floundering regimes, who have brought violence on themselves by delib-

erately refusing to meet the legitimate expectations of their citizenry.

Adding that advancing military technology will permit "throughout the next decade" a reduction in the U.S. need for bases and staging rights in many areas abroad, McNamara predicted, "the whole pattern of forward deployment will gradually change," and the U.S. military presence will disappear in many areas. But, he concluded,

> the irreducible fact remains that our security is related directly to the security of the newly developing world. And our role must be precisely this: to help provide security to those developing nations which genuinely need and request our help, and which demonstrably are willing and able to help themselves.
>
> The rub comes in this: we do not always grasp the meaning of the word *security* in this context. In a modernizing society, security means development. Security is not military hardware, though it may include it. Security is not military force, though it may involve it. Security is not traditional military activity, though it may encompass it. Security is development. Without development, there can be no security.
>
> . . . .
>
> Development means economic, social, and political progress. It means a reasonable standard of living—and the word "reasonable" in this context requires continual redefinition. What is "reasonable" in an earlier stage of development will become "unreasonable" in a later stage.
>
> As development progresses, security progresses; and when the people of a nation have organized their own human and natural resources to provide themselves with what they need and expect out of life—and have learned to compromise peacefully among competing demands in the larger national interest— then, their resistance to disorder and violence will be enormously increased. Conversely, the tragic need of desperate men to resort to force to achieve the inner imperatives of human decency will diminish.

In twenty years, U.S. roles and missions in furthering the development of nations around the globe have not changed, although they have expanded. As one function, the Defense Department attempts to provide a protective shield for a specified country, while helping train and equip local military forces to defend themselves. As another, it assists the under-developed nations, often by helping them utilize economic aid provided through the State Department, in military civic action programs. These programs employ indigenous military forces for nontraditional military projects useful to the local popula-tion—education, public works, sanitation, agriculture, or any-thing connected with economic or social progress. (During 1962–66, for example, through such civic action programs, worldwide, more than 10,000 miles of roads were built or repaired, more than 1,000 schools and hundreds of hospitals and clinics were constructed, and medical and dental care were provided to some 4 million people.)

Another Defense Department mission is to help the State Department convince the other self-sustaining nations of the world that the United States cannot continue to carry a dis-proportionate share of the burden of guarding the Free World's defense perimeter. The success of this effort has been less than impressive. During the past few years, the United States has kept as many men in uniform as all the nations of Western Europe combined—although the latter's population is half again greater.

SUCCESS WITHOUT CHEERS

Any brief history of what the Defense Department has done, or has tried to do, in twenty years of existence will necessarily show that an understanding of its functions has only gradually evolved. Along the way, literally hundreds of debates, some-times involving millions of people, have been devoted to how well the Defense Department has carried out its responsibilities. Complaints notwithstanding, justified or not, about the Department's efficiency in performing its tasks, the important consideration is whether it gets results. On that score, the presence of the Strategic Air Command's bombers and more than an adequate supply of ready long-range missiles have obviously been major factors in forestalling a nuclear World War III. For all the bitter critics of its aid program, its accumulation of little victories through civic action projects far outweighs the occasional, well-publicized mistakes. And, in its series of direct confrontations with Communist aggression—in places ranging from Berlin to Korea to Cuba to Viet-Nam—the Department's persistence, patience, and power have been increasingly more successful. Whether these limited-scale confrontations have involved only the threat to use force or its actual use, the conflicts have not been so mishandled—thus far at least—that they have led to escalation into global war.

Rarely, over the years, has the Defense Department been given much credit for its success in performing these missions, i.e., in preventing nuclear war, halting the escalation in intensity of limited-size conflicts, containing the spread of Communism generally, and doing its assigned work with the least possible imposition on the rest of the nation under the circumstances. But this absence of cheers can be taken to mean that no longer does the Defense Department march to a brass band. To the extent that the muting of martial music indicates that the DOD is doing what it's supposed to do in a somber world—serve as a viable, effective instrument to carry out foreign policy—it can claim that the nation's military forces have seldom been used more successfully than they are today.

VI

Significant Actions in Department History: The Missile Revolution

Although the Defense Department is today in "a period of evaluation when the patterns of the future" are being formed, as McNamara has said, the fact is that it always has been under study. The Department's creation in the first place was, for the federal government, the result of one of many evaluations. Similarly, each significant change since—in the Department's organizational structure, its internal administrative techniques, the size of its forces, and the kinds and capability of its armament—has been the result of a new round of analysis and intellectual soul-searching.

These studies did not, and do not, begin or end at any special time; they run on. They regularly involve audits of past performance, judgments of present trends, and speculations about what is in the Department's future. The relevant examinations (there have been a lot of irrelevant ones) have been directed toward one end—keeping the Department in tune with its environment. As precise understanding of that environment's scope and complexity has grown, the Department's size and versatility has increased.

Each key decision taken in the Department's short history, and each action following the decision, has been predicated, at

Chart 8

DEPARTMENT OF DEFENSE EXPENDITURES BY FUNCTIONAL TITLE

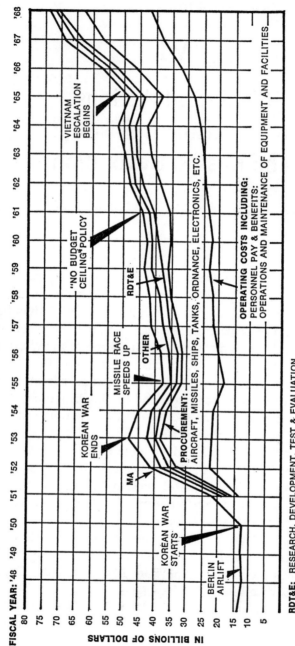

RDT&E: RESEARCH, DEVELOPMENT, TEST & EVALUATION

MA: MILITARY ASSISTANCE

OTHER: INCLUDES MILITARY CONSTRUCTION, FAMILY HOUSING, CIVIL DEFENSE, REVOLVING AND MANAGEMENT FUNDS

Note: subtotals in today's accounting format not available for years prior to 1951.

least in part, on what went wrong, or right, in previous experience. Both the good and the bad are significant to a department that must try ceaselessly, as an Air Force general once said, to keep its plans out ahead of its tactics and its tactics in front of its weapon developments. There is no unanimity about which is most significant in the long list of conflicts that the Defense Department has struggled through to date. Is the U.S. stand in Viet-Nam more important than the stands in Berlin, or in Korea, Lebanon, Cuba, or the Dominican Republic? Did long-range missile development have more impact on military plans than production of the nuclear submarine or surveillance satellites or the electronic computer? The fact is these and many other such moves all were and are important in the over-all framework of what Defense does—and why.

One of the most far-reaching events in Defense Department history, other than unification itself, was the development, in the 1950's, of intercontinental ballistic missiles (ICBM's). Development and operational deployment of the ICBM was a weapons revolution in the military, drastically affecting nuclear deterrence strategy; combatant command planning and operations; the relative value of other weapon systems in the inventory or developing; even the ways Defense manages a weapon's life cycle from birth to obsolescence. Like all revolutions, it left a littered battlefield, which the Department is still trying to tidy up. But this essentially technological contest taught the Department a great deal about how and how not to handle its own affairs.

BEFORE SPUTNIK

At 7:30 P.M., on October 4, 1957, at the Tyuratam Range in Kazakhstan, the Soviet Union fired into orbit the world's first man-made satellite, Sputnik (Russian for "traveling companion"). President Eisenhower later wrote, in *Waging Peace,* "The Soviet scientific achievement was impressive. The size of the thrust required to propel a satellite of this [184-pound] weight came as a distinct surprise to us. There was no point in trying to minimize the accomplishment or the warning it gave that we must take added efforts to ensure maximum progress in missile and other scientific programs." And, Eisenhower added,

> warnings had not been lacking. . . . A Presidential Air Policy Commission had said [in 1948], "It would be unwise to assume . . . that other nations will not have . . . missiles capable of delivering an attack on the United States mainland . . . by the end of 1952. . . . The United States must press most energetically and immediately its basic and applied research and development program . . . [to develop] at the earliest possible date . . . the most effective piloted aircraft and guided missiles and the defense against them."

As Army chief of staff, Eisenhower himself had urged, in February, 1947, before the House Military Appropriations Subcommittee, "in the field of guided missiles, electronics, and supersonic aircraft we have no more than scratched the surface of possibilities which we must explore in order to keep abreast of the rest of the world. Neglect to do so could bring our country to ruin and defeat in an appallingly few hours."

What disturbed the Administration most about Sputnik in 1957 was that the wave of fear it provoked indicated that the U.S. public had not, until then, been very aware of missile developments and research abroad and at home. Still, even in the Defense Department, ICBM development, admittedly, had been slow in gaining momentum. One disgruntled Congressman noted that "major military weapons never spring forth full-blown overnight."

Some important basic research had been done in the United States in the 1930's, especially by physicist Robert H. Goddard (then often scoffed at as "Moon-mad Goddard"). But more formalized government rocket research work did not start until 1942, and serious work on long-range ballistic missile development was not to come until ten years after that. Until fiscal year 1953, expenditures in any one year on long-range ballistic missile programs never came to as much as $1 million. The early work, principally on solid propellant fuels (which burn like cigarettes within the rockets), had been pushed, with military support, by the Office of Scientific Research and Development. From this research had evolved the "artillery rockets" of World War II, air-to-surface (fired from the aircraft) rockets, rocket boosters for aircraft takeoff from shorter than standard runways, other special rocket motors, and the first serious efforts to propel rockets with liquid fuels—efforts that, by the summer of 1945, had produced an Army WAC Corporal rocket that used nitric acid and aniline, but had a short range and could not carry a very heavy warhead.

Then, at the end of the war, the Allied nations had sent scientific teams into Germany to analyze the defeated enemy's technical accomplishments in rockets and missiles, especially the V-1 and V-2 guided missiles fired by Germany at targets in continental Europe and Great Britain late in the war. A number of the best German scientists and engineers had been induced to go to Russia and to the United States. The United States, however, had pressed its recruiting effort less aggressively than the Russians. By late 1946, Russia had identified hundreds of scientists and technicians associated with German missile programs, and was shipping them, along with their research facilities, production plant machinery, instruments, blueprints, missiles, and missile components, back to Russia. Those moves, in turn, had speeded up the development of Soviet scientists and technicians and given them the know-how to bring uncompleted German ideas to practical realization. To U.S. Government intelligence and scientific experts, the advantage achieved by this early Soviet decision to develop and extend German missile technology was already becoming evident in the mid-1950's.

Meanwhile, in the United States there had been only halting, low-level efforts. In 1946, as captured V-2 rockets were used up and development of American-designed and produced rockets began, several potentially useful programs had been started. For instance, that year the Army arranged a "Bumper" program to rebuild and convert V-2's into first-stage booster rockets. The second stage, the WAC Corporal, carried scientific instruments to high altitudes. In its later tests, the vehicle reached maximum speeds of about 5,200 miles per hour and a maximum altitude of some 250 miles. (Standard V-2 performance was 3,600 miles per hour and a 100-mile maximum altitude.) Also, in 1946, the Army Air Forces made its first attempt at developing an intercontinental ballistic missile. Its program, run by Convair (now a division of General Dynamics Corporation), was intended to advance long-range rocket techniques, but economy slashes in the budget terminated it a year later. For the next several years, Convair used its own money to carry on, at low financial levels, studies of what was then known as the MX-774. The Navy, too, had moved out of the laboratory and into the test vehicle stage in the late 1940's, building the first version of its Viking high-altitude scientific research rocket. Finally, in 1950, the Army had begun to develop a 200-mile-range tactical ballistic missile, the Redstone. Its first flight test, in 1953, was only partially successful, but much of the information obtained from this and subsequent Redstone firings was applied to the Jupiter when that program was initiated in late 1955.

A major factor discouraging top Defense and White House enthusiasm for ICBM's was the technical problems existing, not in missilery itself, but in the atomic field. Weight is critical to ICBM design. Generally speaking, it takes about 200 pounds of missile-launching weight to place one pound of warhead on a target several thousand miles away. Because the first atomic warheads weighed 9,000 pounds, a major nuclear warhead weight reduction was required before missiles could be of practical military value. After 1946, the Atomic Energy

Commission (AEC) had embarked on a program of atomic weapon improvement—work speeded up when the President directed the AEC, on January 31, 1950, to emphasize its, until then, low-priority thermonuclear (hydrogen) weapon studies. One objective was to produce both lighter weight and higher yields in a new generation of nuclear warheads, and the AEC was soon showing optimistic evidence that it could meet that objective. During this period, however, the significance of warhead improvement was not applied to ICBM problems. Because of this, and because of the high cost of missile development, priority demands of the Korean War for military resources, and other reasons, long-range ballistic missile development languished. When the Defense Department appointed a director of guided missiles in October, 1950, with authority to start a missile program (of the same high priority given atomic bomb development in the Manhattan Project a decade earlier), the office itself decided against a crash effort, saying it would take a year to institute.

Missile feasibility studies, started by the RAND Corporation in 1949 and completed in late 1950, however, had confirmed the military worth of long-range ballistic missiles. In January, 1951, the Air Force had resumed studies on the MX-774 weapon, redesignated "Atlas." The program still had only a long-term, low-priority objective—that of determining whether a large 5,000-mile ballistic rocket was then technically feasible—but six months later it was formally reactivated. By fiscal year 1953, ICBM annual funding had grown in two years from half a million dollars to $3 million a year.

Then, on June 16, 1953, Secretary of Defense Charles E. Wilson ordered a review of the guided missile program to identify and eliminate duplication. As part of this review, a group of civilian scientists, headed by Dr. John von Neumann, was asked to review the strategic missile portion of the overall rocket-and-missile development spectrum. This Strategic Missiles Evaluation Committee reported in February the highly significant possibility, based on AEC research, of achieving a major technological breakthrough on warhead size. The committee also said that other technical problems associated with the development of ICBM's—such as accurate guidance systems, reliable command and control electronics, powerful enough booster engines, and adequately protective materials to prevent the warhead's burning up on re-entry into the atmosphere from outer space—could be resolved in a few years.

Von Neumann's committee recommended that the ICBM project be completely reoriented to take advantage of advancing warhead technology, which permitted relaxation of guidance, tolerances, and engine propulsion requirements. Within ten days, the Air Force assistant secretary for Research and Development had approved the committee proposal, and, by the following August, major management, organization, and procedural realignments had been completed within the Air Force to accelerate ICBM development. Key among them was the setting up of an autonomous Western Development Division of the Air Force Research and Development Command on the West Coast, in the midst of the nation's major aviation industry complex, under command of Brigadier General Bernard Schriever. (Nuclear tests in the Pacific from March to May that year had proved out the smaller lightweight high-yield thermonuclear weapon, thus confirming the soundness of the von Neumann committee's recommendations.)

By spring, 1955, the Atlas program was expanding rapidly. Spending grew from $14 million in fiscal 1954 to $161 million in fiscal 1955. In February, 1955, a "Technological Capabilities Panel" urged that an IRBM (Intermediate Range Ballistic Missile) program be started, concurrent with the ICBM effort. In June, the Scientific Advisory Committee (the new name of the von Neumann group) recommended that two ICBM developments be run concurrently to assure earliest possible achievement of an operational capability. This was insurance against the fear that an unforeseen technological snag might delay progress. At stake in the now full-scale race with Russia was the favorable U.S. balance of nuclear power; although the contest was filled with engineering unknowns, it was one that the United States could not afford to lose.

In September, President Eisenhower approved assignment of the highest priority to ICBM research and development, and the Titan ICBM was started as a back-up project to the Atlas. At the same time, the President approved a development program for two IRBM's, Jupiter and Thor. Rapid Jupiter development was hoped for, based on Army experience in working with the V-2 and Redstone missiles. Thor's impetus was to come from the Air Force's Atlas experience. The Navy was assigned technical development responsibility for a sea-based Jupiter IRBM.

The Air Force put both its ICBM developments and Thor under the already established Air Force Ballistic Missile Division (the new name given to Schriever's Western Development Division). Hoping to save time, Schriever also launched a "concurrency" program; i.e., rather than waiting until missile development was completed, the training of launch crews, purchase of spare parts, building of operational launch sites, and related tasks were started while the missiles were still in development.* The object was to have these logistics and weapon support elements running at full tilt the minute the first operational missile rolled off the production line. The theory looked attractive in those crisis times. But when mishandled, such an approach can be and was, on some missile programs, expensive.

The Navy created an "Office of Special Projects" to handle its Jupiter assignment. But Jupiter's highly volatile liquid

---

* Normally, support activities do not begin to gain momentum until almost the end of a development cycle, simply because equipment modification and redesign is comparatively minimal then and fewer costly changes need be made in either the production model or the logistics base to support it.

fuel conjured up horrendous visions of one accidental spark instantly turning a whole ship into a blazing fireball, so the Navy also studied a solid-propellant version of the IRBM to cut down shipboard logistics headaches and increase crew safety. In the meantime, Defense reserved $515 million dollars in fiscal 1955 to carry out all these Army-Navy-Air Force ICBM/IRBM programs.

On January 20, 1956, to assure exchange of technical information among the services, as well as provide competent centralized guidance for all the programs, the Scientific Advisory Committee was transferred from the Air Force to the Office of the Secretary of Defense. The Secretary also selected his own special assistant for guided missiles; this official's main task was to keep the Secretary current on all service development progress and see that no program lagged for lack of resources. In February, following an Air Force lead, the Army put its Redstone missile development arsenal under command of a brigadier general, John B. Medaris, and renamed it the Army Ballistic Missile Agency. (Agencies usually have more organizational status than arsenals.)

In September, 1956, a Jupiter-C multistage test vehicle climbed 680 miles high, reached a maximum velocity of 13,000 miles per hour, and traveled 3,300 miles down the Atlantic missile test range from its launch site at Cape Canaveral, Florida. During that same period, Air Force X-17 test vehicle flights proved it possible to prevent air friction from burning up a warhead when it re-entered the atmosphere. In October, the Scientific Advisory Committee endorsed the Navy's proposal that it develop a new, smaller solid-propellant IRBM designed for launch from submarines. Named "Polaris," the program, including six submarines to carry sixteen missiles each, was approved by the Secretary of Defense the following month, and the Navy dropped its work on the liquid-fueled Jupiter program. In November, the Secretary also assigned responsibility for operational deployment of land-based IRBM's to the Air Force and ship-based IRBM's to the Navy. With its option to use long-range missiles in combat fore-closed, the Army reacted with bitter, vociferous objections. The heated complaints ran on for more than a year. (In the end, as noted in earlier chapters, the Army managed only to provoke Congress into tightly centralizing research and development control in the Defense Secretary's office and rewriting the National Security Act to confirm his weapons reassignment authority.)

RESPONSE: IRBM's AND ICBM's

In October, 1957, the month of the Sputnik launching, the President reaffirmed highest priority for both the Thor and Jupiter systems to obtain an IRBM capability at the earliest practicable date, and he ordered both continued until one proved completely successful. (The Army was now in a race not only with Russia but also with the Air Force, some Army leaders hoping that if Jupiter became operational first, it would reestablish their lost claim in the long-range missile business.) Each weapon system had a target operational date of December, 1958, for its first squadron, with a plan to build for each a total of four squadrons with fifteen missiles each. A Navy proposal that Polaris, when operational, be launched from land as well as ships (instead of using Thor and Jupiter) was turned down. In December, an accelerated program of nine Atlas squadrons of ten missiles each was approved. Nearly $1.4 billion was spent on ICBM/IRBM programs in fiscal 1957.

Flight tests of Thor, Jupiter, and Atlas in 1958 exposed a failure of certain turbopump assembly components to pump propellants into the main engine. The flaws were isolated and corrected. Subsequent Atlas flight tests also verified accurate performance of the guidance system and the integrity of the air frame. (Among the successful test flights, one Atlas was placed in orbit in December.) The Air Force, using a good deal of Polaris-developed know-how, began work on a solid-propellant-fueled Minuteman three-stage ICBM. To be guided by a self-contained, all-inertial guidance system, it was designed to carry a nuclear warhead up to 5,500 nautical miles.

In May, the first Royal Air Force students began training on missile operations in the United States under government-to-government agreement that the RAF man and command all Thor units to be stationed in the United Kingdom. (The announcement stirred outspoken complaint and demonstrations from some Britons. They feared that missiles on English soil would make the nation what they claimed it would not be otherwise—an attractive target for Russian nuclear attack.) The Thor guidance system improved during the year, permitting an average impact accuracy better than that originally specified, and, by year's end, Thor was meeting its production schedule.

Polaris, Titan, and Minuteman Stepped Up

In November, the President approved a nine-submarine Polaris program. The initial operational capability date of the first Polaris submarine was moved up to late 1960, and later advanced again to early 1960, with four more submarines to follow at three-month intervals. Congress appropriated $90 million more for the Minuteman program than was in the President's fiscal 1959 budget request, and $609 million more than the President asked for Polaris. ICBM/IRBM spending climbed that fiscal year, 1958, to more than $2 billion.

Flights of the operational prototype Atlas, begun in April, 1959, had little initial success. The planned date for achieving a limited operational capability was slipped again, to September. Malfunctions, which caused four out of five Atlases to explode during takeoff, were corrected, however, by mid-year; and the first launch by an all-military team on September 9, at Vandenberg Air Force Base, California, was successful, proving, among other things, that the concurrency concept worked. Progress on Titan resulted in an approval to increase the number of operational squadrons from four to eleven, each squadron to contain ten missiles. At the same time, plans were pushed to improve each ICBM system's chances of surviving and reacting to nuclear attack. The schemes included launch site dispersal over a wide geographic area, providing individual missile launchers for each missile rather than one launcher for several missiles, and putting the ICBM's in reinforced steel-and-concrete holes in the ground.

Prototype Minuteman missiles were fired successfully from underground silo-type launchers that year. The total planned force of Thor squadrons was cut from nine to four; and construction, installation, check-out, and modification problems in England forced another delay until mid-year in turning over the first squadrons to the RAF. Then, five sites were selected in southern Italy for a total of two Jupiter squadrons of fifteen missiles each. The operational version of Jupiter's ablating nose cone was flown on all missiles fired in 1959 and proved completely satisfactory (in one firing, the nose cone carried biomedical experiments for the National Aeronautics and Space Administration's space research program).

All major objectives of the Polaris program in 1959 were met, including successful check-out of the launching system on the first submarine, the U.S.S. *George Washington*. Successful launches of two Polaris missiles at sea under operational conditions occurred the following year, on July 20. By then, the United States was spending ten times as much each day on ICBM/IRBM developments as was spent in all of fiscal year 1952. Adding the costs of all other missile programs, plus other surface-to-surface rocket weapons, to the nearly $3 billion spent in fiscal years 1959 and 1960 on long-range ballistic missiles, the nation spent almost $7 billion for all missile programs in fiscal 1959, and more than another $6 billion in fiscal 1960.

Some Lessons of the Missile Race

A rough management rule-of-thumb is that it takes seven years, on the average, to go from research to prototype production on a complex weapon system development. In seven years of developing long-range missilery, the United States had gone through a first-generation ICBM/IRBM family (liquid-fueled Atlas, Thor, and Jupiter) into the militarily much more safe and reliable solid-fueled second generation of Polaris and Minuteman. And, by 1961, the production lines of what now called itself the "aerospace" industry were grinding out these missiles at a rate that soon had given the United States a three-to-one operational edge over Russia. The missile race had been won.

Out of this race came considerable knowledge of long-term value to the Defense Department about how and how not to run its affairs, especially the internal ones of advance planning, military hardware requirement justification, research and development, and supply support. In particular, Sputnik had prompted a vastly increased emphasis in Defense on research and development, not just in missilery but in a whole range of promising fields. "R&D" became a much-discussed acronym in the military. The function's importance prompted Congress to pull the top Defense manager for research and engineering up out of the long line of assistant secretaries in the Defense Secretary's office and make him the third most important civilian in the secretariat, ranking behind the Secretary of Defense and the deputy secretary. In effect, on the civilian-run, support side of the house, he became coequal to the JCS chairman on the military side.

Defense spending on and encouragement of R&D stayed in the billions of dollars even after the missile race—the scare it occasioned providing sufficient proof of the threat a nation can face when it fails to nurture and exploit technology.

Importance of R&D

Since research and development are the fountainhead of a great deal of national economic growth, the government prod prompted, in turn, even greater velocity in an already bounding technological revolution. Existing companies expanded and new firms sprang up, all of them with a new kind of character. The service they sold for a profit was creative ability—previously available almost entirely in universities, nonprofit institutions, and government-owned arsenals. And large segments of private industrial inventiveness expanded their market horizons beyond individual and corporate consumers to include the government—a new, exciting, and wealthy customer, demanding products in an area that permitted no second best. Firms that got into the competition found themselves at work on the cutting edge of the economic future, successfully selling ideas before they were even proven by commercial standards. These companies received a double payoff: they found thousands of consumer-market applications for what they developed under government contract, and they found that they could attract more easily than could many non-defense firms the bright scientific and engineering talent that is just as important to a company's future growth as R&D effort generally is to a country's growth.

The public, too, received a double payoff. Theirs came in national security and in the development of newer or cheaper products that helped to raise the standard of living. A few examples, out of many that could be cited, are unbreakable ceramic dishes, stoves that cook with infrared heat, transistor radios, and microminiaturization of "solid state" components in television sets, giving the sets a higher quality and longer failure-free operation. Moreover, by the mid-1960's, some of this newly developed industrial talent was beginning to turn its attention away from defense or space research to solving problems of urban renewal, mass transportation, air pollution, water purification, and a host of related social and economic concerns.

Demand for Management Skills

The missile race also placed a new demand on hard-bitten military leaders—one many of them had in the past found difficult to believe important. Major General W. S. Steele pinpointed this demand in a 1965 speech to the National Capitol Chapter of the Armed Forces Management Association:

> Management skills are an essential resource. Effective, up-to-date managers are needed in every phase of Defense activity; planning, programing, engineering, research, development, procurement, production, human and material resources, public and congressional relations, and in everyday communications. Communications are particularly important. For in addition to the age-old problem of communicating with men, today's Defense manager must face the problems of understanding, at least in general terms, those who communicate with machines and how they do it. The ever-increasing use of computer-based management systems within the Defense environment has created new knowledge requirements for managers, uniformed and civilian alike.

The end of the missile race brought other problems for the military. Of course, the Defense Department did not pause, once missile production lines were rolling, to tote up its mistakes, decide all at once what needed correcting, and start off again. But many problem-solving programs were started, resource management improvements begun, and Defense Department organizational relationships streamlined. Indeed, much had happened in these areas while the race was still on. (For instance, an automatic thought reaction in the military, each time it develops a better weapon, is to begin development immediately of a defense against that weapon. Thus, techniques of antisubmarine warfare and research and development in anti-ballistic-missile missiles were given increased impetus as early as the mid-1950's.)

But, in the early 1960's, a new pattern of change in defense had become obvious. The missile race had been a war, in a sense—and, as in all wars, Defense Department leadership had not been meticulous, let alone energetic, in attempts to save money. With the contest apparently over, management clearly decided it was time to clean up the decision-making process and tighten internal controls for better economy.

A HARDER LOOK AT SPENDING

The new approach to economy was far more sophisticated than simply cutting the budget. In fact, beginning in fiscal 1961, defense spending went even higher, by several billion dollars, than it had ever been previously. But the added expenditure went primarily into limited warfare arms rather than strategic missiles and bombers. What began to happen was that, in all spending categories, the Secretary of Defense and his immediate staff became much more demanding. Where projects had once been approved for funding as much, it seemed, on the hope as on the promise that they would deliver answers, the military were soon being ordered to justify their programs and dollar requests with detailed, carefully thought out, unemotional analysis. With increasing frequency, policy directives included words like "economy" and "efficiency"— both goals often neglected in the previous ICBM rush to save time.

Studies of military resource management during the missile crisis resulted in some interesting and, for the military, often disturbing conclusions. For one, there had been a tendency to let the military alone, giving a service or a project manager or a company or anyone with an encouraging idea free rein to develop it. A concept barely out of the basic-research stage was often formalized, at considerable cost, into a full-blown project and funded all the way through the manufacturing phase. Along with that early commitment and lack of tight control at the top went a lack of close coordination between user and supplier. Thus, even when a concept did turn out successfully, many of its components continued to be improved, at more cost, until they could perform well in excess of what the combat user originally had said he needed. Although such extra development might look like a bonus, careful study revealed that there is a law of diminishing returns in these things. For example, the Defense Department learned that although it took x dollars to achieve a 95 per cent weapon system reliability, it might require that same amount again to boost performance to 97 per cent. And combat commanders complained that, since plans spelling out required size of forces had assumed in the first place that only 90 per cent of the experimental weapons would work in war, those extra dollars were a waste. They argued that the extra money could have been spent better on other things and leveled charges of "goldplating"* at the supplier side of their own house and at industry.

For some time there had been a tendency, especially in Congress, simply to pour money into a program, not as a guarantee of success, but in the hope that money might lure some bright scientist with answers. Moreover, in keeping with the "concurrency" idea, project offices tended to work on a whole weapon system at once instead of only the "pacing" problems, i.e., those components (such as propulsion engines) critical to reaching necessary performance goals. These huge expenditures had reassured many people. But more dollars do not automatically mean more progress. When asked by Congress if his Army missile work would be helped by more defense spending, Werner von Braun had replied, "Some addi-

---

* Elimination of "goldplating" can mean huge savings on big programs, no matter how small the item involved. For instance, using a cheaper metal for the 5 million dog tags it buys each year has saved the Department $100,000 annually.

tional funds for basic and applied research and development for future growth potential would help tremendously in the long run." But, he had added, noting that the five key ballistic missile programs (Atlas, Titan, Polaris, Thor, and Jupiter) could not be speeded up appreciably by an increase in funds, "We don't need excessive amounts of extra money—we certainly don't have to double our present missile budget."

About the only place spending had been challenged strongly was in the General Accounting Office, Congress' watchdog agency on how executive departments utilize appropriated funds. And, unfortunately, the GAO botched its opportunity. Instead of analyzing costs related to program need, its people would return to the scene after a contract was completed and renegotiate the agreement, cutting industry profits in the process. Considering the frightening price the United States would have paid if it had lost the race, it is understandable that the new and highly creative defense industries grew more and more bitter as their profits dwindled from 8–10 per cent (about average for less challenging consumer markets) to about 1–3 per cent in a field that demanded exceptionally high, and costly, talent.

The sum of all this, as Defense Department leadership and, soon, even the management heads of many subordinate military commands saw it, was that in times of weapon development crisis more, not less, control was needed to get the job done on time and to deliver the required combat capability. In the seven years after 1959, the results seemed to justify this decision to tighten top management control of subordinates.

Cost Reduction Program

More than one Secretary of Defense and several hundred thousand persons in the Department had tried to cut costs before. The difference this time was that inherent human motivation was organized to good effect. For every program, a Pentagon project manager was appointed, with delegates in every military camp, post, and station to monitor and encourage the effort. Goals were set; and, for the first time in the Department's fifteen years, a total score on cost-cutting was kept. In 1964, McNamara explained the techniques:

> The program of action, which is helping us to achieve our twin objectives of (a) the required military strength at (b) the lowest possible cost, has three parts:
> 1. Buying only what we need to achieve balanced readiness.
> 2. Buying at the lowest sound price.
> 3. Reducing operating costs through termination of unnecessary operations, standardization and consolidation.

Part 1 includes more precise analysis of weapon requirements for combat effectiveness, increased use of excess inventories, and elimination of so-called goldplating. Part 2 means shifting from the cost-plus contracting used in the missile-race era to buying on the basis of lowest sound price, giving bonuses for equipment performance exceeding contract specification, and utilizing similar industry incentives to do a better job. Part 3 includes base closings, cutting down overhead costs, and other administrative streamlining actions.

After about a year in operation, McNamara's Cost Reduction Program began to take on some of the characteristics of a crusade, with the military and civilian employees of the Department regularly exceeding goals. By fiscal year 1966, Defense was cutting costs and avoiding unnecessary spending at the rate of $4.5 billion a year. In 1966, it estimated annual recurring savings would rise to $6.1 billion by fiscal 1969 and hold for each year thereafter. In fact, the program was so successful that Defense Department critics began challenging the validity of claims for it, labeling them "inflated" and pointing to the difference between real "savings" per item (against what had been spent for the same thing before) and "cost avoidance" (deciding not to buy something new).*

A group of Defense Department auditors, independent of the Cost Reduction Program and responsible for enforcing established criteria on what constitutes savings, in fiscal 1966 rejected 40 per cent of service logistics managers' claimed economies. And a private accounting firm's investigation has concluded that Defense Department cost reductions are "logical and reasonable" and that the program "has achieved the purpose intended." Still, criticism of Pentagon claims has persisted, leading McNamara to answer the belittlers:

> Even with hindsight, we could not have significantly improved on the overall performance of the Cost Reduction Program during the past five years. Certainly, mistakes have been made. In some cases savings have been reported and accepted that should not have been. But in monetary value these are minor indeed [3 per cent to 4 per cent of the cumulative $14 billion saving claimed in the program's first five years]. . . . It is my intention to ensure that there is no relaxation of effort and that further progress is achieved in the year ahead.

Lest this emphasis on cost reduction suggest that the Department was doing a poor management job prior to 1961, it should be pointed out that the effort simply tightened up internal operations; it did not completely revolutionize them. In fiscal 1960, for instance, the Defense Department let approximately 6 million contracts worth $22.9 billion. In fiscal 1966, it let 11 million contracts worth $37.2 billion. Yet, in both years, the percentage awarded industry by competitive bidding, on a price or other basis, was about 93–95.

---

* Both kinds of savings, taken together, were what made the $4.5 billion. The critics complained that cost avoidance could not be considered savings since it was not a reduction from what had been spent before. To this objection one angry Pentagon reaction was, "That's about like my wife demanding a $900 mink coat, my telling her she can have a $50 cloth coat instead —and somebody trying to tell me I didn't save $850!"

The Cost Reduction Program was not the Defense Department management's only approach to achieving economy. A whole series of changed philosophical approaches to procurement included, for example, one that was not really new. The Department began to worry again about what a proposed new weapon would cost during its total life in the military inventory, not just what industry said it would cost to buy it initially. It began to buy more of the kind of quality equipment that had, say, a 20 per cent higher initial purchase price than a substitute, but that worked twice as long before it wore out.

The supply and logistics end of the business was shaken also. Stock inventory control, requisition procedures, and record keeping began to be standardized, automated, and computerized. The advent of huge air transports and "fast deployment logistics ships" brought with them new thinking about where to store supplies and how and when to transport them for economy and efficiency.

Probably the most significant impact of the new management thinking in the early 1960's was in the research and development end of the business. It was here that the missile race had taught most of the hard lessons on what not to do and on what was needed. Since R&D engineers had always been somewhat aloof from the procurement and supply specialists and since neither group had been especially communicative with the combat command users of equipment, the almost inevitable results had been development costs running as much as 4,000 per cent of what original estimates had said they would, engineering designs turning out to be unfeasible for production, too much of some spare parts and too little of others being stocked, and many other related, costly errors. Most could have been avoided had the three elements of control each known what the other was doing.

Steps were taken to bring the whole team closer together. For example, R&D experts began to learn as much about procurement techniques as procurement experts knew. Components once designed with all sorts of supply headaches built in (simply because the engineer didn't understand the support problem) were redesigned or designed at the outset so that maintenance would be easy, not difficult. A host of management controls were set up. This "management tool chest," as some Defense Department executives were soon calling it, was essentially a set of techniques for linking the decision-maker at the top more closely with field level personnel carrying out projects. Most of these tools were printed paper: technical development master plans defining what needed doing on a project and grading progress; cost information; contractor performance evaluation; weapon configuration controls; and cost-effectiveness analysis.

PERT

Probably one of the most important, and certainly one of the best publicized, was called the Program Evaluation and Review Technique (PERT). It was a legacy to Defense from the Navy Special Projects Office, which gave it major credit for their Polaris program being one of the few complex development actions, missile or otherwise, in the military to stay within its original budget and beat its original due date for completion. PERT is, basically, a plan drawn up in advance showing what steps have to be taken to reach a given objective; how each step affects and is affected by the others; which are the most important, i.e., "pacing," milestone actions; and with an estimated cost and completion time for each. Common sense suggests that this is the kind of thinking any good project leader would do before starting to work. But not enough had. Moreover, even when the theory had been followed in general, the precise, detailed planning required to draw a PERT chart had not been attempted.

For example, in 1961, when McNamara cancelled a fifteen-year-old project (that had cost $1 billion) to develop a nuclear-powered aircraft, he noted, in testimony before Congress' Joint Economic Committee, that "throughout its history the program was characterized by attempts to find short cuts to early flight. Only a relatively small fraction of the money expended was applied to the really critical pacing item, namely the development of an efficient reactor with a potentially high performance." A PERT plan, sketched by experts in the field, would have highlighted that need. "Prior planning, and even feasibility testing of 'pacing components,' " said McNamara, "are a lot cheaper than having to reorient, stretch out, or terminate expensive projects after they have been started."

Underscoring the changes in R&D management was a basic conclusion about what the missile race had, or had not, meant in over-all military research and development planning. Developments such as hydrogen bombs and ICBM's add a new dimension to military capability and therefore justify great costs, McNamara testified, but such developments are rare. He pointed out that "the typical development promises, if successful, to achieve a capability that can also be achieved in other ways or represents an improvement of [relatively] modest proportions. In these cases, the urgency is not as great and the employment of a more measured and orderly approach to development and production is fully justified."

The solution, in R&D terms, he added, was a set of three basic decision-guiding policies: first, a "technical building block" approach to gaining new scientific and engineering knowledge; second, careful definition of a project's proposed development, once technology promised that a go-ahead would pay off in improved combat capability; and, third, eliminating parallel projects that would only achieve the same ends. In simplest terms, the "building blocks" are the new technologies and essential components—developed, tested, and proven—necessary to assemble a totally new weapon system. And McNamara went on to say: "We cannot do a proper job of engineering development, least of all operational systems development, unless these building blocks are available. Lack of attention to this principle in the past has been one of the major causes of waste and inefficiency. . . ."

There are four categories of building blocks: research, exploratory development, advanced development, and engineering development. The first category—research—is the fund of basic knowledge across the entire spectrum of science and technology. Defense work here covers literally thousands of individual tasks and projects, each requiring relatively small amounts of money to support, in disciplines such as materials, general physics, chemistry, oceanography, biology, etc. From this realm of ideas, theory, and basic measurements, new devices and inventions needed for development of future weapons will eventually emerge. This building block is handled almost entirely by educational and nonprofit institutions and is monitored at the Defense Secretary's office on a level-of-effort basis, rather than by carefully watching each individual project. Although extremely important for the long term, it is also inexpensive, costing less than 10 per cent of the annual spending total for all R&D building block categories.

Exploratory development emphasizes invention and exploration of various approaches to specific problems, up to the point of demonstrating feasibility with a so-called bread-board and even, occasionally, prototype components and subsystems. Although aimed, like pure research, at expanding technological knowledge, the goal here is also to produce materials, components, and devices that will have directly useful application to new military weapons and equipment. The more than 800 individual projects in this building block add up to about 15 per cent of the entire R&D cost—the average project requiring about $1.3 million annually. About 40 per cent of the work is done by military "in-house" laboratories,

50 per cent is contracted out to industry, and the remainder performed by educational and nonprofit institutions. Work on laser beam devices and boron fiber materials are two of the better publicized examples that fall into this category.

Advanced development includes projects that have advanced to a point where development of experimental hardware for technical or operational demonstration is required to determine whether the item should be designed or engineered for eventual service use. In contrast to engineering development, in which design specifications are employed, advanced development permits use of performance specifications, thus allowing the engineer greater latitude in meeting operational needs and encouraging innovation. A smaller number of projects are funded than in the two previous categories, but their total cost is higher. For instance, $1.25 billion will be spent in fiscal 1968 alone on projects promising enough to have climbed to this building block level. Here, most "pacing" problems, crucial to developing effective operational weapon systems, are uncovered. (For instance, work at this level of effort on vertical-takeoff-and-landing aircraft revealed that a great deal more research and exploratory development was needed, especially on propulsion systems, before such aircraft would be ready for full-scale engineering development.)

Engineering development includes projects being engineered for service use, but which have not yet been approved for production and development. Although only a relative handful of projects are in this category, each one costs several million dollars, and the total adds up to a lion's share of the R&D budget. The final product in each case is a prototype, which then awaits top management approval to go into operational production. The highly publicized anti-ballistic-missile system is probably the best known example in this group.

Total costs for all R&D building blocks, plus $1.2 billion in management and support costs (primarily to operate test and evaluation ranges such as the Cape Kennedy facility in Florida) amounted to $5.8 billion in fiscal 1968.*

Beyond these building block categories, there is another level of R&D known as operational systems development. The slightly more than $2 billion spent on it in each of the past few years is to cover development costs of ironing out engineering "bugs" of systems already approved for operational deployment.

Ideally, when R&D experts are working correctly in their environment, as most of them are, they trade information and opinions continually with intelligence experts (for threat estimates) and strategic and tactical experts (who spell out military requirements for handling the threats).

But there is no set procedural pattern used to evolve weapon systems out of this interaction, any more than a football team uses only one play to score touchdowns. There are sets of prescribed patterns, of course; otherwise, the Defense Department's running of its weapon development programs would break down in confusion. But each set has built into it considerable flexibility for the exercise of individual judgment, initiative, and variation on the main procedural theme, because the object is not to be administratively uniform but to get the right weapon answer.

The case history of any one weapon system development will differ either slightly or considerably, compared to others, depending on the kind and importance of the weapon itself. Policy and procedural doctrine on how development work is to be done is only a guideline. There is still plenty of room to maneuver within that boundary.

For instance, although many of the procedural and man-

* The Defense Department also asked for and received from Congress, as it does every year, a $125 million emergency fund plus authority to transfer another $150 million out of total congressional appropriations for R&D from one project to another later in the year. The idea is to give the Department some flexibility, without having to return for congressional approval each time it wishes to take advantage of a sudden scientific or engineering breakthrough.

agement techniques used in weapon system development evolved during and as a result of the missile race in the late 1950's, many of the more important missile developments themselves often violated several elements of the doctrine. This was especially true when the comparative costs of different missile problem solutions were evaluated. Sometimes the cost of a development wasn't considered at all, simply because the urgency of completing the development was so overriding that the price tag was incidental. More recently, when the Army sought a major technological improvement in their 1¼-ton truck (commonly called the "Jeep"), doctrine prescribed that they should follow what is called a "project definition procedure" because of the engineering unknowns they would theoretically be trying to solve. In fact, they used a two-step, formal advertised bid procedure because, said one automotive engineer, "Until you change the wheel and the internal combustion engine, you just won't get any major technological breakthroughs in trucks."

A new weapon proposal can come from any one or several of many sources. It starts with an idea. The motivation for the idea is either to satisfy a recognized military need by finding appropriate technology or to find a profitable military use for an exciting new technological capability. The latter motivation comes most often from the building blocks, although private funding, especially from heavily defense-oriented industries, produces some as well. Motivation for the former can come from just about anyone, from the combat commands, from industry, from nonprofit institutions, from other government agencies, and from within the R&D side of the Defense Department itself.

As the idea germinates, it is pumped into what is usually called the Operational Requirements Office in each of the military services as a "required operational capability" document. Anyone of authority in Defense can write one, in theory; although the Requirements Office, proficient in such things, usually handles the final draft. "Required" implies more at this stage, however, than is actually the case. At this point, it is largely only the writer's opinion of what is a military deficiency that needs to be overcome. Requirements personnel and planning experts work out several possible approaches to satisfy the "requirement." By study and analysis, the service concerned selects one possible solution to propose to the Office of the Secretary of Defense.

It is at this point that the greatest change in handling evaluation and approval of operational requirements has occurred in recent years. Approval authority to proceed with most requirement-solving programs is now located no lower in the Defense management pyramid than a military department's Pentagon staff (military field commands once had more autonomy), and, in many cases, no new projects start without approval from the Office of the Secretary of Defense.* Moreover, at frequent points along the development path, additional okays are needed. It is not enough simply to delineate the military problem and demonstrate how the proposed system will solve it. All the alternatives that were considered by the service must be identified and explanations given on why the rejected ones were eliminated. Even then, approval is far from assured.

The governing Defense Department Directive 3200.9 says:

Conditional approval to proceed with an Engineering Development will depend on evidence that the concept formulation has proven: primarily engineering rather than experimental effort is

* Present policy is that all new, or major, modifications to existing engineering developments or operational systems developments that will cost more than $25 million in total R&D or $100 million in production will be approved at the Secretary's level, as will the industry contractor selections made later—practically speaking, every project of any current significance. In addition, the services make a regular practice of keeping Research and Engineering and the Joint Staff informally briefed on promising possibilities in the R&D categories of exploratory and advanced development, in the hope that when the time comes to move into full-fledged development for operational deployment, there will be fewer questions to answer and less opposition to combat.

required, and the technology needed is sufficiently in hand; the mission and performance envelopes are defined; the best technical approaches have been selected; a thorough trade-off analysis [against alternative solutions] has been made; the cost effectiveness of the proposed item is better in relationship to the cost effectiveness of competing items on a Defense-wide [i.e., in the other services] basis; and cost and planned delivery estimates are credible and acceptable.

At the Office of the Secretary of Defense level, service analytical success in meeting these criteria will be checked. Where they have fallen short, the Secretary's office will do the justification, or ask the service to do it over, or both. Thus, until approved, a service "requirement" lacks stature and validity, and is best thought of only as a proposal. Formulating these proposals and then "selling" them is the mission of the requirements people in the service, usually with a lot of help from the other functional disciplines on the service headquarters staff and in its subordinate field commands, i.e., the experts in research and development, planning, combat operations, etc. As Air Force Lieutenant General Jack J. Catton, director of Aerospace Programs, noted:

> This means that advocacy is one of our principal functions. Since the Air Force, as advocates, can no longer alone determine the factors essential to a decision about [going ahead with] a weapon system, we have to furnish OSD [Office of the Secretary of Defense], as judge, the considerations which OSD believes most relevant. We have to strengthen them where OSD feels they are weakest, and we try to cast them in terms so as to communicate as effectively as possible.

This is a significant change from where approval power lay in the 1950's and is a major example of what centralization of Defense Department authority has meant.

The most critical decision in the life of a new system, of course, is the first decision that commits major quantities of resources—the decision to begin engineering development.

Prior to that decision, the "advocacy" work involves formal efforts in exploratory and advanced development to lessen the technical risk, studies, analyses, experimental tests, and whatever else is necessary to comply with the six Directive 3200.9 prerequisites noted above and supplemented by a good deal of informal "soft sell" communication from the services to the Office of the Secretary.

If and when approval comes, the weapon system proposal moves into what is known as the "contract definition" stage. A total development plan is put together, including, for potential contractors among others, a detailed work statement. By now, a project officer has been named and has begun pushing the weapon system toward maturity. The work statement is sent out to contractors, previously rated qualified to do the work, along with a request for their bid on what they would charge in time and money (either a fixed price or, because there are still many unknowns, a cost-plus-fee figure) to achieve the specified equipment performance. The replies are reviewed, and rated in almost excruciating detail by an evaluation board, whose five criteria are: approach to the technical problems; company organizational and management approach to the over-all development plan; competency of the industry personnel to be assigned to the project; realism of planning and cost; past company performance on similar projects.*

These analyses are passed up through review echelons until they reach the source selection authority specified when approval for contract definition was granted in the first place. Since the beginning of the contractor proposal evaluation and review, it has been assumed by the military department involved that all firms requested to bid would be able to deliver, given enough time and money. The basic purpose of the

* It should be pointed out this procurement method is only used in a few of the eighteen different ways that the Defense Department is permitted by Congress to procure goods and services; however, it is the source selection system used on important, complex weapon systems. Other procurement techniques are mainly for more mundane items, like groceries.

source selection process is simply to find the contractor or contractors most likely to deliver on time within an acceptable price the minimum equipment performance required. Once contractors are picked, the services and the Office of the Secretary continue to watch the program carefully—demanding progress reports, developing logistics and support plans for the day when the military accepts delivery of finished operational copies, staying current with new technological developments that the original weapon system configuration might profitably be redesigned to accept, and monitoring related problems.

Necessarily, this brief description has hit only the highest spots in a weapon system evolution. The whole routine is so complex that it defies comprehension. It was complex before the missile race began. It became more complex during the race, when the foregoing method of source selection was created. Today, it is even more complex. The entire procedure is a jungle of paperwork, replete with confusing and seemingly contradictory instructions in clauses, subclauses, and sub-subclauses that even the most expert, experienced personnel in the system often find hard to comprehend.

IMPACT OF MISSILES ON STRATEGY

Missiles revolutionized more than just military methods of doing business. No weapon is approved for creation solely because it is technologically fascinating. To survive into production, it must fit into a larger scheme.

Missiles had an impact first of all on strategic planning. Surprisingly, there were no very thorough or comprehensive arrangements to utilize missilery. Military writer Richard Fryklund has commented:

> When the Soviet Union exploded its first nuclear bomb in September, 1949, it was clear to Pentagon planners that the existing

American strategy would soon become suicidal; because as soon as the Soviets built a few bombs and long-range bombers they would be able to punish our cities terribly for any attack on theirs. Knowing, as the Truman Administration did, that the strategy was an impossible one, but that it would take three or four years to change weapons and control systems, Pentagon officers should have been assigned immediately to work out an effective strategy and buy the weapons.

Of course, this was not done. Rather, the Truman Administration built a force for large-scale devastation. By 1954 when our intelligence told us that the Soviets had A-bombs and H-bombs and enough airplanes to carry a number of them to American cities (even if only on one-way revenge missions for an attack by America on the Soviet motherland), the Eisenhower Administration should have seen that there was no rational alternative to a nuclear war strategy based on control and restraint. What that Administration actually did, however, was to plan a war of massive retaliatory devastation and then rely on . . . [only the threat of it to prevent attack and] to save our lives.

In the late 1950's, the Eisenhower Administration did announce that a Russian attack by conventional forces might only result in U.S. use of tactical, rather than strategic, nuclear retaliatory weapons. This announcement somehow made people think that the exchange would be less ominous to world survival. But, considering that tactical nuclear explosives by then were more powerful than the Hiroshima bomb, military strategists, honest at least with themselves, privately contended that any use of any size nuclear weapons by either side would almost inevitably escalate into all-out atomic attack, bent not on wiping out military targets but on wholesale destruction of a nation's cities and society. Fryklund added:

> It was not until late in the first year of the Kennedy Administration that the knowledgeable bettors began shifting their money to a "No-City" strategy. . . . The Services, civilian officials, Congressmen, and the public seemed to believe that to

close the expected gap would solve the nuclear-war problems. They wanted more, or lots more, missiles without a rational plan for using the missiles in time of war. Fortunately, however, it became clear early in 1961 that the gap probably was not going to appear. The strategy and the weapons to go with it could be evaluated on the basis of potential use against specific [military] targets, [rather than on the basis of] their value in a blind numbers race with the Soviets.*

One change, among the hundreds of others big and small, wrought in the military by the nuclear age, is that the choices of what weapons will be used in a contest are no longer military, but, rather, political decisions. In the end, enough strategic offensive missiles (primarily Minuteman and Polaris —both the original models and later, vastly improved versions) were purchased or programed into the inventory for the years following 1962 so that U.S. strategists (the President, the Secretary of Defense, and the Secretary of State) had enough to counterattack, first, against Soviet military targets only; then, enough additional missiles to destroy Russia as a viable socioeconomic civilization if the first counterattack did not end the war; and, finally, enough beyond that to succeed on both plans of attack if the most pessimistic (and unlikely) estimates of what could happen in a nuclear war turned out to be correct.† There were bitter internal debates over this course of action as the decisions were being made and the evolving strategy promulgated. Yet, within three years after numerical superiority in missiles was reached and strategy began to crystallize, it became clear to thoughtful Americans (and even Russians, the Pentagon believed) that there was no longer any rational validity in contemplating the use of nuclear war as an instrument of foreign policy. A corollary

* Richard Fryklund, *100 Million Lives, Maximum Survival in a Nuclear War* (New York: Macmillan, 1962), p. 162, *et seq.*

† None of this capability took into account, at least in planning and procurement of forces, the nuclear capability of the tactical forces, which was very great indeed.

to that was the belief that, as long as both sides maintained a vigilant watch over the moves of the other, neither side would be able to upset that balance.

This thinking assumed no technological breakthrough, from the U.S. viewpoint, in anti-ballistic-missile defensive capability. To guard against the possibility of a scientific development that could be virtually 100 per cent effective in neutralizing or destroying all the enemy's attacking strategic offensive missiles, the United States continued to spend hundreds of millions of dollars each year in research and development (a total of about $4 billion from 1955 through 1966 alone) on antimissile systems to assure, as far as humanly possible, that such a defense would be achieved by the United States first, if it was achieved by anyone. The Department of Defense also improved offensive strength at the same time in, for instance, warhead penetration aids. In each periodic review, the conclusion was regularly reached at highest government levels—at least, as of 1967—that "the best defense is still a good offense."

The Tendency To Mimic

But having adequate antimissile capability and being able to convince the nation that it had it, were two different things, the Defense Department discovered. New debates began, fostered partly by a lack of expert understanding, even in Congress, about the details of the subject and partly by a characteristic national tendency to want to do something either just because it could be done or because someone else (e.g., Russia) was already doing it. In an article, "Planning Our Military Forces," Director of Defense Research and Engineering, and later Secretary of the Air Force, Harold Brown noted:

> Modern weapons need not of themselves inexorably beget more sophisticated, expensive and destructive devices. It is true that

pressures exist which, if unrestrained, would needlessly prolifer-
ate and duplicate weapon designs. There is a tendency to do what
potential opponents are doing, or thought to be doing, or predicted to be able to do. . . . The development community
argues too often for going ahead "because you can do it." This
is a fine reason for mountain climbing, but not for multibillion
dollar development programs.

It has been, and still is, difficult to avoid this pitfall. When
the Russians developed their own atomic bomb, the U.S.
answer was to build the more powerful hydrogen bomb. When
the Soviet Union produced this too, the U.S. answer was to
build more intercontinental-range bombers to carry the weapon
—not because Russian defenses against the bomber were that
much improved, but, because, in the public mind at least,
the Russians were building bombers too. And congressional
pressures on the Defense Department to produce large quantities of already obsolete Atlas ICBM's in 1957–59 were predicated on the same kind of thinking: the United States must
because, allegedly, the Russians were.

The extreme risk in such mimic strategy is that it tends to
force the expenditure of resources for all the wrong reasons.
At the cost of considerable personal criticism and abuse,
Defense Department planners have generally resisted these
pressures. In 1965, when the Pentagon announced that the
Russians would deploy a small anti-ballistic-missile defense
system within two years, an outspoken insistence on an
answering U.S. deployment reached an almost unbearable
crescendo. Secretary McNamara resisted. Eventually, in 1967,
he announced plans for deploying a limited ABM (as the
Pentagon calls anti-ballistic-missile defense), but he made
plain his strong personal opposition to any extension of the
relatively limited program. (See also Chapter X.) From the
very start of this new defensive missile competition, although
he conceded that the Russians apparently believe the deployment of antimissile missiles would reduce the possible extent

of damage to their country in the event of war, he has favored sticking to offensive, rather than defensive, investment. In a 1966 interview with the British Broadcasting Corporation's James Mossman, he stated:

I don't believe they [the Russians] think it would work to the extent of making nuclear war acceptable. The reason I say that is that they have been almost fanatical on the subject of defense for years. Over the past decade or decade and a half they have spent perhaps two and a half times as much as we have spent on air defense [against strategic bombers]. And yet, they must know that that air defense was sievelike, and I mean literally sievelike, because we always had the capability to penetrate it. There was never any doubt in our mind and I don't believe there was any doubt in their minds. At no time during that decade and a half . . . did they ever indicate they thought we lacked a capability to deter their strike against us [by penetrating their defense in retaliation and inflicting unacceptable damage]. And if we had that capability to deter it, . . . they were in effect admitting . . . we could penetrate their defense.

POLICY TODAY: THE 1968 POSTURE STATEMENT

Almost wearily, in testimony before a joint session of the Senate Armed Services Committee and the Senate Subcommittee on Department of Defense appropriations on the fiscal year 1968–72 Department program and 1968 budget, McNamara reiterated the basic ground rules of what he called the "General Nuclear War Problem," saying that

our general nuclear war forces should have two basic capabilities:

1. To deter deliberate nuclear attack upon the United States and its Allies by maintaining, continuously, a highly reliable ability to inflict an unacceptable degree of damage upon any single aggressor, or combination of aggressors, at any time during the course of a strategic nuclear exchange, even after absorbing a surprise first strike.

2. In the event [that deterrent failed and] such a war never-

theless occurred, to limit damage to our population and industrial capacity.

The first capability we call "Assured Destruction" and the second "Damage Limitation." . . . As long as deterrence of a deliberate Soviet (or Red Chinese) nuclear attack upon the United States or its Allies is the overriding objective of our strategic forces, the capability for "Assured Destruction" must receive the first call on all of our resources and must be provided regardless of the costs and the difficulties involved. "Damage Limiting" programs, no matter how much we spend on them, can never substitute for an Assured Destruction capability in the deterrent role. It is our ability to destroy an attacker as a viable twentieth-century nation that provides the deterrent, not our ability to partially limit damage to ourselves.

What kind and amount of destruction we would have to be able to inflict on an attacker to provide this deterrent cannot be answered precisely. However, it seems reasonable to assume that in the case of the Soviet Union, the destruction of, say, one-fifth to one-fourth of its population and one-half to two-thirds of its industrial capacity would mean its elimination as a major power for many years. Such a level of destruction would certainly represent intolerable punishment to any industrialized nation and thus should serve as an effective deterrent to the deliberate initiation of a nuclear attack on the United States or its Allies. . . .

Once sufficient forces have been procured to give us high confidence of achieving our Assured Destruction objective (which the U.S. today has), we can then consider the kinds and amounts of forces which might be added to reduce damage to our population and industry in the event deterrence fails. But here we must note another important point, namely, the possible interaction of our strategic programs with those of the Soviet Union. If the general nuclear policy of the Soviet Union *also* has as its objective the deterrence of a U.S. first strike (which I believe to be the case), then we must assume that any attempt on our part to reduce damage to ourselves (to what they would estimate we might consider an "acceptable level") would put pressure on them to strive for an offsetting improvement in their [attacking] forces. Conversely, an increase in their Damage Limiting capability would require us to make greater investments in Assured Destruction.

McNamara's telling argument here is that what deters nuclear aggression is a potential attacker's certain knowledge that he will be committing national suicide if he attacks, regardless of what damage he may first wreak on the attacked nation. Once both sides achieve that level of destructive capability, according to the theory, any attempts by either to gain an edge and upset the balance will fail, because the other side must react to restore the balance. In an interview with this author, McNamara also said:

> I don't believe any responsible group of people in this country, or any responsible leader, scientific or political or military, believes that any anti-ballistic-missile defense we could presently contemplate (including one that some estimates said would cost $40 billion) would so reduce damage to this nation as to make nuclear war acceptable. We would be lying to the American people if we told them it would.

The issues in the missile race today are of paramount importance—and very hard to evaluate. As Secretary of the Air Force Brown wrote, at an earlier date:

> We may know with reasonable precision how many missiles the Soviets will have in their active force a year or two from now, because they must already have begun work on their deployment. We may have a fair idea how many they will have four or even five years from now, though a less precise idea of what kind of missiles and what their payloads will be. Yet in fact we know very little about how many or what kind of missiles the Russians will have ten years from now, because they probably have not reached a decision themselves. And even if they have, they might change their minds. Consequently, estimates beyond the immediate future enter, at best, a realm of educated extrapolation. . . .
>
> [Thus] our objective in military planning should be to provide

ourselves with capacity to take initiatives of our own, or to make timely responses to the force deployments of others at later times, as their actions inevitably become much clearer to us.

For its record over the past twenty years, in general, and during the period of the missile revolution, in particular, the Defense Department has sometimes deserved black marks for inefficiency and failure to anticipate comprehensively an impending crisis. But in terms of how effectively it has supported the twin foreign-policy objectives of containing the expansion by force of Communism and helping maintain or restore peace in an unstable world, the record shows that, first and foremost, whatever else may have been said about the adequateness of the Department's nuclear strength and how "it should have been" even better, there has been no nuclear war. This fact argues strongly that U.S. nuclear forces have been convincing to the Communists. And, certainly, the psychological effectiveness of this deterrent has been put to the test often enough in the past twenty years.

Under an umbrella of world respect for nuclear prowess by whoever displays it, the U.S. has been able to handle international brush fires, generally with success. During each crisis, military men have held their breath and the public has fretted afterward, about what might have happened "if." But defeat was averted, however narrowly, in Korea in 1950–53, and the ultimate United Nations objective—stalemate—was achieved, tense and uneasy though it was and is, even today. Marines reached Lebanon in time with adequate force, or the threat of it, in 1958, to quiet an uprising that otherwise might have sparked general war throughout the Middle East. A U.S. attempt to aid Cuban exiles in recapturing their home island from the Communists ended in disaster in 1961, but, in subsequent years, a blockade* of Cuba and the rushing of Amer-

---

* Government semanticists prefer the word "quarantine"—a subtlety largely lost to the public. Only missile-carrying ships were prevented from docking at Cuban ports.

ican forces into the Panama Canal Zone and the Dominican Republic to put down threatened or actual armed insurrection demonstrated both the speed and power with which U.S. forces could react once given the order. The toughest test of U.S. military capability to date has been the Viet-Nam escalation, coming as it did just as the Defense Department was completing the build-up of all its forces to fulfill a strategy of flexible response for the whole range of warfare—from guerrilla to nuclear.

In all these challenges, and more than ever in Viet-Nam, most, if not all, of the Defense Department's troubles arise from the requirement that, in the missile age, it mesh with other elements of the national security organization to support foreign policy and the domestic economy. To quote Secretary of the Air Force Brown once again:

> Until greater congruity of purpose exists among nations, military forces will continue to be a foundation of policy. We must be wise enough to manage the interaction between weapons development and defense policy so that our weapons are always responsive to policy and our policy is based on a full consideration of the options made available by technology. This will remain a supreme challenge to policy-makers, who from a position of final responsibility must look at a partially obscure tomorrow and a distant future that seems opaque. They will find, almost invariably, that it is easier to produce military hardware than it is to know what policy to follow.

VII

Interrelationship
with Other Agencies

To support the nation's foreign policy, the military has developed what it calls "a strategy of flexible response." President Kennedy enunciated the philosophy underlying that strategy in a special message on the Defense budget to Congress on March 28, 1961, when he set forth the following "series of essential guidelines and standards to be followed by all civilian and military personnel who work on behalf of our nation's security":

1. The primary purpose of our arms is peace, not war.
2. Our arms will never be used to strike the first blow in any attack.
3. Our arms must be adequate to meet our commitments and ensure our security, without being bound by arbitrary budget ceilings.
4. Our arms must be subject to ultimate civilian control and command at all times, in war as well as peace.
5. Our strategic arms and defenses must be adequate to deter any deliberate nuclear attack on the United States or our allies.
6. The strength and deployment of our forces in combination with those of our allies should be sufficiently powerful and mobile to prevent the steady erosion of the Free World through limited wars; and it is this role that should constitute the primary mission of our overseas forces.

7. Our defense posture must be both flexible and determined.

8. Our defense posture must be designed to reduce the danger of irrational or unpremeditated general war—the danger of an unnecessary escalation of a small war into a larger one, or of miscalculation or misinterpretation of an incident or enemy intention.

At the same time, Kennedy stressed the urgent need for eliminating from the Defense Department waste, duplication, and projects of only marginal usefulness. This, he told the Congress,

> is a long and arduous undertaking, resisted by special arguments and interests from economic, military, technical and other special groups. There are hundreds of ways, most of them with some merit, for spending billions of dollars on defense; and it is understandable that every critic of this Budget will have a strong preference for economy on some expenditures other than those that affect his branch of the Service, or his plant, or his community.
>
> But hard decisions must be made. Unneeded facilities or projects must be phased out. The defense establishment must be lean and fit, efficient and effective, always adjusting to new opportunities and advances, and planning for the future. The national interest must be weighed against special or local interest.

For all the fanfare that announcement provoked (and the several-billion-dollar increase in Defense spending it heralded), the Kennedy policy was not much different than Eisenhower's "New Look" in 1953 or the "balanced-forces" concept of Forrestal in 1948—at least not in intent. What had changed was the judgment of a new President on how much would be required of the nation's military force in lieu of its other national security assets; and how much would be necessary to complement the probable mutual security contributions of its world allies. In simplest terms, the Kennedy judgment was that the Defense Department needed more power, especially for those levels of likely conflict below strategic nuclear war. One major reason for this change was the by then long-standing U.S. success in maintaining a credible deterrent to nuclear attack.

There is a significant limit to a nuclear deterrent's effectiveness. It cannot prevent brush-fire or even rather large-scale conventional wars, since no aggressor possessing a nuclear force could be deterred from posing a lesser danger by its victim's bluffing about nuclear retaliation. In other words, the United States was not likely to inflict nuclear destruction on Moscow, and lose its own cities in return, over a Communist invasion of Formosa, any more than the Russians would risk the possible loss of Moscow to gain a foothold in Latin America. Thus, the United States needed non-nuclear forces capable of handling small crises before they grew into big ones.

The nuclear stalemate had focused national attention on a need to define more exactly the philosophy of a strategy of flexible response beyond the building of a variety of military capabilities to handle a variety of threats. The thorough reappraisal that went into redefining earlier strategy also resulted in a more precise restatement of another generally accepted, basic policy. As early as the 1947 National Security Act, the organization for national security was clearly spelled out as one encompassing not just the military establishment alone. Moreover, combat capability was not considered by any means the sole instrument of foreign policy, important though it is. Nor was, and is, the Defense Department the only adviser to the President on what national security policy and plans should be. Indeed, "policy" itself is not a rock-ribbed dictum from on high about how, specifically, the government is to act, but, rather, a pronouncement of general patterns of behavior that leadership desires.

Policy is the guideline, but it has something less than the impact of the Ten Commandments in dictating exactly what all the government agencies concerned with national security will do at which times in relation to each other in a given world situation. This flexible attitude is necessary; otherwise, the government would find little room to maneuver, to exercise its most important asset—the judgment, experience, and initiative of its talented people. But such flexibility places a great premium on communication of understanding about common intent, mutual goals, and shared interest among the government elements involved in or responsible for a role in national security. The proper meshing of these elements would be tough enough if all the nuances of national security policy were clearly and identically understood by all the hundreds of thousands of authorities in or closely related to government who are charged with seeing that policy is carried out. Unfortunately, such perfect like-mindedness is not humanly possible in government, any more than it is in any other large, complex organization. In fact, the natural inclination of the team is to splinter apart rather than pull together. Each element tends to push its own special interests.

This natural state of individual government agency motivation is, for the President and Congress, not at all unlike the problem the Secretary of Defense faces within his own department, whipping, cajoling, and inspiring its various units into coordinated cohesion. And, as in Defense itself, this "tendency to suboptimize" is a natural breeding ground for contradiction between policy and performance, for confusion in the ranks, for controversy over who should be "team captain" on any given project. National security policy formulation and execution is rarely a precise exercise resulting in a neat, clean rapier thrust into a problem. More often, it is a blunt, sledge-hammer effort, and frequently the right hand and the left fail even to swing in the same direction, let alone in unison.

Although the misfirings that frequently occur are not condoned even among government bureaucrats, who might be expected to defend them, it is understandable that on occasion odd things happen: policy says that the products of space research will be used for peaceful purposes, yet the Defense Department forbids export of space equipment to foreign allies because of its military value; the State Department sells arms to an independent foreign nation to "help stabilize the government," while the U.S. Army is pleading for all the manufacturer's production capacity to equip itself and other allies already in a war; the Defense Department urges an increase in NATO military strength, while the State Department fosters increased trade with East European Communist countries "because the Cold War is thawing"; the Defense Department attempts to increase industry profits to draw more qualified, competitive firms into bidding on military contracts, while the General Accounting Office fights to reduce the size of those profits; the State and Defense departments insist that economic and military aid to poor nations is the key to long-range U.S. security, while Congress turns down this "unrewarding giveaway." When such contradictions arise, it is hardly surprising that the government is accused of talking out of both sides of its mouth.* Theory says that foreign policy recommendations flow up from the State Department to the President and Congress. Once approved or modified, orders flow down to the various appropriate government agencies for the execution of those policies. But, in fact, policy evolves most often—and execution occurs always—as a result of continual interaction among all agencies having, or believing they have, a stake in national security.

RELATIONS WITH THE WHITE HOUSE

How strong a role the Defense Department plays in this awesomely complex tangle depends first and foremost on the Defense Secretary's and the Department's relationship with

---

* Moreover, when the incidence of contradiction begins to outweigh the incidence of consistency in interagency behavior, charges of "a credibility gap" are heard. In fact, that "gap" is not the product of skulduggery, as the charges often imply, so much as it is a product simply of bad management, poor communication, and lack of interagency coordination.

the Presidency, both personally and organizationally. Rapport, or the lack of it, between the two offices affects not only the Defense Secretary's ability to control his own organization, but also his influence in foreign policy deliberations. Moreover, the strength or weakness of that liaison filters down among the Defense staff elements. If "the Boss" is believed closely attuned to his President's wave length, his reputation provides a power base that staff officers use to negotiate vigorously with their counterparts in the State Department and elsewhere. If the Secretary is considered "out of grace" with the White House, his staff subordinates listen more and talk less—or look for some stronger platform, such as Congress, from which to push their favored programs.

"I couldn't accomplish anything over here without Presidential support," said Defense Secretary McNamara once. "It is absolutely fundamental. I wouldn't and couldn't stay here one minute without it."

There have been several examples of how the Secretary can lose his intragovernment effectiveness and tight internal control over the Department when he and the President don't have a close working relationship. In 1948, for instance, Secretary James Forrestal and President Harry S. Truman, never the best of friends anyway, finally fell completely apart (as Forrestal saw it) over the Secretary's insistence that the Defense Department be kept out of politics. Truman was considered an almost certain loser to Republican Thomas Dewey in that year's Presidential election and sought all the help he could find from anyone who could deliver, including his Cabinet officers. Forrestal refused. Worse, to Democratic politicians, he briefed candidate Dewey on the national security situation, a move interpreted at the time as virtual public announcement from Truman's own Administration that he was going to lose the election. Moreover, the military, battling each other and Truman for more funding, paid little attention to the ceiling on military spending. Truman would soon be out, they reasoned, so the ceiling obstacle would not be a problem much longer. (Republicans had indicated they would approve a Defense budget more than twice the $11 billion Truman said he would permit.) And Democrat Forrestal was not likely to remain in office under a Republican. This situation left Forrestal with few effective powers of either persuasion or command in high-level national security deliberations.

His successor, Louis Johnson, saw the Secretary's job as essentially one of carrying out the President's orders with tough determination. He appeared to take little interest in helping formulate policy except when it appeared that some other department, such as State—with which he had a running feud—might be intruding on his bailiwick. While his slashes at military spending stirred the military in some cases to near revolt, those economy decisions stuck because the President stood firmly behind him—until the Korean War broke out. Economy in Defense Department spending was blamed then (although the point was debatable) for permitting that surprise attack, and Johnson, the image of military frugality, became a scapegoat, actually for having carried out Truman's policy so well. Truman was pressured into letting him go.

The next two men to run the Defense Department, Marshall and Lovett, benefited, for a variety of reasons, from an almost kindred closeness to the President and, helped considerably by the military cohesion that a war always tends to inspire, had little difficulty exercising control. Wilson and McElroy worked principally, as had Johnson, at managerial aspects of their responsibility; after all, their primary military adviser was General-turned-President Eisenhower.

Not until Tom Gates, Eisenhower's last Defense Secretary, took over in 1959, armed with clear authority as Eisenhower's Pentagon commander and with the management weapons of the 1958 reorganization, did the Secretary's delegated and legislated powers begin to get full use. That general recognition of the Secretary as the President's "Deputy Commander-in-Chief"—in fact, not just in theory—was continued by both Presidents Kennedy and Johnson. Author Timothy Stanley has noted that "any student of defense and national security must undertake to understand the American Presidency, for here lies the heart of the Nation's decision-making machinery. . . . In considering the President and national security policy, it would be a mistake to stress only his role as the Nation's chief administrator and as Commander-in-Chief of the military forces."

A total of several hundred persons populate the peak of the sprawling organization known as the Executive Office of the President. Few of them devote all their time and attention solely to national security matters, but nearly all make some contribution, even if a relatively minor one. Although the Executive Office, itself, was not created until 1939, some of its subdivisions had been established earlier, either by legislative fiat or Presidential appointment of individuals as "special assistants." Taken together, all the divisions add up to a kind of holding company that monitors for the President important activities within the major agencies under his command. All of them have intricate interrelationships with the Department of Defense.

The Parts of the Presidency

The highest order of interdepartmental business is, of course, handled by the Cabinet, which has existed as a matter of custom and tradition since George Washington was President. It convenes and functions "at the pleasure of the President"; and it is in these meetings that the heads of the twelve executive departments—State; Treasury; Defense; Justice; the Post Office; Interior; Agriculture; Commerce; Labor; Health, Education, and Welfare; Housing and Urban Development; and Transportation—assist the President in deciding policy that affects them all and their work with each other.

Next in order of importance to the Department of Defense,

as to other departments and agencies, is the White House Office. Though no job description says so, the collection of special assistants who staff this office rank higher than do any other agencies or groups in the Executive Office of the President. They achieve rank and respect based on how much confidence and delegated authority the President vests personally in each one and how well that delegation is understood and accepted, especially by top staff members in the executive departments. A special assistant in the White House Office does not acquire power automatically. If, for instance, an aide to the Secretary of Defense appreciates and agrees with the merit of a particular man's being a Presidential special assistant for military or foreign affairs matters, he will work through that man to get White House approval of a project. If he does not, he'll try to have his Secretary of Defense handle the approval matter directly with the President, rather than, as one Pentagon veteran put it, "dealing with that political flak on the White House staff."

In addition to the Cabinet and the White House Office, there are the following to consider:

The Bureau of the Budget. Created by the Budget and Accounting Act of 1921, the Bureau was shifted over from the Treasury to the Executive Office in 1939—a move prompted mainly by the Bureau's acquisition, over the years, of many duties outside strictly budgetary matters. It holds hearings on the various executive department budget requests, and prepares the final budget for submission to Congress. In addition, once funds are appropriated, it reviews requests from the departments for fund apportionment. Probably the most important of its multitude of nonbudgetary functions is to coordinate and "clear" all legislative programs of the executive branch of government, whether they involve appropriations or not. This authority gives its decisions great weight in the determination and administration of national security policy.

The Council of Economic Advisers. Created by Congress in 1946, the Council's primary duty is to keep the President advised on the state of the national economy and to give him expert opinion on where it is headed in the future. Its role as a Presidential adviser is, philosophically, much like the Defense Secretary's in military matters.

The National Aeronautics and Space Council. Chaired by the Vice-President, the Council includes as members the heads of the State Department, the Defense Department, the Atomic Energy Commission, and the National Aeronautics and Space Administration. (NASA, like the Council, was created by Congress in 1958.) Although the U.S. space research program is ostensibly "for peaceful purposes," there is and always has been a great deal of military work in the field. Moreover, the aeronautics portion of this activity covers at least as much if not more technical effort on military aircraft than on civilian airplane developments.

The Office of Economic Opportunity. Set up in 1964, this office oversees certain aspects of the war on poverty, viz. the Job Corps program and other projects to train underprivileged and unskilled individuals. Under certain circumstances—providing trainee facilities, accepting trainees as military recruits, etc.—the Defense Department has assisted the OEO.

The Office of Emergency Planning. Established in 1961, the central purpose of this office is basically the same as that of the National Security Resources Board (NSRB) created in the 1947 National Security Act: to provide the President with an organizational coordination point for military and civilian war mobilization plans and problems. In 1950, the NSRB shared its mobilization responsibilities with two agencies, the Office of Defense Mobilization and the National Production Authority, created that year to direct Korean War mobilization. In 1953, the three were merged into the Office of Defense Mobilization, and it was expanded in 1958 to include civil defense programs as the Office of Civil and Defense

Mobilization. The present name and organization evolved when civil defense policy, plans, and projects were transferred to the Defense Department. Critics today question how much of real value the Office does that is not already done by a combination of various other government agencies.

The Office of Science and Technology. Since 1962, this office has been charged with assuring that science and technology are used effectively in the interests of national security and the general welfare.

The Office of the Special Representative for Trade Negotiations. Another relatively new office, the head of which holds ambassadorial rank, has as its mission the working out of international trade agreements with other nations, agreements that could have either direct or indirect bearing on Defense Department liability or interest in the countries concerned.

The Central Intelligence Agency (CIA). Created, along with the Defense Department and the National Security Council, by the National Security Act of 1947, the CIA theoretically reports to the President through the National Security Council. Actually, the CIA has become for all practical purposes an independent agency, especially since passage of the Central Intelligence Agency Act in 1949, granting it a number of important authorities to protect its confidential nature and permit it to perform independent overseas operations. Thus, it is both a "policy" and an "operating" agency. Its national intelligence estimates are the primary platform on which national security policy decisions are made.

The CIA sits at the top of the government "intelligence community," which includes, among others, the National Security Agency, the Federal Bureau of Investigation, and the intelligence sections in the offices of the Secretary of Defense, the Army, the Navy, the Air Force, the State Department, and the Atomic Energy Commission. The CIA collects, correlates, evaluates, and circulates the data of these groups and has the right to inspect their organization and operation.

There is little likelihood that these continual inspections of effectiveness will produce a reduction in the number of intelligence sections that exist in government at present. Top-level national security decision-makers, like military generals in war, always want as much information as they can get before they have to make a decision, in order to avoid as much as possible that decision's being wrong because of an incomplete set of facts.

Unfortunately for the smoothness of its operation, the CIA is a much-maligned agency, particularly criticized by those to whom secrecy is anathema in a democratic society. It is hampered in defending itself by the very nature of its highly classified activity, which forces it to keep silent when publicly attacked. Actually, for all its "cloak-and-dagger" image, much of its work is simply analysis, in Washington, of published, unclassified documents gathered from all over the world.*

The National Security Council. Since creation of the NSC in 1947, four very different Presidents have occupied the White House. Each has regarded the Council differently. Each has used it to satisfy his own needs and individual attitudes toward its proper relationship to the Presidency. The organization of the NSC and its importance to the formulation of national security policy have changed drastically to meet criteria imposed by the chief executive.

Early proponents of the creation of the NSC, most notably James Forrestal, seem to have had in mind modeling its organization and powers after those of the cabinet in the British parliamentary form of government. President Truman resisted this philosophy, pointing out, correctly, that in the U.S. form of government there was serious question whether Congress had the power under the Constitution to require the President to seek advice from any specific individual groups before he made a decision. Because of Truman's resistance, the more

---

* In this regard, it is like the Soviet intelligence community, which has reportedly stated it can fulfill 95 per cent of its obligation to the U.S.S.R. solely through reading information freely published in the open in U.S. society.

than 300 policy papers produced by the NSC up to mid-1950 failed to carry overriding weight. For one thing, the Council tended to attack major issues with broad generalities and wide statements of principle too imprecise for practical implementation. For another, attendance at Council meetings, originally limited to statutory members, gradually expanded to include many consultants and staff advisers—a trend that encouraged members, and their supporting entourage of advisers, to promote departmental views of problems. Discussions tended to ramble. Action was delayed. Above all, Truman's absence led individual NSC members to downgrade the Council's importance as a corporate body. During the Korean War, the NSC played a somewhat larger role than it had before, but the President continued to look to individuals and to other agencies for advice and recommendations in the national security field.

During the 1952 election campaign, Presidential candidate Eisenhower criticized Truman's use of the NSC. He promised, if elected, to elevate the Council to the position originally planned for it under the National Security Act and to use it as his "principal arm of formulating policy on military, international, and internal security matters." He did just that, by formalizing, developing, and expanding the structure and procedures of the NSC, thereby creating an NSC "system," of which the Council itself was the primary, but by no means the only, significant portion. The NSC system consisted of the central Council, supported by a grid of highly standardized procedures and staff relationships and a complex interdepartmental committee substructure.

Surrounded and supported by the Council were several interdepartmental committees, some of a permanent nature, some *ad hoc,* topped off by the Council's two major subsidiary organizations: the Planning Board—staffed by officials at the assistant secretary level from the Council-member departments and by other advisers—which met every Tuesday and

Friday to prepare proposed policy papers for Council consideration; and the Operations Coordinating Board manned by officials at the executive department deputy secretary or director level—which met regularly on Wednesdays to integrate all aspects of implementing national security policy. The Operations Coordinating Board's principal task was to see that the departments of government responsible for carrying out parts or all of a particular security policy executed that work in concert and harmony.

Supporters praised the neatness and mechanical order of the system, but by the late 1950's, its very routineness was helping to foster controversy. Critics argued that the NSC system was nothing but a huge committee with all a committee's weaknesses. It was, they said, overstaffed, excessively rigid, and capable of bringing order out of chaos only on comparatively minor matters. Like all committees, it tended to compromise on the lowest common denominator among members; its decisions, particularly on larger and more important issues, were couched in vague generalities difficult to understand and harder to implement. What really mattered, however, was that the NSC system was the Eisenhower, and traditional military, way of handling questions as they bubbled up to top authority for resolution. It was not the way of Eisenhower's successor.

Encouraged by the results of a study of the Senate Subcommittee on National Policy Machinery, a study that lasted for more than two years until the fall of 1961, President Kennedy chose to make the NSC a small forum for himself and his chief advisers to use in discussion and debate of a limited number of critical problems. In a very short time, he dismantled the system carefully assembled by his predecessor and replaced it with a loose, flexible, fairly pragmatic set of procedures more suited to his own concepts and methods. Gone was the Planning Board with its highly systematized development of papers; gone the formal, crowded, regularly scheduled Council meetings; gone the Operations Coordinating Board with its elaborate, interdepartmental follow-up on NSC actions. Under Kennedy, the Council became only one of several means by which problems could be solved. It took its place beside special Cabinet committees and informal groups of officials organized temporarily to assist and advise in the national security process. Primary emphasis on both advice to the President and action on his decisions was returned to the regular departments and agencies and their planning and operational staffs. These, reinforced by interdepartmental committees or task forces (and close personal working relationships between the operating heads of departments and agencies), again came to bear the heaviest workload in the national security process.

After Kennedy's death, this personal contact among individuals holding power in the Johnson Administration became even more strongly emphasized. The importance of the NSC diminished even further. It is there, of course, for staff work and coordination of interdepartmental views, or, if the President wishes to use it, for more significant activities. In brief, the Council's importance is what the President in power chooses to make it.

Whatever the relative stature held by each of the foregoing Executive Office agencies and committees, or their individual members, in helping the President deal with national security policy, one significant fact is accepted by all concerned, although sometimes reluctantly. The key point, as one former Executive Office member, Don K. Price, Jr., noted in testimony before the Senate Subcommittee on National Policy Machinery in 1961, is that

> You can't slice policy up neatly among them, any more than among the executive departments. However you define their fields of interest, they overlap not only those of the executive departments they try to coordinate but those of each other. The Budget Bureau is in a broad sense not dealing with different things from the Council of Economic Advisers. Each tries to

help the President by working over the same raw material in different ways. Similarly, there is no way in which you can say in advance just where the interests of the National Aeronautics and Space Council end and the Joint Chiefs of Staff begin, or how they relate to any other interdepartmental committee that may exist in the fields of economics, transportation, communication, manpower, education, science, or strategy.

This "complex interface," as the Pentagon is currently inclined to call it, between the Defense Department and the other executive agencies of government often encourages "doers" in DOD to try to bypass it because of the obstacles it poses to getting a job done. And, complex as the interrelationships of the Defense Department with the Executive Office units are, they are relatively clean-cut compared to the tangled sets of interconnections that it must maintain with its other government partners. The entire Executive Office job description, briefly highlighted here, is essentially only a clue, frightening to many, of the national policy machinery that grinds on below it.

RELATIONS WITH THE STATE DEPARTMENT—AND OTHERS

A 1960 staff report of the Senate Subcommittee on National Policy Machinery stated:

Historically, a President has looked to the Department of State for his principal help in developing and executing foreign policy. But, today, the sphere of the State Department is far narrower than the full range of contemporary foreign relations. As an organization, the State Department can now claim no greater concern in certain aspects of foreign policy than the Defense Department. The interest of Treasury and Agriculture in some areas of international affairs is almost equal to that of State.

Indeed, today, almost every executive department and some eighteen independent agencies are involved with national security policy. Four government agencies and six international financial organizations work in the field of foreign economic aid alone. The net result is this: the planning and execution of national security policy cut across the jurisdiction of many departments and agencies.

A staff report of the same subcommittee, in early 1961, went on to note:

> The means for meeting our foreign-policy objectives now go far beyond those of traditional diplomacy. They embrace economic and military aid, scientific and technical assistance, information programs, surplus food programs, and education and cultural exchange. They invoke work through alliances and international organizations—with all the attendant complications. We have mutual defense treaties with forty-two nations; we are members of four regional defense organizations and an active participant in a fifth; we belong to the United Nations and some two dozen other major international organizations.
>
> Both in its making and execution, moreover, foreign policy has become interdepartmental.

Not only the Department of State and the Department of Defense (with the military services), but also the Treasury, the U.S. Coast Guard (which comes under the Department of Transportation for peacetime functions, and under the Navy for wartime), Commerce, Interior, Agriculture, the Atomic Energy Commission, the Federal Communications Commission, the Export-Import Bank, the Development Loan Fund, the U.S. Information Agency, the U.S. Arms Control and Disarmament Agency, the Selective Service System, the National Aeronautics and Space Administration, and a score of other agencies are all deeply involved in international security activities of one type or another.

Rival claimants from different executive departments with different missions are introduced, therefore, into the policy-making and policy-executing process. Thus, the requirement exists almost as standard practice that power must be shared even though responsibility for the resultant use of that power may not be. And this splintered authority produces a natural breeding ground for even more complexity in the form of coordinating mechanisms, namely committees.

When policy stakes are high and differences in outlook sharp, department heads traditionally have sought to bypass coordinating committees while keeping them busy with secondary matters. And, if such shortcuts are not possible, they have traditionally tried to keep coordination from binding them tightly or specifically to undesired courses of action. The net result has tended to be "coordinating" on the lowest common denominator of agreement, which is often tantamount to no coordination at all.

Roots of Defense Department Strength

Unless carefully policed, the whole national security structure can be, and often actually operates as, a management nightmare. One result, for the Defense Department, is that the Secretary spends less of his time running his own department than he spends dealing with organizations outside it: with the President, Congress, other government agencies, the public, and the military portion (if not sometimes the whole) of other governments and foreign alliances.

Among the agencies of the U.S. Government, as each negotiates to enlarge its sphere of influence or, at a minimum, protect its already established preserves, the Department of Defense has become a formidable adversary—notably so in the last decade. There are a good many reasons for this.

The unparalleled endorsement that Secretary McNamara has received personally from two Presidents is one reason. President Johnson, for instance, in remarks typical of Kennedy as well, has proclaimed McNamara "the finest government servant" he has ever known. To document precisely the effect that such expressions of confidence from the President can have on government deliberations from the highest to the lowest level of interagency staff work is extremely difficult. But it is a powerful force. That many of the Defense Secretary's management techniques have been ordered by two Presidents into use throughout executive government; that two Presidents have compared other Cabinet members on occasion unfavorably to the "get-it-done" Secretary of Defense; that the Defense Secretary has been called on for other duties such as monitoring antipoverty programs, playing a key advisory role in government assistance to a commercial supersonic air transport development, helping the President force aluminum and steel manufacturers to cancel proposed price increases on materials (reportedly to combat inflation in the economy); that the Defense Secretary has been asked to play a leading role in cementing Presidential relations with Congress and arbitrating differences between government "hawks" and "doves" on how the Viet-Nam war should be handled— all these suggest the Secretary's very real, if unwritten, influence in government circles.

Another reason for Defense Department influence is the sheer size and scope of its operations. It is bigger than all the other government departments put together. Where other departments measure their resources in thousands of men and millions of dollars, the Pentagon measures in millions of men and billions of dollars. That financial giantism, coupled with the worldwide scope of defense installations and activities, makes it rare that other government agencies bent on some international program can afford to ignore the Defense Department's presence and resources. In many instances, the Department of Defense functions in a manner not unlike ancient Rome's military legions, which could and did extend not only their control but also Roman culture, economy, and ways of government to large areas of the then known world.

Critics have sometimes complained about the resulting "unwarranted influence" on foreign policy by the Defense

Department. The implication that "Defense, not State, really runs foreign policy" is largely an overplayed indictment, but certainly the need for active Defense Department participation, or at least interest, in all U.S. international activities was inevitable the moment it was decided that the military must help to execute foreign policy all the time, rather than waiting in the wings to be brought out to fight a war only if all other diplomatic efforts failed. It is true that, whereas the State Department once had the field almost to itself in peacetime, today there is a central partnership for advising the President on foreign policy. To quote again from the 1961 report of the Senate Subcommittee on National Policy Machinery:

> The Secretaries of State and Defense are the Cabinet officials most concerned with the government programs that must rank highest on any list of national priorities. They speak for the requirements of national safety and survival.
>
> Today, perhaps the most important problems of national security are joint State-Defense problems, requiring joint action by the two departments for their solution—from the development and execution of military-aid programs, the negotiation of base rights, and arms-control planning, to the overriding problem of properly relating military means with foreign-policy ends.

Inevitably, in recent years, observers have tried to oversimplify this partnership through speculation about which partner is the stronger. Deciding between the two is almost impossible. For one thing, much of the strength, as already noted, is predicated on a human relationship with the President and cannot be measured with precision, if at all. For another, the State Department's work is preponderantly in private negotiations overseas and in politically sensitive behind-the-scenes advisory efforts in Washington. Its only public product that can invite comment is its paperwork. The Defense Department, on the other hand, has far greater visibility. It is a "doer" agency, as much as it is a paperwork mill. It does not merely comment; it acts, moving forces, spending substantial amounts of resources on equipment, hiring and drafting people, and developing new hardware. As a principal tool of national security policy, the Defense Department and its maneuvers are the most frequently displayed evidence of what new policy decisions have meant. It is probably unavoidable, therefore, that the Department's members have acquired a reputation for greater overriding power than they really possess in setting that security policy in the first place.

Yet, if the Defense Department's image is somewhat overblown compared to the facts, its impact on the course of government policy deliberations is still potent. In addition to its rapport with the President, organizational size and worldwide influence, legally established powers, and similar reasons already noted, the Defense Department has one other, unique characteristic that tends to attract the faith and reliance of government decision-makers. Its machinery works well. It has tried harder, with more success, to apply advanced technology to its management problems than has any other agency.

Today, most of this management technology in the Defense Department comes under the heading "Command and Control," which the Department defines as: "An arrangement of personnel, facilities, and the means of information acquisition, processing, and dissemination employed by a commander in planning, directing, and controlling operations." In simpler terms, this means running the show. What is relatively new in it is the application of electronic computers, the most modern communications equipment, and the latest information-collecting devices (infrared sensors, airborne radars, etc.) to give commanders—from the lowest level up to the President—tighter control than ever before on the forces under their command.

This equipment, particularly the computer, has produced, and will produce more, exciting results. In some circles, the phrase "Command and Control" has been used to conjure up visions of computer-operated automatic weapons that find, fix, and finish the enemy with human intervention only at those levels where it has been impossible to eliminate it; visions of the White House running "push-button" wars half a world away, controlling equipment in battle and supplies on the way to war using nothing but electronics to carry out its orders. Grotesque as this notion may seem, there is no question that technology has enabled vast improvements in the speed and accuracy with which military leadership at the very highest levels can receive, handle, analyze, and disseminate information and orders.

Since the challenge to national security leadership is always to separate the valid clues of impending real threat from the ever-present static that shouts immediate crisis everywhere in the world, the more rapid and complete the collection and communication of information, the more reliable that sorting process can be. The military has spent billions, and will continue to do so, on technology to help deliver reliable performance. The use of computers and related equipment now permeates nearly every walk of military life. This equipment is used to control weapons and forces in the field. It is used in accounting systems to handle basic programing, budgeting, fiscal, and funding data; in research and development program control and in collecting and evaluating test data; in upgrading, automating, and integrating the paperwork that is pumped every day through command headquarters at nearly all military echelons.

As in weapon developments, there have been a good many errors and false starts. Much still needs doing. But, in general, command-control systems, appropriately designed and realistically built, have two significant characteristics: (1) as a management tool, they are an accurate reflection of characteristics in the command where they are used, whether it is accounting, research and development, logistics and supply, or combat command; and (2) each system can communicate effectively with every other system to the extent that may be practically necessary (such communication is not necessary, for instance, between the system analyzing test data at the Cape Kennedy missile-testing range and that for a battalion commander in Europe). The command-control system reflects the changes, notably, in centralization of control at the top, which have been firmly established during the last decade in the Defense Department and in the executive branch of government altogether. A participant in command-control development, Esterly Page, has said that the nation has undergone a basic change in the philosophy of command and control resulting in "new emphasis on the requirement for large quantities of finite and precise information to form the basis for consideration at the highest level of problems that previously were considered and sometimes unfortunately decided at a much lower one."

The interlocking relationships today between the Defense Department and other key governmental national security agencies depend on rapid communications and instantly available information. President Johnson has communications with 75 per cent of the 120 independent nations in the world on a "real time" basis (command-control technologists' talk for "right away"). In a crisis situation, the President has a direct line to his Ambassador.* The military command lines run through the commander of the unified command responsible for the crisis area, into the Pentagon's Defense Intelligence Agency, and to the Joint Chiefs, and these are used to supplement the President's own lines as well as to provide information for the military. From the Pentagon, after study and evaluation, the information flows into the White House. Most of the time lag in this flow, and usually it amounts to very little, is in the initial writing of the message and its evaluation at the other end. Even in the most primitive areas of the world, communications equipment can be brought in with a task

* Johnson has four telephones and two teletype machines in his office, as well as two telephones in his car.

force and, with the use of airborne relays, command levels in Washington can be kept abreast of the situation. Communications satellites are expected to make point-to-point long-haul communications even more reliable and secure.

The heart of this worldwide network is the National Military Command System, whose main parts are a command center in the Pentagon (with emergency alternate centers inside a mountain several miles away, in C-135 aircraft in the air, and on two ships at sea) and the various warning, sensor, and communications networks linking these facilities with the unified and specified commands. Secretary McNamara once described its workings in an interview in *Armed Forces Management Magazine* as follows:

> As soon as the intelligence identifies an impending crisis, the National Military Command Center [NMCC] is the focal point to which the Joint Chiefs of Staff and higher authority turn for an immediate review of the situation and for advice as to the available course of action in time of emergency. The Deputy Director for Operations [NMCC], a general/flag rank officer, and the NMCC maintain an around-the-clock evaluation of the worldwide situations with the goal of recognizing incipient problems before they have become crises. The State Department, Central Intelligence Agency, Defense Intelligence Agency, National Security Agency and other Defense agencies are represented in the NMCC and support the NMCC mission of anticipation and evaluating foreign crises. In addition, the NMCC is linked with other key operational centers in the Washington area, including the White House Situation Room, the State Department, and CIA, as well as with the Services and the unified and specified commands. The NMCC has facilities for immediate and comprehensive alert notification.

Probably the best way to illustrate the system's effectiveness is by examining its response to a military incident, one of several score that occur each year.*

---

* In 1964 alone, the workload in this "alerting and controlling agency" consisted of over 340,000 incoming messages and 8,226 outgoing.

On March 10, 1964, U.S. and friendly radars in West Germany detected an aircraft proceeding from West Germany to East Germany on an unauthorized flight pattern. Attempts were made to warn the aircraft, but it was not "listening" on the radar's frequency and penetrated East German airspace. Radars noted the aircraft being intercepted before it faded from the scope. The information—"a possible shootdown of U.S. or friendly aircraft"—was flashed immediately to the NMCC in the Pentagon. Time of the incident: 9:06 A.M., Eastern Standard Time. The information was received in the NMCC at 9:10.

The White House and the Secretary of Defense were informed immediately. In addition, the report was flashed to the State Department Operations Center, the CIA, and the Defense assistant secretariats for International Security Affairs and Public Affairs. At 9:11, the U.S. Commander-in-Chief, Europe, called the chairman of the Joint Chiefs of Staff (through the NMCC) to report that aircraft identification was not known. However, he added, the 9:10 message was accurate because a commercial aircraft in the Berlin Corridor had reported sighting three people parachuting from an aircraft in distress at the time.

Within six minutes the Washington principals knew: (a) an aircraft, U.S. or friendly, had been intercepted; (b) three people had bailed out; (c) the U.S. Commander-in-Chief, Europe, was interrogating friendly powers to determine the aircraft's identity. And within a few more minutes following notification to the White House, the Military Assistant to the President had informed the NMCC that the President had been advised and wished to be informed when the aircraft identity was positively established. The President wanted all the facts not later than 12:00.

The European commander was advised of Presidential interest by the NMCC. By 11:15, the U.S. Commander-in-Chief, Europe, had completed initial investigation and reported to the NMCC, and the following was relayed to the President: (a) the aircraft was an American RB-66 reconnaissance bomber on a low-level navigator training flight; (b) it had become disoriented and flown into East Germany unknowingly; (c) it was believed to have been attacked by Soviet fighter aircraft and to have crashed near Gardelegen, East Germany; (d) the three crewmen had parachuted into East Germany, and the U.S. Military Liaison Mission at Potsdam was attempting to recover them.

While this information was being passed to the White House, the representatives of the Washington agencies in the NMCC were flashing the facts to their officials and supporting staffs. At 12:30, the White House issued a press release declaring the Soviets had shot down a U.S. plane in distress. Later, official protests were made to the Russians. A member of the NMCC, Air Force Brigadier General Paul W. Tibbets, summed up the interplay, political and military, at "the Commander-in-Chief level" as "instrumental in a quick assessment of the incident," and said the incident illustrated that "close interplay on fast moving events is effective in achieving desired results." (In this case, the United States was able first, and accurately, to demand redress.)

Today, the Defense Department has become the focal point in government handling of crises. It is also the chief government expert on how to handle data, whatever its nature, with computers and communications know-how. In utilization of command-control, tight interagency coordination currently exists, particularly between the State Department and Defense.*

* This is not to suggest that mutual understanding is so prevalent that mistakes no longer occur. As long as human beings are involved in decision-making, there will be misunderstanding and, therefore, errors. Technology has provided no guarantee of infallible judgment. One recent example: in March, 1966, "someone" in the State Department approved a sale of 16,000 M-16 rifles to Singapore, while at the same time South Korean allies fighting with the U.S. in Viet-Nam were complaining, correctly, that their troops were still equipped with outdated M-1 weapons.

New Closeness with the State Department

The comparatively new closeness of the State Department and the Department of Defense—and all it implies in terms of internal defense organizational cohesion, the modern-day military role in international affairs, and many related matters (all discussed in previous chapters)—probably emerges most clearly in the evolution of the Joint Chiefs of Staff to top military prominence as a Defense Department component working closely with the State Department. As late as 1949–50, Pentagon staff personnel were expressly forbidden to communicate directly with their counterparts in the State Department, because of alleged suspicions of each other's motives. For that matter, continued service rivalries over roles and missions meant that the Joint Chiefs' debating society often gave the State Department a weak compromise or a confusing set of imprecise contradictions. The central conflict within the JCS rose out of their having (except for the chairman) dual responsibilities (as they still do today): one as members of the Joint Chiefs of Staff and the other as military chiefs of their respective armed forces.

This built-in conflict of interest between a man's obligation to Defense as a whole and to his own service was duplicated in the entire Joint Staff structure. As discussed in earlier chapters, too often the services viewed the Joint Staff as an adversary, withholding their best staff men for their own uses and assigning less than the best to Joint Staff duty. Those given Joint Staff duty were frequently more anxious to sell their separate service programs than to study the needs of total national security. But all this was changed with the 1958 Reorganization Act and the executive orders that immediately followed it.

For one thing, the President shortened the command line from himself to forces in the field. It now ran from the President to the Secretary of Defense and, by Secretarial delegation, through the Joint Chiefs group to the unified and specified commands. With this, and similar emphasis on the joint role of the individual chiefs and the importance of the Joint Staff, the Joint Chiefs' stature in the Defense Department took a dramatic jump. It had taken a long time to reflect in practice what had been the spirit of the original National Security Act. But after 1960, Joint Staff duty for military officers changed from being a bothersome obligation to being an opportunity, and years of joint training exercises, joint schooling, and joint study groups on mutual problems finally paid dividends.

One of the most important dividends was that the State Department now had a single military strategy to plan from, albeit one substructured to cover a host of options and alternative courses of action, depending on the nature of a particular threat. A closer, day-to-day working situation developed almost at once between the Defense and State departments. Efforts to develop that close liaison had been going on, mostly through informal invitations, since 1950, but such military-political contacts became a matter of routine after 1960. In their current operation, no day passes that at least thirty military officers from the Department of Defense are not in the State Department attending meetings. Nothing is done on the military side of national security without the political and economic implications of the move first receiving a thorough airing.

The same teamwork now pervades the whole organization. Proof of how far improvement has come is Defense-State combined operations in Viet-Nam. That conflict marks the first time the JCS as a body has been charged with running a war for the Secretary of Defense. It is the first time, on such a large scale, that the two departments have had to work together continually in the theater of operations, not only fighting the military part of the war, but also waging the "other war" of stabilizing the beleaguered nation's political environment and boosting its economy. Progress in the "other war" has come slowly. But one indication that there is progress has been the increased attempts by the enemy to wreck this essentially civilian development program. In the larger scope of history, the Viet-Nam action may well end up as the major test of State-Defense efforts at building a viable theory for the application of power in the nuclear age.

VIII

The Defense Department Faces the Public and Congress

For all the interagency relationships so important to Defense Department plans and programs, it is outside the national security community that the Defense Department faces an interconnected pair of authorities more important than all the rest with which it deals. They are the public and the public's spokesman in government, Congress.

IMPORTANCE OF PUBLIC OPINION

An influence sometimes overlooked and frequently maligned, public opinion provides a strong check on Pentagon power. Most Defense Department officials devote a great deal of attention to it. They feel as Forrestal did when he said, "This job not only has to be well done but the public has to be convinced it is being well done," and Robert Lovett when he noted, "I have observed over the years that, next to fulminate of mercury, there is no priming charge more effective than a few written words in a responsible magazine to get things moving in military departments."

Cynics often question whether the Defense Department and its component elements really worry that much about public reaction to what they are doing or propose to do. This doubt is easy to understand, because a great deal of the contact the public has with the Pentagon is indirect, impersonal, and frustrating. Yet, to the majority of military leaders, the nation's first line of defense is the internal strength and will of its people, which, in turn, is predicated on understanding and education. This leadership believes that, for the long term, an uninformed or unconcerned or wrongly concerned public is more dangerous to national security than any conceivable external threat.

For example, of the reaction in the United States after the Soviet Sputnik launching, President Eisenhower wrote, in *Waging Peace*: "Most surprising of all . . . was the intensity of the public concern. . . . In the weeks and months after Sputnik many Americans seemed to be seized not only with a sudden worry that our defenses had crumbled but also with an equally unjustified alarm that our entire educational system was defective."

In Sputnik's aftermath, and believing it already had the missile race well in hand, the Administration, the Pentagon, and the military services spent as much effort spelling out how strong their program was as they did working on the program itself. Even then, fearing they had not been entirely successful, they delayed canceling clearly excessive expenditures in missile development duplications because of possible adverse public reaction.

The ways in which the Defense Department reaches the public are as myriad as the many groups that make up the public. In a sense, every Defense employee, in uniform and out, all over the world, is a communicator with one or more of these groups. Harry Howe Ransom, in his book *Can American Democracy Survive Cold War?* wrote:

> American armed services are engaged in world-wide activities, from the operation of diaper services overseas to radio broadcasting networks in foreign lands. At the end of 1962, more than one million American servicemen were on duty in 41 foreign nations around the globe. . . . Pentagon officials, civilian and military, make many more speeches and write several times

as many articles on foreign policy subjects as officials of the Department of State. . . . Through its nationwide links with battalions of individuals and organizations . . . the Defense Department has "a built-in system of communication with the American people unequaled in scale by anything available to other Federal agencies."

Interest in the military message is considerable. At no time in U.S. history, other than during all–out wars, have the activities of the military affected so much of the nation's economy, in general, and its individual communities and families, in particular—and the Defense sphere of influence seems to be ever widening.

The Eisenhower Warning

Probably no better summation of the impact of defense activities has been given than Dwight D. Eisenhower's widely quoted message on leaving the White House in 1961. He said, in part:

We have been compelled to create a permanent armaments industry of vast proportions. Added to this, three and a half million men and women are directly engaged in the defense establishment. We annually spend on military security more than the net income of all United States corporations.

This conjunction of an immense military establishment and a large arms industry is new in the American experience. The total influence—economic, political, even spiritual—is felt in every city, every state house, every office of the federal government. We recognize the imperative need for this development. Yet we must not fail to comprehend its grave implications. Our toil, resources, and livelihood are all involved; so is the very structure of our society.

In the councils of government we must guard against acquisition of unwarranted influence, whether sought or unsought, by the military-industrial complex. The potential for the disastrous rise of misplaced power exists and will persist.

We must never let the weight of this combination endanger our liberties or democratic processes. We should take nothing for granted. Only an alert and knowledgeable citizenry can compel the proper meshing of the huge industrial and military machinery of defense with our peaceful methods and goals, so that security and liberty may prosper together.

Although there is some admitted danger existing in the pressure that the industrial complex as a whole exerts on Defense attitudes and decisions, and although individual companies do try continually to become "chummy" with their military customers, in the interest of sales success, it is doubtful if the collusion implied in Eisenhower's warning could ever develop. For one thing, the large numbers of persons involved in major procurement decisions make it unlikely that even the largest defense manufacturers could ever "buy" their military customers' loyalties to themselves. In addition, the built-in Defense checks on buying desires of any one military group also dictate against the development of an onerous military–industry cartel. Moreover, the great majority of the industry and its military customers are high principled and patriotic. And, as practical insurance that they will remain so, the intense competition between individual suppliers militates against the possibility that any one firm could operate dishonestly in the marketplace for very long.

Channels of Communication

What occurs in the communication between Defense and its industrial suppliers is a continual debating of differences over (a) the proper approach to filling a hardware requirement; (b) changes Defense should make in its procurement machinery so industry could better meet military needs; and (c) how industry must alter its operations to respond more fully to Defense demands. This sometimes angry exchange of views can and does take place in a variety of forums. Among the more notable: the meetings of the Defense–Industry Advisory Council and its subordinate committees—a collection of study groups roughly half Defense experts and half industry experts. These men are specialists in various aspects of the contracting relationship, viz., research and development, procurement practices, contract administration, equipment sales and assistance to overseas allies, contract financing, management of weapon development projects, etc.

Just below this level of deliberation are other significant communication channels. One of the most frequently used today was started by James Forrestal several years before the Defense Department itself was created. Near the end of World War II, Forrestal was instrumental in setting up the National Security Industrial Association (NSIA), a broadly based alliance of industries supplying military requirements. Their original purpose, still consistently pursued, was to provide frank opinions on a wide range of policies and problems. Today, the Pentagon polls this group regularly, for instance, on changes it plans in the Armed Services Procurement Regulations to determine whether industry believes it can live with the changes. Another example of the liaison: prior to launching its cost reduction program in 1961, Defense obtained from NSIA a comprehensive report on how the contracting portions of that program ought to be handled to obtain maximum savings benefits for the military.

Other industry associations that are asked or that volunteer member attitudes and aggravations to the military include the Aerospace Industries Association and the Electronic Industries Association. As their names imply, these two are somewhat more specialized and biased toward one industry's viewpoint in their approaches to the Defense-industry relationship than NSIA. However, they rank close seconds in prestige and maintain a high reputation in Defense, at least in part because they often worry as much about their military customers' problems as they do about what's best for their individual members. The Defense Department also deals with a host of other associations, such as the American Management Association and National Association of Manufacturers, that are recognized nationally, have interests other than defense, and participate in an exchange with military representatives on the theories of management and problems of industrial mobilization.

Unfortunately, a number of other associations, attracted mainly by high defense spending, and not taking the same broad view of national security, also have grown up in the past twenty years. Often constructed, it seems, on whatever gimmick is likely to attract membership dues and the image of power, they cross and criss-cross the whole range of military expenditure. There are associations labeled by military service, by specialized function within a service, or by a specialized function performed in all military departments, such as transportation, communication, and the like. Some make serious attempts to contribute to the national military strength. Others grind away in the military, in Congress, and in the public press, on whatever parochial crusade is deemed "essential" by them or the military group or function they contend they support. Their extreme extensions of this behavior often amount to saying "what's good for us is good for the country." Defense personnel frequently feel dragged into being their convention speakers and panel discussion participants out of apprehension over ruffling politically powerful feathers. Industry provides the bulk of their membership funding, sometimes because it feels it can't afford not to. The whole exercise takes a great deal of time out of military executives' schedules, but little of lasting value results.

Beyond associations, there is a wide range of other military–public contacts. Among those that occasionally creep into public print are: the small business community (which, by law, Defense must assure receives its "fair share" of military contracts); economically distressed areas of the nation (where, again, Congress has provided contract set-asides for potential defense suppliers, provided they can meet the price, quality, and delivery demands in competition with firms from relatively prosperous areas); lobbyists for individual companies, industries, or ethnic groups, which pressure Defense for support or favors; local communities affected either by a base closure or "civic action" programs such as the Army Corps of Engineers' construction of dams, bridges, etc. In addition, there are the educational and research institutions to which Defense turns for support, especially in basic research and development. And there are the nonprofit corporations (often labeled "think tanks"), whose primary product is advice. In theory, their studies are unwarped by the hope of a sale, but, in practice, they sometimes simply tell the military customer what he wants to hear to support his own preconceived conviction.*

Public Information Programs

As the Defense Department has spread its interest and influence over the land, the military has found it necessary to develop communication and understanding with those affected. Not all this exchange of information, opinion, and education is handled by public affairs or information officers, as the Pentagon calls them, but a good deal of it is.

Almost all military installations have at least one public information officer; and the larger the installation or the greater its importance, the larger and individually more specialized the information office. In addition, almost all offices

---

* In other words, the quality of advice from nonprofit groups varies, like that from industry associations. Probably the best of the lot is the RAND Corporation of Santa Monica, California, which numbers among its credits a 1946 study recommending earth satellites for weather forecasting and military reconnaissance; its help to the Air Force in developing the famed "fail-safe" concept for control of the launching of nuclear weapon delivery systems; and its development of the basic outline for the "program package" system of budgeting described elsewhere in this volume.

within a command—especially in the Pentagon and particularly if the office boss is a general, admiral, or high-level civilian—have someone whose job description covers, at least in part, keeping in contact with the press and other representatives of the public.

The focal point for most of this activity is the Office of the Assistant Secretary of Defense for Public Affairs. The function of this office differs from that of any other in the Pentagon. Makers of policy on procedures for lower echelons to carry out, the public affairs officers also take part in day-to-day operations of every other part of the Department. Daily requirements can range from cooperation with the networks to produce a major television show, through sending a grammar school student a Defense pamphlet for a "report" he's writing, to providing flag and honor guards for a school assembly or building dedication, holding regularly scheduled press conferences, producing a monthly paper on Defense procurement practices for industry and labor, providing a local Lion's club with a speaker, or answering the day's quota of some 26,000 letters a year from citizens wanting information on nearly every aspect of military activity.

In calendar year 1966, for instance, the information office in Viet-Nam alone: arranged more than 4,700 in-country flights for newsmen, including ground and air transportation to battle areas; arranged for or conducted more than 7,000 briefings; answered more than 32,000 telephone queries from newsmen; 2nd conducted, in Saigon, daily press conferences, 7 days a week, which a daily average of 130 correspondents attended (out of more than 400 newsmen from 22 nations covering the war).

This huge investment in public information resources is made, the Pentagon claims, simply because, in a democracy, "people have to be informed in order to make right decisions. In one way or another, all public affairs activities, from clearing Defense documents for open release to holding press conferences to accrediting correspondents as representatives of valid publications and media, are directed basically toward one mission: informing the public."

Ground rules for the effort, according to former Assistant Secretary of Defense for Public Affairs Arthur Sylvester, are just two:

First, the safety of our fighting men which, of course, relates directly to the safeguarding of information of value to the enemy.

Second, within the limitations of the first principle, the provision of the maximum amount of truthful factual information to the people of the United States, whether it be sought out by news people or we have to volunteer it.

Admirable as the policy is, however, public affairs personnel are constantly embroiled in pulling and tugging with the recipients of or seekers after their information. One sympathetic writer has noted:

The toughest, most impossible job in government is that of Assistant Secretary of Defense for Public Affairs. Not only must you try to satisfy a hungry press corps which believes it should have access to all information but also you must try to pry news from reluctant, busy Defense managers who distrust the press and generally feel that too much vital information is already being released. It is impossible to satisfy both demands.

Part of the public affairs problem is provoked by internal conflict. Part of that conflict, in turn, has been spurred in the past by military department efforts to aid through press publicity the progress of their pet projects—particularly when the project is having trouble earning top Defense Department approval on its own. News "leaks" by the military, designed to undercut the Defense Secretary's negative view of an individual service proposal, plagued both Forrestal and Louis Johnson. As one attempt to shut off the interminable contending against their decisions, both men moved to reduce the Washington-based public information staffs of the individual services. Some 473 personnel on those staffs were cut, during the 1948–49 era, to a total of 45, with 285 of those service communications experts transferred to working directly for the Office of the Secretary of Defense. Predictably, this move prompted an immediate outcry of "gagging" the military.

Such centralization of public affairs activities eased during the Korean War, and in the ensuing decade, attempts to reinforce control met with only marginal success. The services still found ways to take their cases direct to the public if the climate within the Defense Department was not entirely favorable to their own policies. Generals wrote plaintive magazine articles and books or gave angry speeches. Stories were planted anonymously, often with newsmen more anxious to garner a headline than to present a thorough analysis of a problem. Defense secretaries found that even being completely open and honest about problems was not always an adequate defense against the "leak."

In 1961, however, along with centralization of authority over other elements of Defense, the new Secretary re-established tight centralized control over public release of information. His key point: defense statements should be made by responsible persons, not by an "anonymous report"—and the officer speaking had better support Pentagon policy if he knew what was good for him. The charge of "muzzling the military" was renewed.

There are often good and sufficient reasons why executives, military and civilian alike, can not—or should not—be allowed to speak openly on any subject that comes to mind. For one thing, the speaker's stature may lead the public to believe he is stating official policy when, in fact, he may only be voicing a personal opinion. For another, higher authority may often have a wider view and better ability to assess the impact of a subordinate officer's statement, than does the officer himself.

For instance, early in the Kennedy Administration, one admiral had planned a speech castigating Communism. Following the orders that all military speeches by top personnel be cleared through the Office of the Assistant Secretary for

Public Affairs, he submitted his text and had it turned down. Knowledge of this leaked to the press, and, at once, the "gag" charge was raised. But unknown to the admiral, the President was negotiating for the release of two downed American pilots then held by the Russians. They were released not long after the incident. In all likelihood, the admiral's well-meant but ill-timed speech could have stalled the whole negotiation. "You just don't shoot from the hip in government," said one public affairs officer.

Probably the greatest outcry against the Office of Public Affairs, however, occurred in December, 1962, when the assistant secretary said the government had "a right to lie to save itself." He was referring to the Cuban missile crisis, during which President Kennedy cut short a political campaign swing across the nation (press releases said he had a cold) to return to Washington and personally direct the setting up of the Cuban blockade. It was a tense and potentially disastrous time. The public affairs officer's point was that there are "a very few times in history" when a government must, in effect, mislead the public, in order to strengthen its stand against a potential enemy. That same officer, however, also said, "As is evident every four years, government is the property of the people. And no government can live with a policy built fundamentally on lying to the public."

Good newsmen, of course, expect from public information personnel the most optimistic or favorable description of defense programs and problems. But the obligation of a journalist to his readers is to be an intelligent adversary of government, questioning the validity of everything he hears, and a good newsman probes for a story and always hunts for more views on a problem than those of the first man he interviews. There are, however, different levels of talent in newsmen just as there are different levels of talent in all fields. Some accept as gospel the first thing they hear. Some never believe anything they are told, even when it is clearly factual and accurate. Pentagon public information officers suffer at the hands of these occasional careless, or cynical, reporters. Hence, the advice the Pentagon gives the public at every opportunity is to seek the news from more than one publication and preferably at least two known for having opposing editorial policies. Unavoidably, the Fourth Estate–Pentagon relationship is fraught with mutual suspicion and challenge— but the public willing to probe far enough can be the benefactor of this tension.

A Matter of Security

Centralization of public affairs activities is designed to help keep control of defense in the hands of those charged with running it. But, as witness the almost daily statements in congressional hearings by military officials disagreeing with defense policy and the almost daily analyses of problems by expert, experienced newspaper columnists, there are many ways for controversial subjects to pop into the open. In fact, the stronger the internal Defense disagreement, the easier it is to find individuals willing to express their convictions. A "muzzling" policy, even if it existed, would be foredoomed to failure. Unfortunately, Defense officials who may wish to be completely frank and informative are hampered in their service to the public by more than the understandable tendency of the Fourth Estate to doubt their word. The big problem is security. To protect its position vis-à-vis a potential or an actual enemy, the Defense Department often cannot reveal all it might, even though that full disclosure would enhance the credibility of its action. This dilemma, arising from what the Department would like to do and what it can do, is unavoidable.

THE WAY OF CONGRESS

The way of the Congress is the legislative process, which inherently involves publicity and open debate. Hence, in the American constitutional structure, unlike those of parliamentary systems, specialized standing committees are necessary. . . . The way of the executive branch, on the other hand, is one of discretionary executive action that must have in it a large element of flexibility and—if I may dare use the dirty word—secrecy, if it is to have the energy and achieve the unity of action that the Constitution intended and that we never needed more than we do today.

That statement by Don K. Price, Jr., in testimony before the Senate Subcommittee on National Policy Machinery in 1961, explains why today's world of "Cold War" and "neither war nor peace" has placed extraordinary strains on the tradition of checks and balances among the principal branches of government guaranteed by the Constitution. This warping tension is nowhere more apparent than in the changing relationship between the Defense Department and the Congress of the 1960's. Just as the once distinct line separating the Defense Department's work from the State Department's is now blurred, the challenges to peace following World War II have fouled the once clean-cut understanding between Defense and Congress.

Unfortunately, as many in Congress see it, while the Defense–State relationship has been evolving into one of close coordination, the Congress–Defense relationship has been more and more muddied by conflict. There are many reasons for this apparent deterioration.

Organizational Problems

Congress exercises its powers through the activity of its committees, not through the body as a whole. Yet, apart from the 1946 merger of the Naval Affairs and the Military Affairs committees into a single Armed Services Committee in both the Senate and the House, neither branch has done much to centralize its organization for national security. Conversely, as already discussed, the Defense Department has made a number of significant changes in its force structure, has centralized control over its organization, and has markedly revamped operations and procedures. All these changes have come in answer to new basic assumptions: (a) that force or the threat of it is of no value unless it serves political objectives; and (b) that, in the nuclear age, military force as a means to accomplish political ends must be carefully controlled to prevent its getting out of hand.

Defense organizational changes have continued, seemingly without end, since 1947 and, in recent years, have been supplemented and even overshadowed by improved management procedures looking toward more meaningful and balanced direction of Defense programs, saving money, making better use of resources, limiting the acceleration of expenditures, and minimizing the confusion created by the Department's far-reaching and often diverse purposes. Still, these changes in formal organizational structures and decision-making procedures, however significant, have had comparatively little influence on the shaping of defense policy. This process is, as it has always been, essentially political; defense policy formulation and related budgetary decisions can never be far removed from practical politics.

In marked contrast to the internal adjustments Defense has made in response to political necessity, Congress as a partner in this relationship has been slow to respond. It has not exercised its power as it might. For instance, Congress alone has the right under the Constitution to declare war and involve the nation in combat operations. Yet, in the twenty years since 1947, the nation has fought in two major, but never declared, wars, and has become involved in a whole series of potentially explosive confrontations all over the world—without Congress being able to exercise much leadership, except after the fact.

In addition, over the past few years, Defense has shown a remarkable ability to contest congressional instructions on what kinds of weapons the military should buy and how large the forces should be. With increasing frequency of late, members of Congress have attempted by one method or another to strengthen their decision-making leverage. Yet, in spite of those efforts, probably the best that can be said for the relationship today is that when both the Pentagon and Congress want to do something, it is done. However, when Congress wishes to see a program go forward—even to the point of passing enabling legislation and voting the necessary funds —the Pentagon can effectively stifle a program it does not favor by simply not spending the money (always with White House approval, of course).

For example, the Defense Department held up construction of a nuclear frigate this way in 1965–66, in spite of Congress' having expressly authorized and appropriated the funds. And the decision to deploy an anti-ballistic-missile system was delayed for more than two years (until late 1967) in the same fashion because top Pentagon leadership did not want to go ahead—although Congress, again, had specifically voted a total of nearly $500 million for 1966–67 to begin that deployment.

In instances where Congress objects to a Defense Department program, the Pentagon is often successful in going ahead, anyway, particularly if the program does not require any new budget funds to carry it out. For instance, although congressional members have objected strongly to proposed Defense reorganizations of the National Guard and Reserve forces, the military has nonetheless proceeded with a major part of its reorganization plans. All of which suggests that, although Congress once had had wide powers over determining what the military should be (compared to executive branch authorities through treaties, etc., over what the military should do), there is some question today whether Congress still retains even that authority.

Part of the reason, according to analysts of this disturbing development, is that for Defense personnel, military work—

including testifying before Congress—is a full-time job, but for members of Congress, obligations grow each year increasingly diverse. Even members of the many committees concerned with some aspect of national security can devote only a portion of their time to the subject. Representative Morris K. Udall, of Arizona, estimates that a "typical work week" of 59.3 hours for a member while Congress is in session breaks down as follows: on the floor of the House debating, voting, etc., 15.3 hours; 7.2 hours in legislative research and reading; 7.1 hours in committee; 7.2 hours answering mail; 5.1 hours handling constituent problems; 4.4 hours visiting with constituents in Washington; 3.5 hours on committee work outside of committee meetings; 2.4 hours on political party functions; 2.7 hours on writing chores, speeches, magazine articles, etc.; 2.3 hours meeting with lobbyists and lobby groups; 2.1 hours on press, radio, and television work. In addition, he spends 5.6 days a month in his home district while Congress is in session and has an average of 2.1 speaking engagements outside Washington (other than in his own district) per month. He also reads 5 daily newspapers, more than 8 weekly papers, 5 periodicals, and about 2 nonfiction books a month.

The more thoughtful executives in the Defense Department are as concerned about the effect of these obligations on members of Congress as are the congressmen themselves. Congressional impact on government programs (particularly in saying "no" instead of "yes") can be decisive. In that context, there is probably nothing more dangerous to proper formulation of national security policy than a misinformed or preoccupied congressman.

How the Defense Department Puts Its Case

Defense Department officials spend a great deal of time tending to the needs of Congress. As already mentioned, Congress wields its powers and attempts to work its will on the military primarily through its committees. And where some branches of government have to deal with only one committee, Defense must cope with several. There is a steady flow of business.

One obvious result is the heavy demand congressional committees place on Defense military and civilian officials to testify before them (often when the witnesses would much prefer to remain in the Pentagon handling their routine responsibilities). In the first six months of 1967, for instance, leading Defense executives spent a total of more than 6,000 man-hours in actual testimony before congressional committees. Defense Secretary McNamara alone averaged more than 100 hours a year defending Pentagon programs before Congress during each year in 1961 through 1967—and had to spend roughly four to five hours in preparation for each hour actually spent on Capitol Hill answering questions. Moreover, one congressional committee or another investigated some aspect of Defense operations more than seventy times during 1967, asking often skeptical questions about more than 200 subjects ranging from why the military wanted more than $70 billion to finance its operation during fiscal year 1968 to why the Air Force wanted to build an addition on the Bolling Air Force Base officer's club in Washington, D.C.

The Defense Department's very size, not to mention its impact on all walks of national life, dictates this interest. In some cases, Defense need state its position only once because the inquiry comes from a joint committee made up from members of both houses of Congress. Two that call on Defense frequently are the Joint Atomic Energy Committee and the Joint Committee on Defense Production. At other times, Defense must duplicate its work, repeating its message and facing questions from separate committees—one in each house—covering the same general area of interest. Some examples, again from those that call on Defense often: the

Senate Foreign Relations Committee; the House Foreign Affairs Committee; and committees or subcommittees in each house concerned with government operations, government information, veterans affairs, the merchant marine, space and aeronautics, foreign aid, military justice, construction, etc.

Indeed, any committee that can dream up a reason will attempt to have the Secretary of Defense, preferably, or high-level Pentagon officials testify before it. The Defense Department may have small involvement in the problem being discussed, but its big names are summoned because their presence tends to attract full radio, newspaper, and television coverage nationwide—and such publicity is the lifeblood of politicians.

Whatever the reason, Defense management works hard at its dealings with committees, specifically, and Congress, generally. The Army, Navy, and Air Force each station officers full time on Capitol Hill, primarily to handle personnel matters, such as the tremendous flow of mail to congressmen from their constituents about "Johnny Jones" who was drafted and "hasn't written home in six months," etc. In addition, thousands of letters are forwarded by congressmen to Defense, to request either committee witnesses or answers for voters asking information of every conceivable nature about the military.*

Congressional committees delve into Defense Department matters on three levels: to hear and approve (or reject or modify) military requests for new legislation; to hear and rule on military appropriations requests; and to investigate activities and operations about which congressmen, for one reason or another, may be skeptical and suspicious. On their side, the military spend long hours briefing congressmen, socializing with them, talking to them and their committee staffs—especially prior to the start of hearings to determine

---

* In 1966, for instance, the legislative liaison offices of the Secretary of Defense and the military departments received almost 140,000 such letters, each of which required considerable staff work for a complete, factual answer.

and anticipate the main thrust of an inquiry. Through the Legislative Affairs Office, the Pentagon then works just as hard selecting witnesses able to put the military's best foot forward and giving those witnesses as much background as possible on the kinds of questions they may be asked. It all takes considerable effort.

The most frequent and important confrontation comes, of course, when the military is seeking funds to support its programs. Here, again, there is a time-consuming duplication of effort by military witnesses and congressmen. The annual defense budget request, actually a dollar description of proposed military programs, is the one place where Congress sees at one time all the varied and complex facets of the Department. Clearly, the committees most crucial to Defense are the House and Senate Armed Services committees and Appropriations subcommittees—those committees mentioned earlier, and others like them having looked only at bits and pieces of the total program affecting their parochial interests. And one fiscal year funding request is but a single milestone on a long, tortuous road. Indication of this can be found on the title page of the Defense "Posture Statement" submitted to Congress each year. For instance, the one sent to Capitol Hill in January, 1967, justifying fiscal year 1968 money needs, said it covered "Department of Defense appropriations on the fiscal year 1968–72 Defense program and 1968 Defense budget."

Budget Preparation

Detailed work on the military funding request starts more than a year before Congress finally appropriates the funds. Thus, preparation of the fiscal 1968 budget (covering the period from July 1, 1967, to June 30, 1968), was started in the spring of 1966. At that time, the Defense component agencies began assembling their budget estimates for fiscal 1968 based on national policy guidance from the Secretary of Defense and on the Joint Strategic Objectives Plan of the

Joint Chiefs of Staff (which is the military interpretation of the Secretary's policy guidance).

At the end of a summer-long review, and after many changes, detailed funding requests of the military branches are sent up to the Office of the Secretary of Defense, usually by an October 1 deadline. These requests, supported by a detailed summation of why the funds are needed, are reviewed at the top level. The military services hold briefings, arguing for the fund requests and the programs and plans they represent. Alternative approaches and solutions are analyzed. Choices are made by the Secretary of Defense. Conflicts are resolved. Final decisions are reached by January.

Once approved by the President—who is helped in his analysis not only by Defense Department briefings but also by independent observations from the Bureau of the Budget, among others—the appropriations appeal is submitted to Congress, usually in the latter part of January. There is no required path the budget must follow through Congress. Normally, however, the funding arguments are presented first to the House Armed Services Committee, which sets maximum amounts that can be funded for each program element, and then to the House Subcommittee on Defense Appropriations, which decides how much will be earmarked for each program element within the prescribed ceilings set by the Armed Services Committee.

The same two-step process is repeated in the Senate.* Once the Senate committees have rendered their judgments, conflicts between the conclusions reached by the Senate and House Appropriations subcommittees are resolved in conference—a joint meeting of the two. The recommended budget then goes to the floor of both houses of Congress, is

---

* Except that, through the fortuitous circumstance that Richard Russell is chairman of both the Senate Armed Services Committee and the Senate Subcommittee on Defense Appropriations, at this writing and for some time previously, the two groups ask Defense to argue its case only once, before a joint session of the two committees. Russell is not interested in hearing the same proposals twice any more than Defense is in giving them.

Chart 9

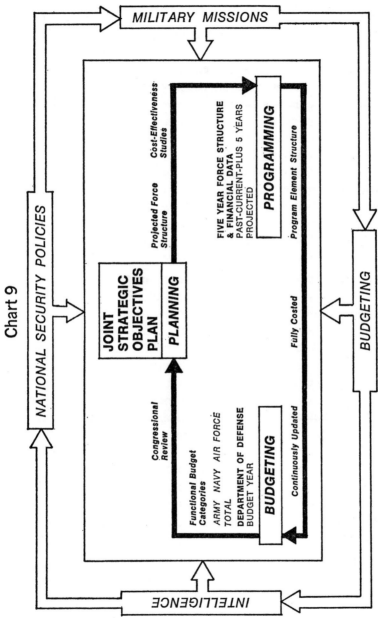

voted on, and passed. Rarely is this whole process completed by July 1 in the year the budget is supposed to take effect. Theoretically, by law, Defense could grind to a halt as of that date. To avoid such a disaster, technically possible, Congress passes an interim resolution each June to the effect that Defense may continue to spend money on each program element in its budget at the same rate as in the previous fiscal year or at the rate requested in the new budget, whichever is less. Once appropriated by Congress, the funds are apportioned to the Defense component agencies by the Bureau of the Budget through the Defense comptroller's office at a time-phased rate throughout the year (usually the rate requested by the military element that originally asked for the money).

As careful analysis will reveal, this life cycle of a budget means that the military usually is handling three budgets at once—spending the funds already appropriated for the current fiscal year, defending on Capitol Hill the budget request for the coming fiscal year, and preparing its budget and spending proposal for the year after that. But, when each of these steps is taken is of secondary importance. Far more significant is the fact that the budget represents the hopes, ambitions, and estimates of the present and future military needs of the nation, as well as the conflicts and resolutions of opinion among a host of middle and top executive management leaders in and outside Defense.

The budget's final resolution each year is the commitment the nation is willing to give to the greatest portion of its national security effort. Thus, as might be expected, there swirls around that budget a continuing, heated argument over what is in it and, more important, why.

The Need for Wisdom

That in this dangerous age, and in its position of coequal status with the executive branch, Congress must perform its role in national defense with wisdom and discretion is, naturally, accepted by everybody. Senate Armed Services Committee Chairman Richard Russell has said: "Under our Constitution, the initiative in the conduct of international relations and the command of our Armed Forces is in the hands of the President. But what the President can and will do in any specific instance is conditioned by Congressional opinion and reaction."

A confrontation between the two, especially when the military is requesting authorization and appropriation of funds for defense, is, according to Russell,

> the moment of truth for those in the Executive Branch who formulate defense programs and those in the Legislative Branch who pass on them.
>
> For several weeks, . . . [congressional committees and subcommittees] will consider volumes of testimony and almost a mountain of supporting data to help them form a judgment on whether the optimum degree of emphasis is being placed on each of several kinds of forces that constitute the military power of the United States. The decisions that are weighed in this process are awesome in their complexity and consequences. In all sincerity, I state my awareness that those who participate need a profound understanding of the lessons of history, a discerning judgment of contemporary events, a prescient knowledge of the future to be confident their choices are wise ones.

Today, many members of Congress tend to feel that the Defense Department, concentrating heavily on cost effectiveness, is not paying due heed to the role of Congress. As Representative Udall has pointed out, "in any final casting-up, it is well to remember that the representative assembly is one of the great creations of free men and that its historic mission is not efficiency in government but the maintenance of freedom."

In matters of conflicting evaluations, particularly in areas of policy and force structures, the Defense Department, many congressmen think, is increasingly inclined to delete or delay programs recommended or directed by Congress, or to implement them in a manner not intended by the legislative body. On this subject, House Armed Services Committee Chairman Mendel Rivers once complained: "The Congress and the Department of Defense must act as partners in the matter of national security, but I think there are times when the Department of Defense forgets that Congress exists for reasons other than to provide a blank check."

To those intimately acquainted with both sides of this troubled partnership, it is obvious that the relationship between the two remains better than usually reported, but certainly not so harmonious as it has been in the past. It is also obvious, of course, that both are working hard to achieve their common objective of having the best military forces possible for the security of the country. But Congress is inclined to go to greater lengths, more expeditiously, and at commensurately greater cost than the current Defense regime, whose philosophy of "cost effectiveness" dictates a slower decision-making process and a holding of defense resources (predicated upon systems analysis) to spending only for those programs absolutely necessary to meet recognized threat contingencies. In contrast to Defense leadership, the Congress clearly feels that a surplus of military hardware, even if it means waste, is preferable to a shortage that may possibly mean disaster.

Many veteran congressmen believe the United States is measurably stronger today and more adequately prepared to meet its responsibilities as a result of past aggressive actions of Congress, taken upon its own initiative, above and beyond the recommendations of the executive branch. Congressman George Mahon, Chairman of the House Subcommittee on Defense Appropriations puts this belief bluntly:

> My position is that if Congress is due any credit, and I think it is, the credit comes principally not from increasing or decreasing defense budgets but from redirecting, re-emphasizing, and accelerating key defense programs. The important role of Congress

has been in the downgrading of marginal projects or low priority projects and the acceleration of high priority projects having a direct relation to our ability to survive.

In spite of its sometimes extreme aggravation with the way Defense does or does not do what it wants, Congress generally has been restrained in legislating too much detail into its defense laws and instructions. Although there are congressional critics of Defense Department behavior who would like to dot every "i" and cross every "t," most legislative leaders have nearly always left a degree of flexibility for Defense executives in the laws passed. Chairman Russell, for instance, "looks upon Congress and [his] Committee as highly potent weapons," yet at the same time recognizes their limitations. He feels that Congress has infinite power to grant or deny funds, but is generally skeptical of its ability to legislate efficiency into the management of the Department of Defense. "It is difficult," he says, "to make wisdom a matter of law."

EFFECTS OF THE VIET-NAM WAR

In an academic and in a very real sense, the U.S. involvement in Southeast Asia has opened to new scrutiny the basic tenets of defense strategy, planning, and operations; the use of the military as an instrument of foreign policy; and the principles and practices of the American armed forces spelled out in the earlier chapters of this work. It has also brought new and nerve-straining dimensions to Defense Department relationships with other government and international agencies, with Congress, and with the public.

Of the purely military picture, Deputy Defense Secretary Cyrus Vance said, in October, 1966:

The ability to support our forces in Southeast Asia and have them perform in such magnificent fashion is the acid test. I think it has been an extraordinary achievement to be able to put some

350,000 men into Southeast Asia in such a short period of time and keep them fully supplied.

That is not to say we are right 100 per cent of the time. You never are in this business, but looking at the test of Viet-Nam over all, it is a superb achievement.

By early 1967, performance was proving the ability of the Joint Chiefs in the Pentagon and unified commands in the field to function well as a team. The strategy of flexible response was also proving itself, as was the validity of the build-up in the early 1960's of conventional war forces. Even the heavy investment in men, money, and matériel for Southeast Asia drained only about 30 per cent off total U.S. military strength world wide. Despite severe strains on U.S. production lines, supply inventories, transportation, and warehouse facilities, the logistics base had shown that it had enough strength and flexibility to deliver.

But although the military picture by itself was reassuring, many congressional leaders, both in their own right, and as representatives of the American public, were voicing dismay over many aspects of the U.S. commitment to Southeast Asia. To the extent that the ultimate aim of the North Vietnamese could be construed as the undermining of congressional support for "an interminable war" so that the United States would pull out, leaving South Viet-Nam to Communist domination, the Communists appeared to have gained a tactical and even strategic advantage. Increasingly, the White House and the Pentagon were finding they had to fight as strongly with words on Capitol Hill to retain congressional support as they had to fight with bombs and bullets against the Viet Cong.

In this respect, the Viet-Nam war had become a powerful pressure affecting Defense Department relationships with Congress and the public in ways and to a degree that cannot yet be assessed. It was provoking bitter and plainly deep-rooted, but largely inconclusive, arguments on points ranging from which branch of government had the right to formulate foreign policy down to what kind of procurement techniques should be used to buy military hardware in a pseudo-peacetime economy.

The final effects of these unfinished debates, involving Defense, Congress, and the public in new tensions as well as in new attempts to define interrelationships and responsibilities, are for the future to determine—if, indeed, any real redefinition ever does come out of the present turmoil. Certainly no clear, long-term pattern has emerged as yet, for instance, from the White House pronouncement in mid–1967 that it did not even need the authority of the Senate's "Gulf of Tonkin" Resolution (establishing "the sense of Congress" that the United States should stand behind its real or implied promises to support the free peoples of South Viet-Nam) to escalate the nation's military commitment in Southeast Asia. In fact, the executive branch claimed that it had possessed sufficient authority long before the Gulf of Tonkin Resolution in the Senate-approved U.S. membership in the Southeast Asia Treaty Organization (SEATO). For many in Congress the implication in that statement has raised a serious question about government separation of powers. Has the Congress, through its approval of the several-score military assistance treaties that the United States has signed, abrogated its own constitutionally granted authority to "make and declare war"?

IX

Conflicts and Controversies: Their Source and Sense

General Marshall reportedly once said, "Don't ask me to agree in principle; that just means we haven't agreed yet." Throughout the Defense Department's short history there has been little disagreement with the principle that fighting the Cold War effectively demands a total commitment from the nation's diplomatic, economic, and military resources. A few persons might argue, but most would agree with Robert Lovett's 1960 statement before the Subcommittee on National Policy Machinery of the Senate Committee on Government Operations:

> our system of government and our way of life have come under direct and deadly challenge by an implacable, crafty and, of late, openly contemptuous enemy of both.
>
> We need not waste much time in attempting to prove this point. If the public statement "We will bury you" [by former Russian Premier Nikita Khrushchev in 1959] does not carry the message to us, then words have lost their meaning. Attempts to explain away this blunt warning of intention by calling it jovial, or by saying that it really does not mean a big military funeral but just a little economic one is a form of jocularity too close to the jugular to lighten my heart.
>
> If we are not prepared, after that statement and the evidence of the past several years, to admit that we are in a struggle for

survival involving military power, economic productivity, and influence on the minds of men in political, scientific, and moral fields, then we have truly succumbed to the hard sell of the soft attitude.

Few have objected, either, to maintaining in peacetime a powerful military force—kept continually updated by the best new equipment that the technological revolution has to offer, tempered only by very loose limits on what the nation can afford to spend. In nearly every one of the Defense Department's twenty years, Congress has made clear its willingness to give the military even more funds than the Pentagon's top leadership asked for, provided those funds could be put to good use. Nor has there been much argument, in general terms, with the principle that in its own security interest the nation should provide military and economic aid to other countries.

Knowing only this much, an observer who had not read the news headlines of the past two decades might assume that the Defense Department's evolution to its present state has been relatively calm. But, as almost everyone does know, the organization has been torn, battered, and badgered by conflict and controversy throughout its history, and no doubt will continue to be. The source of nearly all this turmoil has not been what, in sweeping language, needs doing, but how best to do it. What is the true, comprehensive description of the threat? What parts of the ominous challenge are most serious today? Tomorrow? Where is totalitarianism likely to emerge, or poverty to explode into revolution next? What should the response be to prevent trouble? To squelch it? Which weapons, forces, and weapon developments clearly demand top-priority treatment at any given point in time? How much funding for defense is enough? How accurate are the intelligence estimates? The long-range plans? Is there enough cushion for contingency and error?

Often overlooked, especially by critics of Defense Department behavior, is that the Department's leaders deal in tomorrow. Much can be learned from experience, of course, but it is risky to assume that merely by doing right the next time what was done wrong the last time, mistakes will no longer be made. The main business of the Defense Department is to decide today what the military force structure and functions should be seven, eight, or even ten years from now. More than a score of years ago, an Air Force general said in a perceptive speech:

> National safety would be endangered by an Air Force whose doctrines and techniques are tied solely to the equipment and processes of the moment. Present equipment is but a step in progress, and any Air Force which does not keep its doctrines ahead of its equipment, and its vision far into the future, can only delude the nation into a false sense of security.

The Defense Department does not have any ultimate, inarguable profit-and-loss statement, as does commercial business, except final success or failure in war, and the military's first function is to prevent war, if at all possible. Consequently, the "Who is right?" among the experts can be answered only by evaluating performance against inference. Did the presence of two B-29 bomber groups in England during the Berlin Airlift prevent the Russians from going to war to enforce their blockade? Was the President's threat to enlarge the war in Korea the reason the Communists finally agreed to negotiate? Were the billions spent to finance duplicate missile development programs in the mid-1950's the reason that race was won? Will the strong American presence in Southeast Asia prevent the spread of Communism there—and, for that matter, does this effort really make that much difference to America's security?

Lacking an irrefutable, it-did-or-it-didn't statistic, the answers to these and similar questions are again a matter of subjective, if informed, judgment. And what all this means is that a controversy, once started in Defense, can run on indefinitely. There is nearly always opportunity for an expert whose advice was not followed to contend, after the fact, that the result would have been the same, or better, if his opinion had been accepted. Perpetuating the conflict of ideas is the fact that judgment often is mixed up with presumptive instinct. As Forrestal, who fought through as much of this as most other stewards of Defense put together, once said, "A great many decisions, both in business and in government, have been reached more on emotional than on intellectual levels." And where the result of judgment or emotion or both has been bad, the opposition invariably renews its insistence that the original concept was wrong. Actually, the decision could have been right, as could the policy, with only the execution wrong or poor.

The Defense Department, like private industry and private individuals within any organization, has made, and continues to make, mistakes. But private enterprise is protected from the glare of public scrutiny much of the time. Moreover, a 1 per cent error in a private firm is usually not devastating to the company; the same percentage of error in the Department of Defense can cost millions of dollars—and that kind of mistake, even if it does not concern life-or-death matters, deserves, and, predictably, will get, strong comment from nearly everyone who hears about it.

INTELLIGENCE PROBLEMS

Even if it were possible to separate predictive judgment from emotional bias, there would remain a fountainhead for continuing error and argument—incomplete collection or lack of thorough understanding of intelligence information.

Authorities generally agree that misunderstanding of intelligence information regarding Pearl Harbor in 1941 was a major cause of the Japanese attack's being a successful surprise. A factor contributing to unawareness of what was about to happen in Korea in 1950 was misunderstanding of a Central Intelligence Agency report prior to the attack stating, in effect, that the attack was about to come. And a Pentagon expert had said that one need only examine the history of deliberations over NATO strategy "to discover that our inability to assess accurately the capabilities of General Purpose Forces [on both sides] can . . . have potentially dangerous consequences." He was referring to calculations that assumed the Soviet Union's divisions—some 160 to 175—each had an effectiveness roughly equal to a NATO division. But the true picture proved different from this pessimistic one, as studies of specific factors that make a division an effective fighting force were compared. These included, among other things, comparative ratios of combat-ready versus reserve troops, of firepower, of battlefield mobility and "staying power," of logistics support, and of training techniques and effectiveness.

The result of the initial overstatement of enemy strength was not an increase in conventional forces but a decrease, on the premise that any attempt to catch up was futile. The result, in practice, turned out not to be insurance and safety, but smaller forces and greater risk. "The same kind of error," according to the expert spokesman, "was also being made in several other areas." The history of war is filled with many examples in which one side could have attacked or defended successfully had it known the enemy's true strength, but did not because it overestimated that strength.

Internal Defense Department conflict over such intelligence estimates has produced, as a by-product, still another conflict. Inherent in all military strength is the use of numbers and statistics. As noted earlier, the primary tool that technology has produced (and improved amazingly in the past few years) for storing and analyzing numbers is the computer. Many have claimed for this electronic marvel the ability to perform almost superhuman feats of comparison and evaluation. Scientists, mathematicians, and engineers, including those who developed the computer, have without question worked wonders by the rigorous use of numbers. But, unfortunately, in spite of the fact that management deals in uncertainties, which cannot be measured as precisely as a physics formula, there has been a noticeable tendency in many defense circles of late to suspend the use of logic when given a number—that is, to assume that, if a solution has a number on it, it is correct. Those in a position to know claim that more bad policy has been written because somebody used the wrong number than for any one reason. Wise management leaders are aware that if you pump garbage into a computer, it will pump garbage back out; thus, the challenge still remains with expert judgment.

Additionally, use and misuse of the computer in the Defense Department—which employs more of them than any other organization in the world to assist it in just about every phase of its work—has added to, not alleviated, the problem of communicating valid, complete information. This phenomenon of the mid-twentieth century, itself contributing further to controversy, has been called the "Information Explosion." General Howell M. Estes, Jr., commented, in a speech at the national symposium on Better Management Information and Reporting, in 1966, that

> because we didn't know exactly what questions to ask [the computer] we ask far too many. . . . The important point is that the potential offered by this revolution in computer handling of information will never be realized without a wholly new approach to management and to the management information that each management level will require. . . . The question—how to manage management information—*must* be asked. And we must have at least a reasonable set of possible answers very soon, before we are all engulfed, inundated and strangled in an unremitting flood of information—too much to even be able to

determine how much of it we could very well have done without. . . .

Someone [has] asserted that man can always pull the plug on the machine before the machine could take control of man . . . [but one computer expert has answered that] with a machine doing millions and billions of calculations a second, the man will have been overwhelmed and bypassed long before he can even know it is time to cut off the power. Information, including management information, is growing by the microsecond and even the nanosecond. We cannot turn off the flow. We had therefore better learn to control it—and we are already running late.

With the need to estimate an enemy's strength accurately, any decision-maker's acquisition of too little correct information or too much irrelevant information can lead him to wrong conclusions. A practical case in point: during McNamara's first two or three years in office, his seemingly revolutionary ways of doing business stirred up tremendous amounts of anger and argument. McNamara's immediate staff attributed nearly all this aggravation to a basic, and predictably temporary, human reluctance to make change. The Secretary himself said, "People don't naturally do things the most difficult way; so, if you propose change, they assume it is criticism of the way they've been doing things." But that emotional reaction was only a partial cause of conflict. Also a spur to controversy over the newly instituted program packages, systems analysis, and all the other changes was the fact that the Secretary and his relatively young, bright civilian assistants were getting more and better data faster than were the old-line military officers that were asking them for program approvals. The generals and admirals had already fought two wars while some of McNamara's key civilian aides were still growing up to draft age. "It was tough," admitted a Pentagon admiral, "having these kids prove you wrong all the time."

The threads of all these factors—the changing nature of the struggle, the slowness of some to see the significance of that change, the shortage of sufficient relevant information and the deluge of redundant data, and the judgments based on or tempered by instinct and emotion rather than fact— run through nearly every argument on any specific subject in the Defense Department, adding at least to the heat of disagreements over problems, if not to the substance. The most important debates, based on fundamental differences in viewpoint, seem likely to remain unending. To evaluate what they are today, and what they may be tomorrow, it helps considerably to review how and why they were argued in earlier times.

COMBAT EFFECTIVENESS: THE ROLES-AND-MISSIONS ARGUMENTS

As a matter of policy, rather vaguely stated in the earlier years, it has always been understood in the military that the armed forces were likely to face and have to counteract a variety of threats, from guerrilla insurgency to nuclear holocaust. If all the military planners in all the services had been working cooperatively in an atmosphere uncluttered by controversy, it is reasonable to assume that they could have divided up the spectrum, deciding who would handle each part of it. Each service would have specified what forces and weapons it needed to handle its part of the total problem. But that was, and is, far from practical.

As late as 1961, McNamara observed:

we found that the three military departments had been establishing their requirements independently of each other. I think the results can fairly be described as chaotic: the Army planning, for example, was based primarily on a long war of attrition, while the Air Force planning was based, largely, on a short war of nuclear bombardment. Consequently, the Army was stating a requirement for stocking months of fighting supplies against the event of a sizable conventional conflict, while the Air Force stock requirements for such a war had to be measured in days, and not very many days at that. Either approach, consistently followed, might make some sense. The two combined could not possibly make sense. What we needed was a coordinated strategy seeking objectives actually attainable with the military resources available.

That statement is significant as much for what it does not say as for what it does. Forrestal had called for a balance in the variety of military forces at least as early as 1948. But the separate and autonomous services were bitterly divided over what "balanced" should mean to each of them in relation to the others. The proper "balance" was so strongly contested that a description of individual military roles and missions was not even included in the National Security Act—partly because it was recognized that they would probably change, and the need to rewrite the law each time they did would mean a pesky, if not actually dangerous, delay. Dissension was already so strong that any cut-and-dried wording could have resulted in near military mutiny.

After World War II, for instance, there were great gaps in agreement over the roles each service should play in amphibious operations, strategic bombing and reconnaissance, submarine warfare, and protection of shipping. The Marines considered amphibious warfare their primary responsibility, while the Army claimed it should have the necessary forces for sustained operations beyond the beachheads, and Marine Corps size should be cut back to only that necessary to take and secure just the beach. Also, said the Army, if its advice were followed, the Marine Corps could be absorbed into the Army, and Defense would realize some economies. Needless to say, this did not set well with the Marine Corps, which had difficulty even accepting the Navy as its foster parent, let alone the Army as a brother. Strategic bombing, said the newly created Air Force, should be solely its responsibility. The Navy saw this as a direct threat to its large carrier fleets with their complements of combat aircraft, which, in World War II, had replaced the battleship as the Navy's major attack unit. Moreover, the Navy insisted it needed land-based aircraft to support its missions in antisubmarine warfare and protection of shipping. The Air Force countered that it should have the aircraft if they took off from land, with the Navy sticking strictly to carrier-based air operations. The biggest argument of all was over delivery of the atomic bomb, considered by many in the military, Congress, and the public alike to be The Weapon. Although conceding that the Air Force had a primary interest here, the Navy still claimed that strategic bombing launched from large carriers was feasible, and the Navy "should not be prevented from this type of operation when the situation called for it."

The vitriol spewed into public view over the relative merits of the Air Force strategic bomber versus the Navy aircraft carrier. The Air Force, on the threshold of converting its entire airplane inventory to jet-engine power, had decided to adopt the B-36 bomber. An intercontinental heavy bomber, it was designed for attack-and-return missions from the United States to any spot in the northern hemisphere. In terms of the then current state of aviation technology, however, it had many questionable characteristics, all of which the Navy promptly pounced on. A prime motivation in the Navy's antibomber campaign was that, almost concurrently with the Air Force decision, the Secretary of Defense had canceled Navy plans to build a huge (by 1948–49 standards), aircraft carrier designed to carry jet-powered aircraft. Faster and heavier than most aircraft then in the defense inventory, the planes that would fly off the carriers' decks would in some cases also be able to carry the atomic bomb. The Air Force, supported by the Army, told Congress that canceling the Navy carrier was a wise decision since the Navy would have been "building an expensive weapon for which there would be no logical employment in any foreseeable war" and that the carrier constituted "a waste of Defense Department funds." The Air Force also pointed out that "the only logical enemy would be Russia," which had a negligible surface fleet, and that, therefore, the Navy was gearing itself to fight a nonexistent force.

As told in some detail in the opening chapters of this volume, there swirled around the year-long congressional hearings over these contentions in 1949 storms of protest, threatened officer resignations, and deprecations by both the Air Force and the Navy of the other's reasoning and even its combat capability in general. At the end, the supercarrier cancellation stood. Congress tabled a decision on the B-36— and forgot about it altogether within two years, when the arrival of B-47 jet bombers made it obsolete.

Later, in the middle of the Korean War, the Army was pulled directly into similar debate. Overriding emphasis and budget expenditures by both the Air Force and the Navy on their assumed strategic responsibilities, coupled with a budget ceiling, had resulted, according to the Army, in Air Force neglect of its air support obligations to the Army. Failing to get what it thought was adequate effort from the Air Force, the Army began to develop its own heavy fast aircraft, primarily for battlefield reconnaissance and logistic airlift missions. Soon, a good many Army planners were calling for Army development of Army-owned aircraft to perform even more missions than close air support and interdiction. They foresaw providing their own logistic airlift both to the combat zone and within it. The Army also formed an experimental "Sky-Cav" combat unit designed to perform cavalry-type missions under nuclear-war conditions using a variety of helicopter and fixed-wing aircraft. The Air Force objected to all this, claiming it usurped their rights in the tactical and logistic aviation fields. (In the 1960's, the debate is still going on.)

Still another argument welled up over who should have the

right to develop and control a whole new blossoming family of missiles—land-based, sea-based, short-range, intermediate range, and intercontinental. This argument began to get out of hand in late 1956. Hoping to end the disputes, the Secretary of Defense issued a "clarification of roles and missions" memorandum, purportedly updating the accords theoretically reached in 1948. It did not disturb the Marine Corps and Navy missions at all. But Army aviation efforts were ordered back within the limits of battlefield reconnaissance and transportation, and the Army was instructed not to develop missiles with a range greater than 200 miles. The Army was given responsibility for air defense of points on the map; the Air Force, for air defense of geographic areas. The Army was told that it did not need any more long-haul logistic airlift than the Air Force already had, and therefore should stop asking for it—unless "currently approved strategic concepts" changed.

In general terms, during all these squabbles, where separate service functions and combat capabilities supposedly interlocked, the tendency was to neglect those links. Where the weapon system had glamour and could command or attract large amounts of budget appropriations, each service concentrated on it, especially if the weapon function was to deliver an atomic warhead. The emphasis was on competition, rather than on complementary effort toward a common combat capability goal.

Another argument also cropped up: had the intercontinental ballistic missile, which at the time was considered invulnerable, made the bomber as a strategic weapon obsolete? In addition, nuclear warheads on the ends of missiles, whether strategic or tactical, opened up a whole new round of controversy over what strategy ought to be. Especially in the Army, there was increasingly outspoken insistence that expenditures first for nuclear power and bombers, then for missiles, had left the modernization and improvement of traditional conventional war forces in outmoded disarray. Ground forces spokesmen argued that the nation had put all its military eggs into the atomic basket and had left itself no options other than nuclear war if it became involved in a serious conflict. For many persons, the implications in these arguments raised fears of a strategy of "brinksmanship," with the United States rushing to the cliff-edge of nuclear holocaust if the Communists anywhere started shooting anything at anybody.

THE ISSUE OF ECONOMY

Disturbing as the debates on strategy, roles and missions, and ownership of weapons were, they did not constitute the whole of service conflict in earlier years. Interconnected with all these arguments was the fight for dollars. Funds needed to buy hardware and support missions were always, according to the military, short. Higher-level approval—particularly in the Pentagon and the White House—of how much the military wanted was regularly a cut below what was asked, the result of estimating what the economy could afford and what the taxpayer would stand for.

The Defense Department's first two commanders-in-chief, Truman and Eisenhower, both seriously concerned with balancing federal budget spending against tax income, supported, in broadest terms, a military policy of substituting quality for quantity. Forces were reduced in number and in terms of matériel, and the loss in combat strength (according to advocates of this approach) was equalized or better by increasing firepower, improving command and control, and adding mobility. Translated into weapons, this meant atomic power and aviation or missile delivery systems. It also meant emphasis on speeding up the technological revolution.

During this period, much as the budget ceiling pressured the services into frustrating dollar-short positions, the services also tended to aggravate their own problem by refusing to change their approach. For instance, although the Army complained bitterly that it was not receiving enough funds to modernize, it was spending a large portion of what funds it did receive on missiles and antimissile missile systems, neglecting many other weapons that modernization seemed to demand.

Political Considerations

There were certain continuing contests, mostly between the Pentagon and other authorities in government, that involved dollars, but also fit into a category best characterized by a general who said, "In the final analysis, the major decisions about the course we pursue are political decisions which are strongly influenced by the mood of the people."

Over the years, the military has tried to reshuffle and streamline the Reserve and the National Guard forces, one objective being to merge them into a single force of reserve units, not only to cut costs but to improve the quality of training and readiness. To date, whether the approach has been to merge the Guard into the Reserve or the Reserve into the Guard, Congress has vehemently and successfully objected. One reason is that these units involve part-time soldiers who are full-time voters. A merger would mean fewer training facilities required. Federal dollars going into some local constituencies would stop; and some congressmen would no longer be able to campaign, at least in part, on their alleged abilities to pump federal dollars into the hometown economy.

Universal military training is another program that the Pentagon has pushed from time to time, especially in the first several years of the Department's existence. It, too, has been bluntly turned down by Congress, forcing a continuation in peacetime of the wartime draft.

Another Defense effort notable for being in continual trouble due to its political and economic overtones has been the Military Assistance Program. In theory, MAP, as the military calls it, has been a cornerstone of collective Free

World security, and it actually existed even before enabling legislation for it was passed by Congress in 1950. The concept behind it has always been that the United States would provide a protective atomic umbrella; contribute to the local, conventional forces of allies; and, where the local nation had the will but not the means to oppose aggression or maintain stability, supplement that will with contributions of U.S. equipment, technical advice, and similar assistance.

Since 1950, the United States has invested approximately $35 billion in the equipment and training of other Free World military forces. Although setting up the machinery for this complex, worldwide program was difficult, obtaining the resources to run the program started off with relative ease. It has grown steadily more difficult. In the beginning, substantial stocks of excess military equipment left over from World War II were available in storage depots all over the world for use in the program. In addition, Congress unhesitatingly provided whatever funds were requested to buy new stocks, pay for training, etc. The bulk of this effort—some 79 per cent of the annual appropriation—went, at first, to Europe. As European allies got back on their feet, that percentage dwindled—now it is approximately 3–4 per cent of the total annual appropriation. Yet, the size and complexity of the Military Assistance Program has not changed. It has merely shifted to new geographic locations, primarily the Middle and Far East.

But congressional attitudes toward the program have changed. In the early stages, MAP expenditures were running $5–6 billion a year. The total is now less than $1 billion a year. In the meantime, weapon complexity and economic inflation have added to equipment price tags and the excess stocks once available from the military departments for the price of repair and refurbishing are all gone. In spite of these cost increases, congressional opponents of what they have called "a giveaway which earns us only disrespect" have gradually hammered down the size of the MAP appropriation every year. The military readily admits that it has sometimes made errors in judgment on where to put how much of what kind of aid, but it insists, too, that, over-all, the program has given the United States the best return on its investment of any of its defense dollars.

A Changing View of Costs

With the arrival of the McNamara team in 1961, the ground rules, if not the substance, of many of these dollar controversies began to change. Official policy that the nation could afford "whatever is necessary" meant that the military departments no longer let their priority-rated list of weapon and force structure requests be influenced, in advance, by assumptions based on how large a budget each service might receive. In addition, the strategy of flexible response earned general military acceptance. For years, of course, over-all military requests had consistently been based on the nation's need for a wider range of answers to aggression than simply nuclear-powered forces. The new point, however, was that the combination of Administration pronouncements about strategy and funding meant that, henceforth, programs would be argued on their individual merits in performing a function and that cost would be important only in terms of whether one weapon could perform the same function as well, or better, at a lower price than another, regardless of which service developed the weapon.

This was not an original blueprint. Strategy, funds, and the comparison of one with the other had always reflected the Department's internal sorting out of who had the power. But now, through reorganization, administrative order, and gradual adjustment in service relationships, the Secretary of Defense had finally obtained clear command of the Department; approval for and the paying out of spending power had shifted from the services to his office. He had become the focal point for conflict and controversy, as no Secretary had been before. Along with the acquisition of authority had gone the inevitable assumption of added responsibility. (Inherent in the program-package approach to budgeting, for instance, is the fact that only the Secretary of Defense and his staff are in a position to compare, without service bias, the relative merits of the Minuteman strategic missile developed by the Air Force and the Navy-developed Polaris strategic missile, or to evaluate a mixture of the two together.)

Debates continued, naturally, on the proper weapons and force structure for antisubmarine warfare, strategic bombing, aircraft versus missiles, and conventional versus nuclear capability. A change for the better, however, had come into the texture of the argument—a change from service-oriented opinion to function-oriented Joint Staff debates. And, at the same time that the color of the uniform became less important, the civilian gained full-fledged—some thought, too dominant —membership in the debating society. Whereas the complaint by Defense Department higher authority, in the Pentagon, the White House, and Congress, had once been the resistance of the military to civilian control, now many in the military were objecting that overriding civilian power had wiped out respect for military judgment. Admirals, generals, and their political, civilian friends in Congress, as well as the public, contended that the military had been relegated to second-class citizenship in the Pentagon.

DECISION-MAKING CONTROVERSIES

McNamara's order to streamline traditional methods of military staff work also caused unhappiness. The old way, he said, was taking too much time, and producing too much compromise and not enough decision. As Assistant Secretary of Defense (Administration) Solis Horwitz explained in 1965,

[McNamara] believes that one of the great difficulties, whether in the government or in industry, is the inability or lack of desire to make decisions. If a problem involves conflict, the tendency is not to decide the problem. The tendency is to shove it under the carpet and avoid the conflict; or alternatively, to arrive at a decision which satisfies everybody. Often, as I'm sure you know, a decision which satisfies everybody actually decides nothing at all.

According to former Deputy Secretary of Defense Roswell Gilpatric, however, "When he arrived, Mr. McNamara felt we had to move quickly. Unfortunately, the system just couldn't move that quickly. During the period before we were all geared up to the new tempo, the new philosophy, there was bound to be confusion and complaining."

Robert Lovett had warned the government in 1960 that it needed a clearing out of the progress-choking bureaucratic underbrush that it had accumulated over the years. He said:

The often forgotten fact [about] our form of government, and its machinery, [is that it] has had built into it a series of clashes of group needs. They appear to have been originally designed to protect the individual citizen and to keep any one group or department . . . from getting too dominant. This device of inviting argument between conflicting interests—which we can call the "foul-up factor" in our equation of performance —was obviously the result of a deliberate decision to give up the doubtful efficiency of a dictatorship in return for a method of protecting individual freedom, rights, privileges, and immunities.

When Government was small, the "foul-up" system must have worked very well; when Government became large, it probably worked fairly well. But Government has now become gigantic at the very moment in history when time itself is not merely a measure, or a dimension, but perhaps the difference between life and death.

Under McNamara's new management system, the Defense Department organization chart lost much of its significance. The new Secretary preferred dealing with individuals—anyone who showed a willingness to accept responsibility and act—rather than working through channels. He treated his assistant secretaries (civilian) and the secretaries of the military departments as, in business terminology, his divisional executive vice presidents, and the mantle of his authority went with them when they called on military officers with their probing questions and questioning suggestions. It was a new experience for the services, and some officers resented suddenly having to deal with the Secretary of Defense through an intermediary, particularly if the man was a civilian. It was easy to exaggerate irritation into "proof" that military authority had been downgraded. A good deal of this fresh conflict consisted of simple peevishness.

There was one serious charge, however—that the civilian Secretary of Defense was making military decisions. Again, Lovett had warned of this possible risk, telling Congress in 1960:

> Civilian and military executives alike should stick to the fields in which they have special training and aptitudes. If they do, the chance of making the machinery work well is excellent. One of the few humans as exasperating as a civilian businessman who suddenly becomes an expert on military strategy and tactics is the military adviser who magically becomes an expert in some highly sophisticated production problem in which he has no background of experience.

It is dangerously easy to oversimplify the stresses of this military versus civilian relationship. For instance, the Joint Staff and military men who serve as leaders or participants in joint military deliberations—and whose stature climbed in the new setup vis-á-vis the officers in the military departments—adapted to the change more quickly than their counterparts in the services. They endorsed, more than they criticized, the new routines—leading some McNamara detractors to insist that they were "muzzled" and could not express their true feelings. Yet the number and heat of their disagreements, with each other and with McNamara, did not decrease. Far from it; but their disagreements were reflections of honest differences on the issues themselves. These officers are no longer wrapped up in the disharmony that, in the past, had tended not only to distort the facts of a problem, but to weaken enthusiasm for implementing agreements reached.

Even today, however, officers complain that the civilian Secretary of Defense, on occasion, makes decisions contrary to their recommendations, and add that his conclusion is really a military judgment that they do not consider him qualified to make. For example, the Secretary's decision that the Air Force and the Navy should buy one fighter aircraft, the F-111, to perform a variety of tasks for both services, rather than each service buying its own, was an order they felt fit this indictment. At the Secretarial level, cost saving was claimed as a primary motivating factor. But some officers, even in the Joint Staff, felt that the decision was more the result of the Secretary's military conclusion that different kinds of specialized aircraft were not needed. He believed, they said, that the course to follow was to have one or at most only a few different types of airplanes to perform a variety of missions. Another protest against "military judgments by the civilian Secretary" hit McNamara's cutback on the number of helicopters the Army wanted to equip a division designed to be virtually air-mobile on the battlefield. Also, in the military mind, Secretarial reluctance to deploy an antimissile missile defense, contrary to the unanimous request of the Joint Chiefs, has been regarded as a decision taken as much on the basis of his personal military analysis as on his desire not to spend money unnecessarily.

What has concerned informed and thoughtful observers is the significance of too much civilian interference with the military authority at top Defense levels. Former high-level Pentagon executive, Wilfred McNeil, addressing the Industrial College of the Armed Forces, in 1964, said:

> Our national defense is as much a matter of strong and dynamic ideas as it is weapon systems, bases and manpower. If we lack a wealth of ideas, our wealth of the material means of defense will be meaningless. These ideas much be cultivated at every level of our defense system. They must be encouraged and must flow with relative freedom to the very top levels of Government where they can compete for acceptance.
>
> Recently, there seems to be a dangerous tendency in our defense to try to anticipate what is wanted from the top and then supply it. In this kind of "give me what I want" atmosphere we lose many valuable ideas and the benefit of many points of view, each based on a particular perspective and framework of experience. And, perhaps of greater importance, well trained and incisive people are discouraged from further attempts at unpatterned thinking. . . . Civilian control is a principle, of course, that underlies our military forces. [But] the present tendency to increasingly greater civilian control, over both defense planning and execution, must be tempered by an increasingly skilled and competent Officer Corps. The need was never greater for fully professional men. There is a great value in the inherent conservatism of the military, and a necessity for the realism of the true professional.

Clearly, this Pentagon veteran was warning that a Defense Secretary treads in hazardous territory when his orders to the military amount to instructions on what equipment they are to use and how they are to plan their campaigns—unless his decision is based on something other than his own notion of military effectiveness. And, of late, many officers, especially recently retired ones, have argued that "the pendulum is swinging too far," i.e., that the basically military aspects of defense planning and policy are being decided by civilians unschooled in the art of war strategy and tactics.

McNamara's position in this controversy, to quote a statement that he made in testimony before Congress' Joint Economic Committee in 1963, has been that "it is not primarily the primacy of the civilian versus a military authority, but rather the primacy of an individual, military or civilian, who bears the total responsibility and can see the total problem in all of its aspects." And, by law, the Secretary of Defense, who, Congress specified, must be a civilian, is responsible for the actions of the entire Department, including its military actions. Subordinates in the organization, civilian and military alike, for all the authority that might accompany their collective experience and intelligence, are legally only advisers to the Secretary of Defense.

It would be misleading to leave the impression that the significance of this conflict lies entirely in the opposition, one to another, of military and civilian authority. More important is that the scope of a military adviser's military opinion has broadened, as has the civilian's. In 1964, speaking to an audience in Chicago, General Maxwell D. Taylor made this point plain:

> As for the corporate body of the Joint Chiefs of Staff, I can certainly testify that it has not been bypassed during my tenure of office as Chairman. . . . As I look at my own schedules and those of my senior colleagues, replete as they are with consultations at the White House, State Department, and elsewhere throughout the Government, I cannot feel that the views of the military are not being adequately represented in the policy-making councils of the Government. If we are not carrying the day in all the arguments, it is more likely that our cause may not always be right or that our persuasiveness may not always be effective, rather than that there is a deliberate desire to disregard the military facts of national life.
>
> If such a disregard existed it would be a most serious matter. If as Clemenceau is reported to have said, "war is too serious a business to be left to the generals," it is equally true today that the maintenance of peace is too serious a business to be left to any single class of society or agency of our Government. Flex-

ible and adequate policy-making in times like these calls for a sophisticated blending of all components of our national strength —political, economic, ideological, as well as military.

And McNamara himself has noted: "Planning for military action must be complemented today by international political and psychological factors not normally, by many past standards, a part of strategic or tactical planning. . . . Today's senior military officers must take these into account. Many are developing extraordinary ability to do so."

For his analysis to be rational and his advice to be practical, the military officer today must be versed in fields once far removed from his direct interest. Similarly, the civilian has had to change also, be he adviser to or Secretary of Defense. Not only have the traditional civilian areas of expert knowledge—diplomacy, economics, politics—become more closely linked with military deliberations than ever before, but, also, the technological revolution has raised challenging questions about the relevance of military experience even in largely military matters. Possessing as they do today many weapon systems untried in combat and yet three, four, and even five generations removed from those used in World War II and in Korea, the most expert of military strategists must question whether their experience applies to contemporary doctrines concerning the use of force.

A prominent military affairs writer, Samuel P. Huntington, noted in 1963, in an article in *Daedalus*:

Military leaders and military institutions were less powerful in the Truman administration that they were during World War II. They were less powerful under Eisenhower than they were under Truman. They are less powerful now . . . than they were under Eisenhower. This constant decline in power and influence of the military profession is the single most important trend in civil-military relations during the past fifteen years.

He also found that "most of the significant writings on strategy produced after World War II were produced by civilians.

. . . Experts such as Brodie, Kaufman, Kissinger, Wohlstetter, Schelling, and Kahn took the lead in articulating theories of stabilized deterrence, limited war, tactical nuclear war, arms control and civil defense."

Interestingly, there is, today, the broadest kind of information exchange between and among all the military and civilian groups that allegedly have been at each other's throats. After several years of working together, they have developed, in general, a mutual trust and awareness of each other's strengths and weaknesses as individuals. Their personal, informal relationships are an intangible but extremely important aspect of this discussion, which no clinical analysis can hope to capture. Perhaps the most fair and accurate observation that can be made is that, if civilians have occasionally stepped over the line into properly military domains, it is hardly surprising.

One conclusion is certain: Whatever the personal feelings of the individuals, military and civilian alike, about how they work together, there is little chance that they will be allowed to grow complacent over seeking the proper balance in their relationship; public and private scrutiny will not permit it. Moreover, by now they themselves know, or have begun to realize, that they are all in business together and that they will succeed or fail as a team.

X

Forecast for Tomorrow

In his inaugural address to the nation on January 20, 1961, President John F. Kennedy said, in part,

> man holds in his mortal hands the power to abolish all forms of human poverty and to abolish all forms of human life. And yet the same revolutionary beliefs for which our forebears fought are still at issue around the globe—the belief that the rights of man come not from the generosity of state but from the hand of God. We dare not forget today that we are the heirs of that first revolution. . . .
>
> . . . .
>
> But neither can two great and powerful groups of nations take comfort from their present course—both sides over-burdened by the cost of modern weapons, both rightly alarmed by the steady spread of the deadly atom, yet both racing to alter that uncertain balance of terror that stays the hand of mankind's final war.
>
> . . . .
>
> Since this country was founded, each generation has been summoned to give testimony to its national loyalty. . . . Now the trumpet summons us again—not as a call to bear arms, though arms we need—not as a call to battle, though embattled we are—but a call to bear the burden of a long twilight struggle . . . against the common enemies of man: tyranny, poverty, disease and war itself.

Kennedy's call inspired many around the world who heard or read it—including, of course, many in the Department of Defense. The Department, in the short years of its existence, had already become one of the main instruments, though not the only one, for carrying on that "long twilight struggle." Its efforts had not been totally rewarding. Since the Department had been set up, the United States had been drawn into two major wars and a series of comparatively minor, but no less critical, clashes. No solution nor end to the Cold War had been found, in spite of its awesomely high costs in men and matériel. With the notable lack of general Allied support for, or sometimes even understanding of, U.S. objectives against Communism and oppression, and with nations that the United States had helped to independence and security subsequently, in the words of one commentator, "abusing our good name, our good record, and our honorable purpose," it was hard for many people to see that there had been much progress in the struggle.

Yet, especially for those in the Defense Department who had lived close to the challenge over the years, it seemed, at the time of Kennedy's inauguration and on into the embattled mid-1960's, pointless to be pessimistic. (As British Prime Minister Winston Churchill had once said, "I am an optimist; there does not seem to be much use in being anything else.") In his February, 1965, statement to Congress on the state of military affairs, Defense Secretary McNamara included the following observations:

> Although the change in the leadership of the Soviet Union and the detonation of a nuclear device by Communist China were two of the most widely noted developments on the international scene during the past year, a more fundamental though less heralded change has been taking place which, over the long run, could be of much greater significance to our national security. . . .
>
> On the Free World side, the nations of Western Europe,

as well as Japan in the Far East, began to get back on their feet politically and economically, and today, the United States is no longer the only important economic and political power. On the Communist side, the absolute control of the Soviet Union has been successfully challenged, and now not only Yugoslavia, but also China, Albania and, to a lesser extent, other Communist nations of Eastern Europe, are following policies directed to their own national interests. Long frozen positions are beginning to thaw and in the shifting currents of international affairs there will be new opportunities for us to enhance the security of the Free World.

In January, 1967, he added:

In Europe, as I noted two years ago, long frozen positions are beginning to thaw and there is an intensified search—on both sides of the Iron Curtain—for new arrangements which might better serve the security needs of all concerned. . . . Another trend of longer term significance is the growing awareness among the nations of Southeast Asia and the Western Pacific that their future security and well-being depends importantly upon their ability to work together in strengthening the military, economic and political cohesion of all the non-Communist nations in the area. . . . This continuing clash between the two Communist giants [China and Russia] is one of the most significant developing trends on the current international scene. . . . The outcome of that struggle could have a profound effect far beyond China's borders.

Too often in the past, such statements have been labeled "superficial" and "naively optimistic" by those who too readily criticize the Defense Department. One of the most persistent obstructions, or at least distractions, to Defense Department personnel in performing their business effectively has been the Department's failure to enlist whole-hearted support from other elements of the government and the nation— a failure due, at least in part, to those elements listening more than they should to criticisms of the Defense Department that are uninformed and superficial. Too often, there is a tendency, particularly by those not intimately involved in Defense Department problems, to search for simple, black-and-white answers to complex questions that can have only gray solutions—or worse, to waste everybody's time and energy demanding solutions to problems already solved. The truth is that a good deal of perceptive judgment by hundreds of bright, dedicated individuals has produced marked, though often hectic, changes in the Department during its short history. And, as has been previously stated, for all the fuss over real or imagined errors, the Defense Department has so far achieved its over-all goal of preserving the national security.

As this book was going to press Washington was surprised by the announcement that Secretary McNamara would leave the Department of Defense sometime in 1968 to become President of the World Bank. In January, 1968, President Johnson named Washington lawyer Clark M. Clifford as successor.

Looking today at the future, former Deputy Secretary of Defense Cyrus Vance says: "We have tried to weigh all the rational and valid alternatives in making decisions. I believe the resulting force structure which we have developed is sound. Thus, no matter who comes into Defense, it is unlikely there will be any major, dramatic change in the Defense program." (Vance's observation is doubly important in view of the speculation on the possible meaning of the McNamara departure to future Defense operations. If Vance is correct, there will be little if any change in *what* Defense has to do. Whatever change comes, it will be in the *way* Defense does it, depending on whether the new Secretary endorses the McNamara management theory of tight leadership direction or believes more in delegating authority to others.) Although he may be correct that no major, dramatic change in Defense is to be expected, and although it may be true, as proponents claim, that the Department's successful, restrained use of power is slowly convincing potential aggressors that military force is not a profitable tool for imposing their will on others, yet, in this author's opinion, it is well to recall the prophetic view of the first Secretary of Defense, James Forrestal, who once said that "The great danger in any country is for people to believe that there is anything absolute about security. Air power, atomic bombs, wealth—by itself none of these can give any security . . ."

Certainly, no unclouded crystal ball is needed to see that the Pentagon is already snared in difficulties—and at a time in history when, as Defense Secretary McNamara has noted, "The margin for error is shrinking." The proliferation of nuclear weapon developments among largely independent-minded nations, in spite of the best U.S. efforts at collective security agreements and disarmament treaties, is proof enough of that cold warning. Moreover, holding democracy's sway over the globe is a task still largely undone.

Even within the Defense Department itself, the long, difficult struggle to build organizational economy, efficiency, and effectiveness has a considerable way to go. Indeed, the Department's very nature suggests that this effort will never be completed, largely because of the unending difficulties in dealing with the often contradictory and always inseparable elements of cost and effectiveness.

For all these reasons, although the prospect for the future in the Department of Defense may not indicate drastic or fundamental program changes, new developments can be expected in the areas of budget ceilings, the arms race, personnel policy, internal organization, and the interrelationships of the Defense Department with other agencies of government involved in determining national security strategy.

RENEWED BUDGET CEILINGS?

For a time, from 1961 to approximately 1966, mid-level military leadership was heartened considerably by Presidential policy declaring that the nation could afford whatever was necessary for national security. As stated, it sounded like the lifting of the "ceiling" on defense spending that they had long blamed for the failure of some of their pet—and, they said, essential—projects to receive funds. As a corollary to the policy of spending whatever was needed, it was also claimed that new cost-effectiveness studies, systems analysis, and the Five-Year Force Structure Plan and Program Package Budget analysis would pinpoint the necessary with far more precision than had been possible in the past.

Initially, these new approaches to budgetary matters seemed to work well in practice. As experience was gained, however, an increasing number of signs began to appear around the mid-1960's that a "no-budget-ceiling" attitude was no more apt to hold sway in the Defense Department tomorrow than it had yesterday. This is not to say that the program-package approach to military funding and force structure analysis was not a valuable contribution to making sound decisions. It was. But it soon became clear that these planning techniques, shorn of their high-sounding names, were neither altogether new, nor panaceas either.

Wilfred McNeil, who was Defense comptroller for the Department's first thirteen years (remaining longer than any other top Pentagon official in any such high-level post), pointed out some remaining problems as early as summer, 1961, when he testified before the Subcommittee on National Policy Machinery of the Senate Committee on Government Operations:

> No matter how precise the planning may have been; no matter how determined management [was] so that budget planning would not encounter a last-minute rush, it is almost certain that something in this day and age will come along and upset it. . . . From a long-range viewpoint, we must have a total national strategy in which each element is in proper balance. Resources must be allocated on that basis and the allocation shifted in line with shifts in over-all strategy.
>
> Fortunately or unfortunately, the allocation cannot be entirely

on a scientific basis. Allocations usually must be a matter of judgment. While we may see some differences in interpretation of certain aspects of the total problem from one administration to another . . . the threat is multifaceted and of a long-term nature, and . . . the strategy and its implementation must be geared to the long pull. . . .

Furthermore, defense requirements cannot be viewed in isolation. The benefits of additional dollars spent for defense are weighed by any administration against the benefits of additional dollars spent for other governmental purposes, and against the additional burden placed on the taxpayer, or the additional debt which future generations would be required to bear.

It is not simply a matter of figuring requirements and adding up their costs. The defense program must be judged in context with the Government program as a whole, and in the light of other desirable objectives, particularly in the fiscal and economic areas. . . .

. . . .

Many people, even though associated with the defense program for a long period of time, come to think of military requirements as finite quantities. This is a misconception. Virtually all military requirements stem from decisions on major force levels, and decisions on the levels of readiness of these forces.

The determination of the forces required for national security and their level of readiness at any particular time is a complicated and by no means exact process. Decision as to the course of research and development and weapons themselves, if rapid advances are to be made, are, in part, a matter of judgment. . . . The package plan . . . seems to contemplate a very high degree of preciseness and ability to perceive successful weapons development and suitability. Certainly past experience would indicate that is not true, although certainly it is all right as a goal to look as far ahead and as precisely as one can.

Recently, with increasing disillusionment, observers have begun to argue that Defense Department mesmerization by the program-package technique has turned national attention away from important substantive issues that need continual scrutiny. If anything, these critics claim, faith in or fear of the packaging formula has tended to silence challenges to the basic policy decisions underlying the arithmetic. For example, what has been justified under the "we-can-afford-anything" philosophy has obscured the continued existence of the "guns-or-butter" dilemma, which is no less serious a problem today than it was in 1953 when President Eisenhower said:

> Every gun that is made, every warship launched, every rocket fired signifies, in the final sense, a theft from those who hunger and are not fed, those who are cold and are not clothed. This world in arms is not spending money alone. It is spending the sweat of its laborers, the genius of its scientists, the hopes of its children. The cost of one modern heavy bomber is this: a modern brick school in more than thirty cities. It is two electric power plants, each serving a town of 60,000 population. It is two fine, fully equipped hospitals. It is some fifty miles of concrete highway. We pay for a single fighter plane with a half-million bushels of wheat. We pay for a single destroyer with new homes that could have housed more than 8,000 people.*

In sum, the amount of investment in defense is determined not only by estimates of the size of potential threat and the size of military forces necessary to counter that threat, but also by the willingness and ability of the people, through Congress, and the economy to support such an investment. Defense budget formulation had produced a tight limit on military spending before the Korean War. When that conflict ended, a similar budget ceiling was imposed on the Department, and held until the missile race began. There were signs in the mid-1960's that pressure to cut Defense Department funding was beginning to reassert itself. Among the indications of this change was the rising tide of complaints from the public, as reflected in Congress, over foreign-aid expenditures

* As quoted in Eisenhower, *The White House Years: Mandate for Change, 1953–1956*, p. 145.

and over keeping strong forces in Europe. And, in May, 1966, Secretary McNamara told the United States and the Free World, "A nation can reach the point at which it does not buy more security for itself simply by buying more military hardware—we are at that point."

The big jump in the U.S. military commitment to fight in Viet-Nam softened some of this defense-economy pressure, but it will almost certainly harden again when that war ends or levels off. Many Defense Department programs not related to the Viet-Nam conflict were feeling the pinch even during the escalation. Their ability to keep going was hampered by the continually increasing cost of increasingly complex weapon systems and also by an inflationary spiral, in which more and more dollars were required to continue doing the same things. Defense Department leaders tried to silence complaints about rising military costs by pointing out that, as a percentage of the gross national product, almost the same amount was being spent on national security that had been spent earlier. Their arguments did little to appease those who insisted that the government had failed to reverse the inflationary trend of defense spending.

In this atmosphere, the services, bumping here and there into what they term a "new budget ceiling," are already raising again their old objections to the ways civilian leadership in the Pentagon, the White House, and Congress is trying to reduce defense costs. They say that these economy moves involve stretching out development and production of hardware to lessen the cost in any given year and cutting the amount of equipment that they are permitted to buy. Thus, reduction of costs means that, because one new fighter aircraft may now be as expensive as two of the old fighters it is replacing, the military is permitted to buy only one to replace two—albeit one carrying greater firepower. In essence, say some officers, "our military strength is being cut even though the threat we have to face has not been reduced."

WHAT PRICE THE ARMS RACE?

One hope for an answer to budget and preparedness problems is in the potential benefits of the United States Arms Control and Disarmament Agency (ACDA). Fundamentally, the goals of ACDA and the Department of Defense are identical and intertwined: the avoidance of war, particularly nuclear war, and the security of the nation. The stereotyped image, in the minds of some military men, of the ACDA as a group of idealists willing to gamble with the nation's survival is, of course, fatuous. The arms control agency is conscientiously searching for ways, through negotiations with other countries and research into surveillance concepts and equipment, to lessen world tensions.

Although forward strides have been made in conceptual studies and equipment development, probably the primary obstacle to ACDA success has been the extreme difficulty in finding common ground in arms control negotiations for agreement among nations as to the manner in which the provisions of an agreement can be policed. Most experts would agree that, for stringent arms control, the world would be better off if the most advanced weaponry known to man were the bow and arrow; certainly, in light of the difficulties involved in inspection and enforcement, the effects of clandestine activities on the part of any treaty signatory would have far less import than in the thermonuclear age. It is not that the military and ACDA do not recognize the merit of arms control. Rather, they harbor the suspicion that all signatories would not honor the provisions of agreement.

For all the practical pessimism that wells up around disarmament talks, ACDA's work is in the same spirit as that of the eighteen-nation Disarmament Committee established in 1962. Made up of five NATO nations, including the United States, five Warsaw Pact nations, including the Soviet Union, and eight nonaligned nations, the group meets in Geneva,

Switzerland, and, although it is not a U.N. body, reports the results of its discussions to the U.N. General Assembly. The most encouraging facet of the Disarmament Committee's tangibly unproductive talks is, in the words of the salesman's adage, "If you can keep him talking, he can't say, 'No!' and slam the door in your face." But this negative success, and even the positive successes of government efforts in the past— the 1963 international treaty banning nuclear testing in the atmosphere, the setting up of a "hot line" between Washington and Moscow to prevent the launching of nuclear weapons "by mistake," and the treaty agreeing to use outer space only for peaceful purposes—seem weak, ineffective brakes on the rapid pace of the arms race.

The most serious aspect of that race is the spread of nuclear weapons. Today, there are only five nations possessing a nuclear capability. Says ACDA Director William Foster, "As additional nations achieve this capability, it puts increased pressure on their neighbors and ultimately we could have 15 or 20 nuclear weapons nations about which we [would] have to be concerned." And, as shattering to world peace as that trend would be, it is not the only disarmament problem. There are a number of nations that the United States insists ought to re-evaluate their own security needs, especially in the underdeveloped parts of the world. Most of them do not have great resources, but they do have great ideas about the weapons necessary to protect their internal security. As a result, they seek and continue to buy highly sophisticated weapons, which have more value as prestige items than as necessities for security. "These things escalate," says Foster, "when one nation acquires such sophisticated weaponry, its neighbor feels that it must also." Such miniature arms races succeed only in undercutting already fragile economies, but the United States has been notably unsuccessful in (a) convincing these nations that they do not need the weapons; (b) preventing U.S. allies, particularly France and Britain, from selling the hardware to these nations if the United States does not; and (c) preventing Communist countries from selling the equipment if the Free World does not.

To the extent that disarmament efforts fall short of goals, investment in the insurance of strong military forces must remain high. In 1961, a new government leadership turned its attention to strengthening forces other than the strategic nuclear arm, while continuing to pay the heavy procurement price of buying operational intercontinental ballistic missiles —and the price of defense went up another $7–8 billion a year compared to what had been spent in 1958–59. This boost came even though no weapon revolutions were boiling at the moment, as there had been during the missile race, and Pentagon top management was cautious and demanding about detailed substantiation before approving a military spending request. Most signs indicate the price will continue to climb.

Many scientists and engineers agree that no one nation ever gains a decisive lead over another in technological knowledge. For all the new discoveries in the past few years, the world scientific community has managed to share technical data among its members reasonably well. A nation gains advantage depending on what its political leadership decides to do with that knowledge. Thus, most often a breakthrough comes not in the technology itself, but from the direction in which that technology is pushed by managers.

Today, the Cold War technology contest in selection and counterselection of weapons is being waged almost solely between the United States and the Soviet Union, with Europe running generally a poor third and the Chinese Communists only beginning to appear on the horizon. Out of this international military competition has come an arms race costing billions of dollars, with money spent on new and newer generations of equipment, each rapidly outdated by a more expensive and more powerful successor.

The questions for the future that the decision-makers must

ask themselves are many and frightening. What new investment will threaten to unbalance the balance of power? Will
the next wind sprint in the race come from Soviet development of an effective antisubmarine weapon system? Will it
come as a byproduct of space-born technology? From developments in chemical, bacteriological, or radiological weapons
—commonly called the "germ-warfare" or "silent-bomb" business? From advances in laser beams? Or command-and-con-
trol systems? Or electronic countermeasures to neutralize the
effectiveness of those communications systems? From greater
advances in known missilery? Or bombers? Or both?

As Defense Secretary McNamara has stated, the currently
planned U.S. offensive force of missiles and bombers has built
into it a hedge against several different contingencies, including, first, the possibility that "a Soviet ballistic-missile defense
might be greater than [predicted] by the intelligence estimates;
and, second, that the Soviets might embark upon any one of
several possible offensive build-ups, including variations in
their target doctrine, variations in the technological sophisti-
cation of their weapons systems, and variations in the speed
of deployment of those systems."

Since the race first began after World War II, fundamental
differences have become apparent, according to former Defense Deputy Secretary Roswell Gilpatric, in a recent article
in *The New York Times Magazine,* "in the Soviet and U.S.
responses to each other's strategic weapons programs. The
United States sought to emphasize and to invest more of its
resources in offensive capabilities, whereas the Soviets have
always stressed defensive measures."

The nation's whole deterrence strategy has been built on
having, and letting the world know that the United States
would have, enough offensive power left after a nuclear attack
to retaliate and destroy the attacker. One offshoot of that U.S.
strategy, at least since McNamara became Defense Secretary,
has been the release to the public of what were once consid-

ered highly classified comparative strength figures. In his fiscal 1968 funding request to Congress, for instance, Mc-Namara announced, with considerable supporting detail, that the United States had 934 intercontinental ballistic missiles to 340 for the Soviet Union, 512 submarine-launched ballistic missiles to 130 for the Russians, and 680 intercontinental range bombers to only 155 in the Soviet arsenal.

Gilpatric also wrote that, "as the Russians built up stronger defenses, the United States added to the numbers of its strategic forces and provided them with the capacity to penetrate Soviet defenses. At the same time we learned that beyond a certain level of defense, the cost advantage lies increasingly with offense." It has been estimated that, after a certain point is reached in the weapons inventory—a point both sides have long since passed—for every $10 the Soviets invest in more defenses, the United States need spend, comparatively speaking, only another $1 in offense weapons to negate completely the whole $10 defensive build-up cost. The importance of this cost advantage for the offense will, it is obvious, affect more and more the decision-makers' weighing of budgetary and security factors.

ABM Deployment

Disarmament, the high cost of the arms race, and the quandary of picking appropriate weapons to develop and deploy are still at work helping to shape the Defense Department's future. Nowhere is this more clear than in the profound worry over the recently announced U.S. decision to put an anti-ballistic-missile defense system into operation. The ABM debate has been going on in the Pentagon for several years. When the Russians began limited deployment of such a system around a few of their military bases and cities, an immediate demand went up, both within and without the Pentagon, that the United States should move its own system out of the decade-long test, evaluation, and improvement stage into production.

Like all important defense questions, this one involves many complex "whats" and "ifs." A basic consideration, of course, is: what will an antimissile missile system be used to protect against? The presently planned Nike-X deployment will, it has been announced, cost the nation $5 billion over five years. According to Secretary McNamara's statement, this light (or "thin," in military terminology) ABM system is "Chinese-oriented." Almost all officials, civilian and military, who have studied the system agree that it would very likely prevent the Chinese from hitting American cities with ICBM's, at least in the 1970's. (According to intelligence estimates, the Chinese will have an operational ICBM by 1970.)

However, few experts believed the publicly announced reason for McNamara apparently—and suddenly—changing his mind and approving ABM deployment in September, 1967. Their reasoning that the announced deployment is not really simply Chinese-oriented was the same reasoning McNamara himself used on ABM deployment generally, i.e., if China really is bent on building a strong offensive nuclear force at a cheap price, it could easily outdistance a "thin" ABM by the early 1980's.

Thus, they argue, the protection at best is temporary and as much Soviet-oriented as Chinese-oriented. Military leaders both in Europe and the United States saw the McNamara announcement as simply his surrender to the order of President Johnson—an order prompted in turn by congressional and military pressures based on a conviction that the United States could not afford, at this stage, with the stakes so high, to place its future security in the logic and honesty of Communist diplomats at a negotiation table. What it all meant, according to many observers, was that those searching for viable means to disarmament had lost another, and possibly their most important, round. British Defense Minister Denis Healey put this reaction bluntly: "It is essentially a surrender in the United States to irrational pressure which will only feed the mad momentum of the arms race."

The faith some persons seem anxious to place in the system itself may prove unfounded. An antimissile missile system still means trying to hit an attacking bullet with another bullet —an extremely difficult matter. And, whatever its promised effectiveness, deployment of an anti-ballistic-missile system carries with it added hazards. McNamara declared, "The danger in deploying this relatively light and reliable Chinese-oriented . . . system is going to be that pressures will develop to expand it into a heavy Soviet-oriented . . . system." The costs of a heavier system, designed to protect American cities and military target areas against full Soviet missile attack, could be anywhere from $10–20 billion to as much as $40 billion. But, in McNamara's view, any of these expenditures for varying degrees of civilian protection would only force the Russians to build enough ICBM's to make sure that they could penetrate the U.S. ABM system, thus rendering the hope of saving lives a tragic illusion. Moreover, the upward spiral in the arms race that would result might, in his view, eliminate hope for any arms limitation agreements.

Any short description of the debate over antimissile missile systems invites oversimplification. In brief, however, on the one hand, the military, including some of McNamara's top advisers on the Joint Chiefs of Staff, argue for the deployment of a heavy ABM system to defend against Soviet attack. McNamara, on the other hand, contends that there are cheaper, equally effective ways to assure the survival of sufficient nuclear retaliatory forces—and the continued credibility of U.S. nuclear war deterrence. Roswell Gilpatric's article, cited above, stressed McNamara's underlying conviction:

> It is the virtual certainty that the Soviets will act to maintain their deterrent which casts such grave doubts on the advisability of our deploying the system for the protection of our cities

against the kind of heavy, sophisticated missile attack they could launch in the 1970's. In all probability, all we would accomplish would be to increase greatly both their defense expenditures and ours without any gain in real security to either side.

An even better measure of how strongly Secretary McNamara feels on this issue can be found in the words of warning with which he accompanied his announcement of the U.S. ABM deployment. He departed from the prepared text of his speech, which had been carefully checked, word by word, by the Pentagon, the White House, and the State Department, to add, in explicit opposition to any expansion of this limited program, "I know of nothing we could do today that would waste more of our resources or add more to our risks."

If, after all, the decision is to go ahead with a heavy defense against the Russians, what, apart from dollars, will be the cost? If the United States installs ABM's to protect its population to whatever possible extent, should not its European allies also be given the system? In their turn, would not the Iron Curtain satellites insist on the same thing from the Soviet Union? And, in either of these cases, who would pay? Would a U.S. deployment, and the almost certain heightening of U.S.–Soviet tensions, help Chinese Communist attempts to disrupt a budding U.S.–U.S.S.R. rapprochement? When would the new cycle of billion-dollar expenditures end? What might be the impact on the nuclear "have-not" nations, who would be asked to stay out of the field even though Russia and the United States were building up rather than cutting down their nuclear arsenals?

This issue is one of the most serious facing the Defense Department today—so serious that the United States has appealed to Russia to negotiate the whole question. As of late 1967, the effort to start negotiations had produced little, if any, promise of success.

PERSONNEL: QUALITY VERSUS QUANTITY

In finding its way around the problem of mounting costs, the Defense Department has significantly revamped in the personnel end of its business. Both the cost and the quality of people, military and civilian alike, have always deeply concerned the Pentagon and its congressional overseers. Department leaders consider human talent the organization's single most important asset. At the same time, people are the most costly single element in yearly Defense Department expenditures, receiving annually almost 30 per cent of all military appropriations, for salaries, training, etc. Costs in dollars for people have climbed relentlessly as equipment has become more complex, requiring more expensive training—and an increasingly higher caliber—of professionals to operate and maintain it.

That trend promises to continue. Air Force Lieutenant General T. P. Gerrity reported, in a 1965 speech, regarding officer cadre training alone:

We have been called the world's biggest campus. Ninety-eight per cent of the 14,000 officers we will commission [in 1965] will have at least an undergraduate degree. Ten thousand of our people hold advanced degrees and the number is constantly growing. In my own field, for example, we offer the M.A. degree in systems and logistics management. . . . This is because the logistician of the near future will have to be able to handle such complex managerial tools as economic analysis, computer-based information systems, mathematical models, and the application of probability statistics to decision-making under uncertainty.

The same know-how requirements and individual learning opportunities exist in the noncommissioned officer ranks and among the civilian personnel of the Defense Department.

Yet, there are clear signs that neither the military nor Congress has faced up squarely or comprehensively to the problem that this trend has repeatedly presented in the past fifteen years: how best to get the most out of personnel at the least cost. Nowhere is this more evident than in personnel turnover. For a long time, the military has admitted privately, and sometimes stated publicly, that it is not getting the most out of its expensively acquired and expensively kept work force. One major reason is that, by any private-industry standard, this costly talent does not stay on the job long enough for the Defense Department to receive a satisfactory return on its personnel investment. Politically appointed civilians rarely remain, or can afford to remain, in top Pentagon posts for more than three to four years. And the majority of military personnel—drafted or otherwise—leave the Defense Department after no more than about six years of service. Even among career officers, assignments change after three to four years of duty in one spot—the gross formula, in an age of specialization, being to give everyone a broad enough background for the opportunity to become a general some day.

For a variety of reasons, a great many persons leave the military just about the time that they are becoming proficient in their tasks, and the extremely expensive cycle of recruiting-training-assignment must start all over again. Apart from the high price paid to keep that cycle running, the military incurs the additional expense of inefficient operation. Virtually all military veterans are certain that a costing-out of the annual amount of judgment errors produced by inexperienced personnel would rival in dollars the cost of the personnel themselves.

Some efforts have been made to correct this waste. For instance, steps have been taken to prevent an officer's career from being hurt if he chooses to specialize in one field rather than to generalize. Also, more and more civil servants (who tend to stay in one location working at one specialty for long periods of time) have been given assignments once held by uniformed personnel, especially in research, development, and logistics—again, to stabilize the work force and capitalize on the expertise of experience. Moreover, considerable investment has been made in recent years—in terms of better pay, more fringe benefits, improved educational opportunities, etc. —to make a military career more attractive. Unfortunately, over all, any Defense Department attempts to make more sense out of its personnel utilization must battle powerful, ingrained, and sometimes highly emotional obstructions.

The first attempts to reconcile military necessity with the suspicious public attitude toward military service were housed in proposals, beginning shortly after World War II, for universal military training (UMT). Such a notion has been regularly and vociferously shouted down every time it has cropped up. The stopgap alternative, re-enacted into law by Congress every two years since 1948, has been the continuation of the Selective Service System. As late as 1966, Defense Secretary McNamara noted:

> As matters stand, our present Selective Service System draws on only a minority of eligible young men. That is an inequity. It seems to me that we could move toward remedying that inequity by asking every young person in the United States to give two years of service to his country—whether in one of the military services, in the Peace Corps, or in some other volunteer developmental work at home or abroad.

Overlooking the Peace Corps aspect of this suggestion, critics blasted the nation's military leader "for trying to establish UMT." The idea, however, was not new. In his final Korean wartime report, General George Marshall pointed out that, in the future, political pressures would have great influence upon military budgets, especially if the costs were high, and that to maintain a large professional armed force would be very costly. To help ease the budget burden, he proposed a small professional army of volunteers backed by a large reservoir of trained men who would be called into active service in an emergency. He denied, at the time, that this concept called for maintaining a mass army in peacetime (which seems to be Congress' chief objection), pointing out that of some 14 million men mobilized during World War II, "less than 1½ million had actually been assigned to the infantry of the Army and the Marines. The remainder were largely engaged in . . . fighting a war of machinery."

Two decades later, Defense Department efforts to consolidate and streamline the manpower reserves that it already maintains (the Reserves and the National Guard) still come up against bitter opposition. General Wallace Greene, former Commandant of the Marine Corps, says:

> The day is here when the militia and even the draft will not offer a satisfactory answer. The military is becoming more and more a highly technical profession, not just for the old-timers but for the youngsters. Our outstanding 19-year-olds of today are more than men who fight well. They are crew chiefs who can keep in operation multimillion-dollar aircraft loaded with complex equipment. Or the boy we assign to our NATO forces who is so highly motivated he learns to speak French better than his thirty-eight superiors, so well in fact that he could pass for a Frenchman not just in language but in knowledge of country and customs. The importance of that kind of person is more vital today than the atomic bomb or any piece of hardware.

How this old but increasingly significant problem of utilizing manpower will be solved looms large for tomorrow's Defense Department.

PREDICTED: ANOTHER ROUND OF REORGANIZATION

The regularly recurring problems of how best to organize and run the Department of Defense lead typically, with each new administration, first to a sweeping out of old routines and a reshaping of old organizations. For a time, the newly oiled decision-making machinery works better. But, as time passes, the innovators become administrators leary of new ideas, comfortable and confident in their now familiar management methods. It is not a new problem. Admiral Alfred Thayer Mahan wrote in 1903:

> Since armies and navies have existed, there has been a constant struggle on the part of the military element to keep the end—fighting or readiness to fight—superior to mere administrative considerations. This is but natural, for all men tend to magnify their office. The military man having to do the fighting considers that the chief necessity; the administrator equally naturally tends to think the smooth running of the machine the most admirable quality. Both are necessary; but the latter cannot obtain under the pressure of war unless in peace the contingency of war has dictated its system. There is a quaint, well-worn story, which yet may be new to some readers, of an administrator who complained that his office was working admirably until war came and threw everything out of gear.

Three times in twenty years the Defense Department has faced crises of major proportions—in the Korean War, in the technology race of the late 1950's, and in the Viet-Nam conflict. Three times the organization and procedural routines that have gone into the contest had been set up in advance to handle it. And three times innovators within the organization have had to invent new chains of contact, of communications and command, to manage the high-priority problems inherent in each crisis.

Each new reorganization and procedural revamping has possessed two main characteristics: further centralization of authority at the top and an attempt to eliminate bureaucratic obstructions between the top and the authorities in the field closest to the problems. The basic objective is to assure that ideas bubble up to the top fully analyzed by all pertinent staff elements, and that the bubbles rise to the surface quickly so that opportunities do not degenerate, through inattention, into problems. In the past, both centralization of authority and elimination of red tape have fallen, at the outset of each cycle, under the general heading of reorganization. It appears likely that they will do so again. The Defense Department also appears about due for a new round of such efforts.

The Canadian armed forces are attempting to gain both speed and thorough staff work—and economize at the same time—by doing in one sweeping move what the Pentagon has long been approaching gradually: creating a single military staff at its top level. Canadian Defense Minister Paul Hellyer has said, "As long as there are three organizations, Army, Navy, and Air Force, you will need a fourth to control them. In our generation," he insists, "complete unification is the only answer."

Canada's success has led to some embarrassment among the defenders of decentralization and the *status quo,* who insist that such innovations won't work. But many within the Defense Department have long favored similar moves. In 1953, Secretary Lovett proposed that the U.S. Defense Department do many of the things that Canada has done since then to achieve this unification goal. In a letter to President Truman, he said:

> There are, in my opinion, far too many levels of headquarters in the Military Services, thus adding to the overhead and inevitably causing delay. Furthermore, each headquarters sets up a chain reaction of demands for housing, transportation, etc., thus adding to the cost. Special groups have been investigating this area for some time in connection with the utilization of manpower and I think the effort to reduce the number of headquarters must be given every assistance by the senior Defense officials.

Comments like Lovett's—and they are being made more and more frequently of late—are usually reliable indicators that initiative and innovation are beginning to reassert themselves in defiance of what the speakers consider stultifying administrative routine. The new administration that took over in 1961 was noted for its emphasis on giving responsible individuals authority to crash through the bureaucratic underbrush to get the job done. But signs have begun to crop up that what were once new ideas are now organizational routine and have started to grind unacceptably on a new crop of innovators. One indication that the creative element in Defense Department management is upset are the complaints heard that "no new starts" are being made in military development and deployment of a bigger and better next generation of hardware. Another sign is the relatively recent surge of comment by the military and by the industry suppliers that they are being drowned in paperwork (by latest count, directives numbering more than 20,000—and still climbing—with which reports to various superiors must comply, compared to "only 3,000 in 1961"). Bitter complaints are also made that there are more than 800 new "management systems" of one kind or another under which the military and defense industry must operate.

One more clue that change is in the air shows up in the increasing objections to the number of "concurrencies" that an individual must obtain before he receives the green light to go ahead with a proposed solution to a problem. Finally, there is a kind of inverse clue in the greater frequency with which top management defends itself and its previously glamorized decision-making techniques. Typical of this attitude is the introduction to an article on management planning schemes in the Defense Department's January, 1967, *Defense Industry Bulletin:*

> PPBS stands for Planning-Programming-Budgeting Systems. These words have so pervaded Government in the last year that the letters used by themselves have come to suggest a magical panacea for all management ills. This is unfortunate. When a basically good idea is translated into a "buzz" word [the typical mark of a management innovation reaching middle age], it often suffers from distortion and misinterpretation. If it fails to solve all problems or live up to its inflated billing, it is abruptly discarded. Usually a critic is readily available to pronounce the epitaph—"I told you it wouldn't work in the first place."

Notwithstanding all these signs portending change, the real question is whether the Viet-Nam crisis will force action—as earlier crises have produced other reorganizational action. If it does, further strengthening of the already informally recognized and real powers of the Joint Staff can be expected. At the same time, there could well be some reshuffling in the Defense Secretary's civilian secretariat, most of it done under the banner of streamlining and standardization. Finally, some staff offices in the military services will be prime candidates for elimination from the Pentagon organization chart.

Clearly, some reorganization is needed. Recently, one general commented that, "as a firm foe of creeping bureaucracy," he could "not agree that we are now doing a good job of managing the total defense program. Layers of management staff and reams of ineffective paper work may look good from the outside, but don't make for good management." He pointed out that the principle of delegation of responsibility and decentralization of management functions in large organizations has been thoroughly tested and proven, and said, "I find it difficult to give high marks to a trend in the opposite direction."

SHIFTING EXTERNAL RELATIONSHIPS

Significant as questions in the internal Defense Department future are, the Department plainly faces even more important challenges in its relationships with other government agencies and other elements in the nation, as well as with the military forces of other nations. And because the Defense Department has only one (albeit powerful) vote, the problems arising from these relationships will be even more difficult for its leaders to solve. As has been spelled out earlier, the Defense Department is not by any means the sole agency of government nor the only element in the body politic involved in national security. Often, when the Defense Department has become the leading protector of security, it has done so because other groups have failed to achieve an objective. Such things are easy to see with hindsight, but less easy to forecast in particulars. The merging of divergent national interests into a coordinated national security team is far more intricate and perplexing than the arduous building of teamwork among units within the Defense Department itself.

Governmental leaders must fight the battle of trying to divide their time properly between planning for the future and putting out the fires that flare up each day. Management tends to be trapped by the daily, and preoccupation with the headaches of today can lead to ill-defined policy for tomorrow. That, in turn, leads to confusion and inconsistent action among subordinate agencies responsible for executing policy actions efficiently, and, inevitably, failure at the top is compounded by failure at lower levels. Lacking sound cohesive guidance, executive middle management specialists try to fill the vacuum by striving to take over for themselves a larger share of the total program—and, in effect, set policy by performance. The result, always, is an exercise in wasteful contradiction and confusion, and can, sometimes, even lead to the government tragedy of two capable agencies canceling out, rather than complementing, each other's efforts.

Senator Henry Jackson has written, in his concluding statement to the Subcommittee on National Policy Machinery of the Senate Committee on Government Operations in November, 1961:

> The requirements of national security press ever more strongly on our resources. Can we establish a proper scale of priorities that separates the necessary from the not really essential? . . .
>
> Presidential control over foreign policy and defense programs becomes more difficult. How may the globe-girdling programs of the national security departments and agencies be harnessed on behalf of the Presidential purpose? How can we assure their efficient execution?
>
> Standards of performance adequate for quieter times will no longer do. The Presidency, the State and Defense departments

and the rest of our government must now meet new tests of excellence.

Jackson also reported: "Faulty machinery is rarely the real culprit when our policies are inconsistent or lack sustained forward momentum. The underlying cause is normally found elsewhere, in the absence of a clear sense of direction and coherence of policy at the top of the Government." He went on to say:

The State Department is not doing enough in asserting its leadership across the whole front of foreign policy. Neither is it doing enough in staffing itself for such leadership. State also needs more respect for comprehensive forward planning. The Department as a whole attaches too little importance to looking ahead in foreign policy and is too wedded to a philosophy of reacting to problems as they arise.

Today, many budding or limping programs and projects cry out for the stimulation of long-range planning and coordination and human motivation. The lack of good planning, with resultant follies in execution, more than any other single factor, has been responsible for growing congressional reluctance to spend money on foreign aid, military and economic alike—two of the most important national security programs. The apparent lack of priorities for fighting this "other war" results in a sprinkling of help all over the world. In few places is it massive enough to do much good, and one result is that the whole program has gone sour.

At the same time that the roles of the State and Defense departments have become bewilderingly interwoven, Congress, the watchdog of the executive branch of government and the approving authority for all its actions, with its splintered committee structure, appears less and less well equipped to comprehend totally, let alone cope intelligently, with all the powerful defense influences in American politics and in the national economy. A divided, superficially informed, and disputatious Congress often demands actions inappropriate to the problems or finds itself acting only after the fact of White House, Defense Department, or State Department impact on the nation and the world. In this situation, the Defense Department already has been used, by design or default, to settle labor-management differences, control prices, air political campaigns, and semisocialize certain industries. The products and byproducts of the Defense Department in technology, management, and many related areas, are, potentially, of unparalleled value to the country, but their development calls for a careful watch by a coordinated Congress lest those assets inadvertently force the suspension of the very freedoms that the whole Defense Department effort is supposed to preserve.

Thus, it appears that the vital issues in the Defense Department's future external relationships are primarily problems of what other agencies, Congress, and the public should be doing for national security. Few people are better aware of the awesome implications of this than the man who finds himself occupying the position of Secretary of Defense. Certainly, every one of them has advised, as did George Marshall when he accepted the Nobel Peace Prize in 1953, "For the moment, the maintenance of peace in the present hazardous world situation does depend in very large measure on military power, together with Allied cohesion . . . but [for the long term] we must, I repeat, we must find another solution." Failure to pursue world peace offensives as vigorously as arms preparedness is now supported almost guarantees for the United States and its Defense Department an unending future of risk and violence.

Appendix I

Secretaries of Defense

JAMES V. FORRESTAL, Secretary of the Navy from May, 1944, until he took office as the first Secretary of Defense on September 17, 1947, served as head of the new National Military Establishment until March 27, 1949. He was admitted to the Naval Hospital, Bethesda, Maryland, on April 2, 1949, in a state of exhaustion, his condition "directly the result of excessive work during the war and post-war years." He died May 22, 1949.

LOUIS JOHNSON, a former Assistant Secretary of the Army, was sworn in as Secretary of Defense on March 28, 1949, and served until September 19, 1950. He died April 24, 1966.

GEORGE CATLETT MARSHALL, General of the Army, World War II Chief of Staff of the Army, former Secretary of State, and President of the National Red Cross, was sworn in as Secretary of Defense on September 21, 1950, and served until his retirement on September 12, 1951. He died October 16, 1959.

ROBERT A. LOVETT, Under Secretary of State under General Marshall, and Deputy Secretary of Defense under General Marshall, succeeded the General as Secretary of Defense on September 17, 1951, serving until January 20, 1953.

CHARLES E. WILSON, President of General Motors, was sworn in as Secretary of Defense on January 28, 1953, and served until October 8, 1957.

NEIL H. McELROY, President of Proctor & Gamble Company, was sworn in on October 9, 1957. He resigned December 1, 1959.

THOMAS S. GATES, JR., former Secretary of the Navy and Deputy Secretary of Defense, was sworn in on December 2, 1959, and served until January 20, 1961.

ROBERT S. MCNAMARA, President of Ford Motor Company, was sworn in on January 21, 1961.

CLARK M. CLIFFORD, Washington lawyer, named in January, 1968, to succeed Robert S. McNamara.

Appendix II

Deputy Secretaries of Defense

STEPHEN T. EARLY served as Under Secretary of Defense from May 2, 1949, until August 9, 1949, when that position was abolished. He continued to serve, as Deputy Secretary, from August 10, 1949, to September 30, 1950.

ROBERT A. LOVETT, Deputy Secretary from October 4, 1950, to September 16, 1951, had previously served, during World War II, as Assistant Secretary of War for Air, from April, 1941, to December, 1945.

WILLIAM C. FOSTER served as Deputy Secretary from September 24, 1951, to January 20, 1953. During World War II, he served as Under Secretary of War on Procurement for the Army Air Forces.

ROGER M. KYES, Deputy Secretary from February 2, 1953, to May 1, 1954, prior to his appointment had been an official with General Motors since 1948.

ROBERT B. ANDERSON, Secretary of the Navy from February 4, 1953, until he was sworn in as Deputy Secretary on May 3, 1954, served until August 4, 1955.

REUBEN B. ROBERTSON, JR., Deputy Secretary from August 5, 1955, to April 25, 1957, had previously served as Vice Chairman of the Committee on Business Organization of the Department of Defense (Task Force of the Hoover Commission).

DONALD A. QUARLES, Deputy Secretary from May 1, 1957, to his death on May 8, 1959, had previously served as Assistant Secretary of Defense (Research and Development) from September 1, 1953, to August 14, 1955, and as Secretary of the Air Force from August 15, 1955, to April 30, 1957.

THOMAS S. GATES, JR., Deputy Secretary from June 8, 1959, to December 1, 1959, was Secretary of the Navy from April 1, 1957, to June 7, 1959, and Under Secretary of the Navy from October 7, 1953, to March 31, 1957.

JAMES H. DOUGLAS, JR., Deputy Secretary from December 11, 1959, to January 20, 1961, was Secretary of the Air Force from May 1, 1957, to December 10, 1959, and Under Secretary of the Air Force from March 3, 1953, to April 30, 1957.

ROSWELL L. GILPATRIC served as Under Secretary of the Air Force from October 29, 1951, to February 5, 1953; Assistant Secretary of the Air Force from May 25, 1951, to October 29, 1951; and Deputy Secretary of Defense from January 24, 1961, to January 20, 1964.

CYRUS R. VANCE, former Secretary of the Army, was sworn in as Deputy Secretary of Defense on January 28, 1964, succeeding Mr. Gilpatric.

PAUL NITZE, former Secretary of the Navy, succeeded Mr. Vance on July 1, 1967.

Appendix III

The Joint Chiefs of Staff

CHAIRMAN*	*From*	*To*
General of the Army		
Omar N. Bradley, USA	August 16, 1949	August 14, 1953
Admiral Arthur W. Radford, USN	August 15, 1953	August 14, 1957
General Nathan F. Twining, USAF	August 15, 1957	September 30, 1960
General Lyman L. Lemnitzer, USA	October 1, 1960	September 30, 1962
General Maxwell D. Taylor, USA	October 1, 1962	July 3, 1964
General Earle G. Wheeler, USA	July 6, 1964	To Date

* Position created by 1949 Amendment to the National Security Act of 1947.

Appendix IV

National Security Act of 1947

Be it enacted by the Senate and House of Representatives of the United States of America in Congress assembled,

SHORT TITLE

That this Act may be cited as the "National Security Act of 1947." [This statement of the short title is part of the first section of the Act of July 26, 1947, ch. 343, 61 Stat. 495. The remainder of that section is the table of contents, which is omitted . . .]

DECLARATION OF POLICY

SEC. 2. In enacting this legislation, it is the intent of Congress to provide a comprehensive program for the future security of the United States; to provide for the establishment of integrated policies and procedures for the departments, agencies, and functions of the Government relating to the national security; to provide a Department of Defense, including the three military Departments of the Army, the Navy (including naval aviation and the United States Marine Corps), and the Air Force under the direction, authority, and control of the Secretary of Defense; to provide that each military department shall be separately organized under its own Secretary and shall function under the direction, authority, and control of the Secretary of Defense; to provide for their unified direction under civilian control of the Secretary of Defense but not to merge these departments or services; to provide for the establishment of unified or specified combatant commands, and a clear and direct line of command to such commands; to eliminate unnecessary duplication in the Department of Defense, and particularly in the field of research and engineering by vesting its overall direction and control in the Secretary of Defense; to provide more effective, efficient, and economical administration in the Department of Defense; to provide for the unified strategic direction of the combatant forces, for their operation under unified command, and for their integration into an efficient team of land, naval, and air forces but not to establish a single Chief of Staff over the armed forces nor an overall armed forces general staff. [Section 2, Act of July 26, 1947, ch. 343, 61 Stat. 496, as amended by section 2, Department of Defense Reorganization Act of 1958, 72 Stat. 514; 50 U.S.C. 401.]

TITLE I—COORDINATION FOR NATIONAL SECURITY

NATIONAL SECURITY COUNCIL

SEC. 101. (a) There is hereby established a council to be known as the National Security Council (hereinafter in this section referred to as the "Council"). [The National Security Council was incorporated into the Executive Office of the President by Reorganization Plan No. 4 of 1949, 63 Stat. 1067.]

The President of the United States shall preside over meetings of the Council: *Provided,* That in his absence he may designate a member of the Council to preside in his place.

The function of the Council shall be to advise the President with respect to the integration of domestic, foreign, and military policies relating to the national security so as to enable the military services and the other departments and agencies of the Government to cooperate more effectively in matters involving the national security.

The Council shall be composed of—

    (1) the President;

    (2) the Vice President;

    (3) the Secretary of State;

    (4) the Secretary of Defense;

    (5) [Formerly the Director for Mutual Security. All the functions of the Director for Mutual Security, including his functions as a member of the National Security Council, were transferred to the Director of the Foreign Operations Ad-

ministration by section 2(a), Reorganization Plan No. 7 of 1953, 67 Stat. 640. The office of Director of the Foreign Operations Administration and the functions of the Director in his capacity as a member of the National Security Council were abolished by section 303, Executive Order No. 10610, May 9, 1955, implementing section 525, Mutual Security Act of 1954, 68 Stat. 856.];

(6) [Formerly the Chairman of the National Security Resources Board. Most functions of the Chairman, including his functions as a member of the National Security Council, were transferred to the Director of the Office of Defense Mobilization by section 2(a), Reorganization Plan No. 3 of 1953, 67 Stat. 634. The functions of the Director of the Office of Defense Mobilization as a member of the National Security Council were transferred to the Director of the Office of Defense and Civilian Mobilization by section 4, Reorganization Plan No. 1 of 1958, 72 Stat. 1800. The title of this office became Director of the Office of Emergency Planning by the first section of the Act of September 22, 1961, Public Law 87–296, 75 Stat. 630.]; and

(7) the Secretaries and Under Secretaries of other executive departments and of the military departments, when appointed by the President by and with the advice and consent of the Senate, to serve at his pleasure. [The former memberships of the Chairman of the Munitions Board and of the Chairman of the Research and Development Board terminated when those offices were abolished by section 2(b), Reorganization Plan No. 6 of 1953, 67 Stat. 638.]

(b) In addition to performing such other functions as the President may direct, for the purpose of more effectively coordinating the policies and functions of the departments and agencies of the Government relating to the national security, it shall, subject to the direction of the President, be the duty of the Council—

(1) to assess and appraise the objectives, commitments, and risks of the United States in relation to our actual and potential military power, in the interest of national security, for the purpose of making recommendations to the President in connection therewith; and

(2) to consider policies on matters of common interest to the departments and agencies of the Government concerned with the national security, and to make recommendations to the President in connection therewith.

(c) The Council shall have a staff to be headed by a civilian executive secretary who shall be appointed by the President, and who shall receive compensation at the rate of $——— a year. [The compensation of the executive secretary of the National Security Council is now governed by section 105 of title 3, United States Code, which authorizes the President to fix the rate of basic compensation of the Executive Secretary at a rate not to exceed that of level II of the Federal Executive Salary Schedule ($30,000). See section 5313 of title 5, United States Code.] The executive secretary, subject to the direction of the Council, is hereby authorized, subject to the civil-service laws and the Classification Act of 1949, as amended, to appoint and fix the compensation of such personnel as may be necessary to perform such duties as may be prescribed by the Council in connection with the performance of its functions.

(d) The Council shall, from time to time, make such recommendations, and such other reports to the President as it deems appropriate or as the President may require. [Section 101, Act of July 26, 1947, ch. 343, 61 Stat. 496, as amended by section 3, National Security Act Amendments of 1949, 63 Stat. 579, and section 501(e)(1), Mutual Security Act of 1951, 65 Stat. 378; 50 U.S.C. 402.]

CENTRAL INTELLIGENCE AGENCY

SEC. 102. (a) There is hereby established under the National Security Council a Central Intelligence Agency with a Director of Central Intelligence who shall be the head thereof, and with a Deputy Director of Central Intelligence who shall act for, and exercise the powers of, the Director during his absence or disability. The Director and the Deputy Director shall be appointed by the President, by and with the advice and consent of the Senate, from among the commissioned officers of the armed services, whether in an active or retired status, or from among individuals in civilian life: *Provided, however,* That at no time shall the two positions of the Director and Deputy Director be occupied simultaneously by commissioned officers of the armed services, whether in an active or retired status.

(b)(1) If a commissioned officer of the armed services is appointed as Director, or Deputy Director, then—

(A) in the performance of his duties as Director, or Deputy Director, he shall be subject to no supervision, control, restriction, or prohibition (military or otherwise) other than would be operative with respect to him if he were a civilian in no way connected with the Department of the Army, the Department of the Navy, the Department of the Air Force, or the armed services or any component thereof; and

(B) he shall not possess or exercise any supervision, control, powers, or functions (other than such as he possesses, or is authorized or directed to exercise, as Director, or Deputy Director) with respect to the armed services or any component thereof, the Department of the Army, the Department of the Navy, or the Department of the Air Force, or any branch, bureau, unit, or division thereof, or with respect to any of the personnel (military or civilian) of any of the foregoing.

. . . .

(d) For the purpose of coordinating the intelligence activities of the several Government departments and agencies in the interest of national security, it shall be the duty of the Agency, under the direction of the National Security Council—

(1) to advise the National Security Council in matters concerning such intelligence activities of the Government departments and agencies as relate to national security;

(2) to make recommendations to the National Security Council for the coordination of such intelligence activities of the departments and agencies of the Government as relate to the national security;

(3) to correlate and evaluate intelligence relating to the national security, and provide for the appropriate dissemination of such intelligence within the Government using where appropriate existing agencies and facilities:

Provided, That the agency shall have no police, subpoena, law-enforcement powers, or internal-security functions: *Provided further,* That the departments and other agencies of the Government shall continue to collect, evaluate, correlate, and disseminate departmental intelligence: *And provided further,* That the Director of Central Intelligence shall be responsible for protecting intelligence sources and methods from unauthorized disclosure;

(4) to perform, for the benefit of the existing intelligence agencies, such additional services of common concern as the National Security Council determines can be more effectively accomplished centrally;

(5) to perform such other functions and duties related to intelligence affecting the national security as the National Security Council may from time to time direct.

(e) To the extent recommended by the National Security Council and approved by the President, such intelligence of the departments and agencies of the Government, except as hereinafter provided, relating to the national security shall be open to the inspection of the Director of Central Intelligence, and such intelligence as relates to the national security and is possessed by such departments and other agencies of the Government, except as hereinafter provided, shall be made available to the Director of Central Intelligence for correlation, evaluation, and dissemination: *Provided, however,* That upon the written request of the Director of Central Intelligence, the Director of the Federal Bureau of Investigation shall make available to the Director of Central Intelligence such information for correlation, evaluation, and dissemination as may be essential to the national security.

(f) Effective when the Director first appointed under subsection (a) has taken office—

(1) the National Intelligence Authority (11 Fed. Reg. 1337, 1339, February 5, 1946) shall cease to exist; and

(2) the personnel, property, and records of the Central Intelligence Group are transferred to the Central Intelligence Agency, and such Group shall cease to exist. Any unexpended balances of appropriations, allocations, or other funds available for such Group shall be available and shall be authorized

to be made available in like manner for expenditure by the Agency. [Section 102, Act of July 26, 1947, ch. 343, 61 Stat. 497, as amended by section 4, Act of October 15, 1949, ch. 695, 63 Stat. 880, and the Act of April 4, 1953, ch. 16, 67 Stat. 19; 50 U.S.C. 403.]

OFFICE OF EMERGENCY PLANNING

[Section 103 of the National Security Act of 1947, 61 Stat. 499, provided for a National Security Resources Board. The functions of the National Security Resources Board were transferred to the Chairman of the National Security Resources Board by section 1, Reorganization Plan No. 25 of 1950, 64 Stat. 1280. Reorganization Plan No. 3 of 1953, 67 Stat. 634, abolished the National Security Resources Board, created the Office of Defense Mobilization, and transferred all functions of the Chairman of the National Security Resources Board (excluding certain functions abolished by section 5), as well as certain additional functions, to the Director of the Office of Defense Mobilization. Reorganization Plan No. 1 of 1958, 72 Stat. 1799, as amended by the Act of August 26, 1958, Public Law 85–763, 72 Stat. 861, abolished the Office of Defense Mobilization and transferred its functions to the President and established the Office of Civil and Defense Mobilization. The Act of September 22, 1961, Public Law 87–296, 75 Stat. 630, further amended Reorganization Plan No. 1 of 1958, *supra,* by deleting "Office of Civil and Defense Mobilization" and inserting "Office of Emergency Planning" in place thereof and provided that any reference in any other law to the Office of Civil and Defense Mobilization would be deemed to refer to the Office of Emergency Planning.]

SEC. 103. (a) The Director of the Office of Emergency Planning, subject to the direction of the President, is authorized, subject to the civil-service laws and the Classification Act of 1949, to appoint and fix the compensation of such personnel as may be necessary to assist the Director in carrying out his functions.

(b) It shall be the function of the Director of the Office of Emergency Planning to advise the President concerning the coordination of military, industrial, and civilian mobilization, including—

(1) policies concerning industrial and civilian mobilization in order to assure the most effective mobilization and maximum utilization of the Nation's manpower in the event of war;

(2) programs for the effective use in time of war of the Nation's natural and industrial resources for military and civilian needs, for the maintenance and stabilization of the civilian economy in time of war, and for the adjustment of such economy to war needs and conditions;

(3) policies for unifying, in time of war, the activities of Federal agencies and departments engaged in or concerned with production, procurement, distribution, or transportation of military or civilian supplies, materials, and products;

(4) the relationship between potential supplies of, and potential requirements for, manpower, resources, and productive facilities in time of war;

(5) policies for establishing adequate reserves of strategic and critical material, and for the conservation of these reserves;

(6) the strategic relocation of industries, services, government, and economic activities, the continuous operation of which is essential to the Nation's security.

(c) In performing his functions, the Director of the Office of Emergency Planning shall utilize to the maximum extent the facilities and resources of the departments and agencies of the Government. [Section 103, Act of July 26, 1947, ch. 343, 61 Stat. 499, as amended by section 3, Act of October 15, 1949, ch. 695, 63 Stat. 880, and section 50, Act of September 3, 1954, ch. 1263, 68 Stat. 1244; 50 U.S.C. 404.]

TITLE II—THE DEPARTMENT OF DEFENSE

ESTABLISHMENT OF THE DEPARTMENT OF DEFENSE

SEC. 201. (a) [Repealed and restated in sections 131 and 133 of title 10, United States Code. The language of section 133 appears under section 202, below.

[§ 131. Executive department

[The Department of Defense is an executive department of the United States.]

(b) [Repealed by section 307, Act of September 7, 1962, Public Law 87–652, 76 Stat. 526.]

(c) Section 158 of the Revised Statutes, as amended, is amended to read as follows:

"SEC. 158. The provisions of this title shall apply to the following Executive Departments:

"First. The Department of State.

"Second. The Department of Defense.

"Third. The Department of the Treasury.

"Fourth. The Department of Justice.

"Fifth. The Post Office Department.

"Sixth. The Department of the Interior.

"Seventh. The Department of Agriculture.

"Eighth. The Department of Commerce.

"Ninth. The Department of Labor." [Section 201(c), Act of July 26, 1947, ch. 343, as added by section 4, National Security Act Amendments of 1949, 63 Stat. 579.]

(d) Except to the extent inconsistent with the provisions of this Act, the provisions of title IV of the Revised Statutes as now or hereafter amended shall be applicable to the Department of Defense. [Section 201(d), Act of July 26, 1947, ch. 343, as added by section 4, National Security Act Amendments of 1949, 63 Stat. 579.]

SECRETARY OF DEFENSE

SEC. 202. (a) [Repealed and restated, along with subsections (b), (d), and (f), in section 133 of title 10, United States Code.

[§ 133. Secretary of Defense: appointment; powers and duties; delegation by

[(a) There is a Secretary of Defense, who is the head of the Department of Defense, appointed from civilian life by the President, by and with the advice and consent of the Senate. A person may not be appointed as Secretary of Defense within 10 years after relief from active duty as a commissioned officer of a regular component of an armed force.

[(b) The Secretary is the principal assistant to the President in all matters relating to the Department of Defense. Subject to the direction of the President and to this title and section 401 of title 50, he has authority, direction, and control over the Department of Defense.

[(c) The Secretary shall report annually in writing to the President and the Congress of the expenditures, work, and accomplishments of the Department of Defense during the period covered by the report, together with—

[(1) a report from each military department on the expenditures, work, and accomplishments of that department;

[(2) itemized statements showing the savings of public funds, and the eliminations of unnecessary duplications, made under section 125 of this title;

[(3) a report from the Reserve Forces Policy Board on the reserve programs of the Department of Defense, including a review of the effectiveness of chapters 51, 337, 361, 363, 549, 573, 837, 861, and 863 of this title, as far as they apply to reserve officers; and

[(4) such recommendations as he considers appropriate.

[(d) Unless specifically prohibited by law, the Secretary may, without being relieved of his responsibility, perform any of his functions or duties, or exercise any of his powers through, or with the aid of, such persons in, or organizations of, the Department of Defense as he may designate.]

(b) [Repealed and restated in section 133 of title 10, United States Code. See subsection (a), above.]

(c)(1) [Repealed and restated, along with clauses (2), (4), (5), and (6), in section 125 of title 10, United States Code.

[**§125. Functions, powers, and duties: transfer, reassignment, consolidation, or abolition**

[(a) Subject to section 401 of title 50, the Secretary of Defense shall take appropriate action (including the transfer, reassignment, consolidation, or abolition of any function, power, or duty) to provide more effective, efficient, and economical administration and operation, and to eliminate duplication, in the Department of Defense. However, except as provided by subsections (b) and (c), a function, power, or duty vested in the Department of Defense, or an officer, official, or agency thereof, by law may not be substantially transferred, reassigned, consolidated, or abolished unless the Secretary reports the details of the proposed transfer, reassignment, consolidation, or abolition to the Committees on Armed Services of the Senate and House of Representatives. The transfer, reassignment, consolidation, or abolition concerned takes effect on the first day after the expiration of the first 30 days that Congress is in continuous session after the Secretary so reports, unless either of those Committees, within that period, reports a resolution recommending that the proposed transfer, reassignment, consolidation, or abolition be rejected by the Senate or the House of Representatives, as the case may be, because it—

[(1) proposes to transfer, reassign, consolidate, or abolish a major combatant function, power, or duty assigned to the Army, Navy, Air Force, or Marine Corps by section 3062(b), 5012, 5013, or 8062(c) of this title; and

[(2) would, in its judgment, tend to impair the defense of the United States.

If either of those Committees, within that period, reports such a resolution and it is not adopted by the Senate or the House of Representatives, as the case may be, within the first 40 days that Congress is in continuous session after that resolution is so reported, the transfer, reassignment, consolidation, or abolition concerned takes effect on the first day after the expiration of that forty-day period. For the purposes of this subsection, a session may be considered as not continuous only if broken by an adjournment of Congress sine die. However, in computing the period that Congress is in continuous session, days that the Senate or the House of Representatives is not in session because of an adjournment of more than three days to a day certain are not counted. [Clause (3) of section 202(c) was repealed and restated in section 303, Act of September 7, 1962, Public Law 87–652, 76 Stat. 525.]

[SEC. 303. (a) For the purposes of this section, any resolution reported to the Senate or the House of Representatives pursuant to the provisions of section 125 of title 10, United States Code, shall be treated for the purpose of consideration by either House, in the same manner as a resolution with respect to a reorganization plan reported by a committee within the meaning of the Reorganization Act of 1949 as in effect on July 1, 1958 (5 U.S.C. 133z and the following), and shall be governed by the provisions applicable to the consideration of any such resolution by either House of the Congress as provided by sections 205 and 206 of that Act.

[(b) The provisions of this section are enacted by the Congress—

   [(1) as an exercise of the rule-making power of the Senate and the House of Representatives, respectively, and as such they shall be considered as part of the rules of each House, respectively, and supersede other rules only to the extent that they are inconsistent therewith; and

   [(2) with full recognition of the constitutional right of either House to change the rules (as far as relating to the procedure in that House) at any time, in the same manner and to the same extent as in the case of any other rule of that House).

[(b) Notwithstanding subsection (a), if the President determines it to be necessary because of hostilities or an imminent threat of hostilities, any function, power, or duty, including one assigned to the Army, Navy, Air Force, or Marine Corps by section 3062(b), 5012, 5013, or 8062(c) of this title, may be transferred, reassigned, or consolidated. The transfer, reassignment, or consolidation remains in effect until the President determines that hostilities have terminated or that there is no longer an imminent threat of hostilities, as the case may be.

[(c) Notwithstanding subsection (a), the Secretary of Defense may assign or reassign the development and operational use of new weapons or weapons systems to one or more of the military departments or one or more of the armed forces. However, notwithstanding any other provision of this title or any other law, the Secretary of Defense shall not direct or approve a plan to initiate or effect a substantial reduction or elimination of a major weapons system until the Secretary of Defense has reported all the pertinent details of the proposed action to the Congress of the United States while the Congress is in session.

[(d) In subsection (a)(1), "major combatant function, power, or duty" does not include a supply or service activity common to more than one military department. The Secretary of Defense shall whenever he determines it will be more effective, economical, or efficient, provide for the performance of such an activity by one agency or such other organizations as he considers appropriate.]

. . . .

[§ 3010. Organization

[The Department of the Army is separately organized under the Secretary of the Army. It operates under the authority, direction, and control of the Secretary of Defense.

[Section 3012(b) (third sentence), title 10, United States Code:

[The Secretary [of the Army] is responsible to the Secretary of Defense for the operation and efficiency of the Department.

[Section 5011 (first two sentences), title 10, United States Code:

[The Department of the Navy is separately organized under the Secretary of the Navy. It operates under the authority, direction, and control of the Secretary of Defense.

[Section 5031(a) (third sentence), title 10, United States Code:

[The Secretary [of the Navy] is responsible to the Secretary of Defense for the operation and efficiency of the Department.

[Section 8010, title 10, United States Code:

[§ 8010. Organization

[The Department of the Air Force is separately organized under the Secretary of the Air Force. It operates under the authority, direction, and control of the Secretary of Defense.

[Section 8012(b) (third sentence), title 10, United States Code:

[The Secretary [of the Air Force] is responsible to the Secretary of Defense for the operation and efficiency of the Department.

[Section 136 (c) and (d), title 10, United States Code:

[(c) Except as otherwise specifically provided by law, an Assistant Secretary may not issue an order to a military department unless—

[(1) the Secretary of Defense has specifically delegated that authority to him in writing; and

[(2) the order is issued through the Secretary of the military department concerned, or his designee.

[(d) In carrying out subsection (c) and sections 3010, 3012(b) (last two sentences), 5011 (first two sentences), 5031(a) (last two sentences), 8010, and 8012 (b) (last two sentences) of this title, the Secretary of each military department, his civilian assistants, and members of the armed forces under the jurisdiction of his department shall cooperate fully with personnel of the Office of the Secretary of Defense to achieve efficient administration of the Department of Defense and to carry out effectively the authority, direction, and control of the Secretary of Defense.]

.   .   .   .

[§ 124. Combatant commands: establishment, composition; functions; administration and support

[(a) With the advice and assistance of the Joint Chiefs of Staff, the President, through the Secretary of Defense, shall—

[(1) establish unified combatant commands or specified combatant commands to perform military missions; and

[(2) shall prescribe the force structure of those commands.

[(b) The military departments shall assign forces to combatant commands established under this section to perform the missions of those commands. A force so assigned is under the full operational command of the commander of the command to which it is assigned. It may be transferred from the command to which it is assigned only by authority of the Secretary and under procedures prescribed by the Secretary with the approval of the President. A force not so assigned, remains, for all purposes, in the military department concerned.

[(c) Combatant commands established under this section are responsible to the President and to the Secretary for such military missions as may be assigned to them by the Secretary with the approval of the President.

[(d) Subject to the authority, direction, and control of the Secretary, each military department is responsible for the administration of forces assigned by that department to combatant commands established under this section. The Secretary shall assign the responsibility for the support of forces assigned to those commands to one or more of the military departments.]

.   .   .   .

JOINT CHIEFS OF STAFF

SEC. 211. [Repealed and restated in sections 141 (a)–(d) and 142 of title 10, United States Code.

[§ 141. Composition: functions

[(a) There are in the Department of Defense the Joint Chiefs of Staff consisting of—

[(1) a Chairman;

[(2) the Chief of Staff of the Army;

[(3) the Chief of Naval Operations; and

[(4) the Chief of Staff of the Air Force.

[(b) The Joint Chiefs of Staff are the principal military advisers to the President, the National Security Council, and the Secretary of Defense.

[(c) The Commandant of the Marine Corps shall indicate to the Chairman any matter scheduled for consideration by the Joint Chiefs that directly concerns the Marine Corps. Unless, upon request of the Chairman for a determination, the Secretary of Defense determines that such a matter does not concern the Marine Corps, the Commandant shall meet with the Joint Chiefs of Staff when that matter is under consideration and, with respect to it, the Commandant has coequal status with the members of the Joint Chiefs of Staff.

[(d) Subject to the authority and direction of the President and the Secretary of Defense, the Joint Chiefs of Staff shall—

[(1) prepare strategic plans and provide for the strategic direction of the armed forces;

[(2) prepare joint logistic plans and assign logistic responsibilities to the armed forces in accordance with those plans;

[(3) establish unified commands in strategic areas;

[(4) review the major material and personnel requirements of the armed forces in accordance with strategic and logistic plans;

[(5) formulate policies for the joint training of the armed forces;

[(6) formulate policies for coordinating the military education of members of the armed forces;

[(7) provide for representation of the United States on the Military Staff Committee of the United Nations in accordance with the Charter of the United Nations; and

[(8) perform such other duties as the President or the Secretary of Defense may prescribe.

[§ 142. Chairman

[(a) The Chairman of the Joint Chiefs of Staff shall be appointed by the President, by and with the advice and consent of the Senate, from the officers of the regular components of the armed forces. He serves at the pleasure of the President for a term of two years, and may be reappointed in the same manner for one additional term. However, in time of war declared by Congress there is no limit on the number of reappointments.

[(b) In addition to his other duties as a member of the Joint Chiefs of Staff, the Chairman shall, subject to the authority and direction of the President and the Secretary of Defense—

[(1) preside over the Joint Chiefs of Staff;

[(2) provide agenda for the meetings of the Joint Chiefs of Staff and assist them in carrying on their business as promptly as practicable; and

[(3) inform the Secretary of Defense, and, when the President or the Secretary of Defense considers it appropriate, the President, of those issues upon which the Joint Chiefs of Staff have not agreed.

[(c) While holding office, the Chairman outranks all other officers of the armed forces. However, he may not exercise military command over the Joint Chiefs of Staff or any of the armed forces.]

JOINT STAFF

SEC. 212. [Repealed and restated in section 143 of title 10, United States Code.

[§ 143. Joint staff

[(a) There is under the Joint Chiefs of Staff a Joint Staff consisting of not more than 400 officers selected by the Joint Chiefs of Staff with the approval of the Chairman. The Joint Staff shall be selected in approximately equal numbers from—

[(1) the Army;

[(2) the Navy and the Marine Corps; and

[(3) the Air Force.

The tenure of the members of the Joint Staff is subject to the approval of the Chairman of the Joint Chiefs of Staff, and, except in time of war, no such tenure of duty may be more than three years. Except in time of war, officers completing a tour of duty with the Joint Staff may not be reassigned to the Joint Staff for a period of not less than three years following their previous tour of duty on the Joint Staff, except that selected officers may be recalled to Joint Staff duty in less than three years with the approval of the Secretary of Defense in each case. The number of such officers recalled to Joint Staff duty in less than three years shall not exceed 30 serving on the Joint Staff at any one time.

[(b) The Chairman of the Joint Chiefs of Staff in consultation with the Joint Chiefs of Staff, and with the approval of the Secretary of Defense, shall select the Director of the Joint Staff. Except in time of war, the tour of duty of the Director may not exceed three years. Upon the completion of a tour of duty as Director of the Joint Staff, the Director, except in time of war, may not be reassigned to the Joint Staff. The Director must be an officer junior in grade to each member of the Joint Chiefs of Staff.

[(c) The Joint Staff shall perform such duties as the Joint Chiefs of Staff or the Chairman prescribes. The Chairman of the Joint Chiefs of Staff manages the Joint Staff and its Director, on behalf of the Joint Chiefs of Staff.

[(d) The Joint Staff shall not operate or be organized as an overall Armed Forces General Staff and shall have no executive authority. The Joint Staff may be organized and may operate along conventional staff lines to support the Joint Chiefs of Staff in discharging their assigned responsibilities.]

Bibliography

As might be expected from the size and importance of the Department of Defense, thousands of books and articles have been written in the past twenty years on different aspects of its activities. The specific sources helpful in research for this book are too vast to enumerate.

Articles appearing in *The New York Times, The Washington Post,* the Washington, D.C., *Evening Star,* the *Civil Service Journal,* and the *Armed Forces Management* magazine, have been useful. In addition, government publications—committee hearings and reports—and unpublished material from my personal records and experiences have added to the final form of this book. The following references will lead the serious and thoughtful student to new material.

ALBION, ROBERT G., and CONNERY, ROBERT H. *Forrestal and the Navy.* New York: Columbia University Press, 1962.

ARNOLD, HENRY H. *Global Mission.* London: Hutchinson & Company, 1951.

BORKLUND, C. W. *Men of the Pentagon.* New York: Frederick A. Praeger, 1966.

DONNELLY, CHARLES H. *United States Defense Policies Since World War II.* Prepared for Congress at the request of Congressman Melvin Price. House Document #100. Washington, D.C.: Government Printing Office, 1956.

DYER, FREDERICK C., and JOHN M. *Bureaucracy vs. Creativity.* Coral Gables, Fla.: University of Miami Press, 1965.

EISENHOWER, DWIGHT D. *Crusade in Europe.* New York: Doubleday & Company, 1948.

————. *The White House Years: Mandate for Change, 1953–1956.* New York: Doubleday & Company, 1963.

————. *The White House Years: Waging Peace, 1956–1961.* New York: Doubleday & Company, 1965.

FRYKLUND, RICHARD. *100 Million Lives: Maximum Survival in Nuclear War.* New York: The Macmillan Company, 1962.

HAMMOND, PAUL Y. *Organizing for Defense: The American Military Establishment in the Twentieth Century.* Princeton, N.J.: Princeton University Press, 1961.

HUNTINGTON, SAMUEL P. "Power, Expertise, and the Military Profession," *Daedalus* (Fall, 1963).

JACKSON, HENRY M. (ed.). *The National Security Council.* New York: Frederick A. Praeger, 1965.

KAUFMANN, WILLIAM W. *The McNamara Strategy.* New York: Harper & Row, 1964.

KISSINGER, HENRY A. (ed.). *Problems of National Strategy.* New York: Frederick A. Praeger, 1965.

MCNAMARA, ROBERT S. Statement to a joint session of the Senate Armed Services Committee and the Senate Subcommittee on Department of Defense Appropriations on the Fiscal Year 1968–72 Defense Program and 1968 Defense Budget, January 23, 1967.

MILLIS, WALTER, with MANSFIELD, HARVEY C., and STEIN, HAROLD. *Arms and the State: Civil-Military Elements in National Policy.* New York: Twentieth Century Fund, 1958.

NEUSTADT, RICHARD E. *Presidential Power: The Politics of Leadership.* New York: John Wiley & Sons, 1960.

Organizing for National Security. Hearings of the Subcommittee on National Policy Machinery of the Senate Committee on Government Operations. Vol. I. Washington, D.C.: Government Printing Office, 1961.

RANSOM, HARRY HOWE. *Can American Democracy Survive Cold War?* Garden City, N.Y.: Doubleday & Company, 1964.

STANLEY, TIMOTHY W. *American Defense and National Security.* Washington, D.C.: Public Affairs Press, 1956.

TACHERON, DONALD G., and UDALL, MORRIS K. (eds.). *The Job of the Congressman: An Introduction to Service in the U.S.*

House of Representatives. Indianapolis, Ind.: Bobbs-Merrill Company, 1966.

TAYLOR, MAXWELL D. *The Uncertain Trumpet.* New York: Harper & Row, 1960.

TRUMAN, HARRY S. *Memoirs by Harry S. Truman.* Vol. II: *Years of Trial and Hope.* New York: Doubleday & Company, 1958.

TUCKER, SAMUEL A. (ed.). *A Modern Design for Defense Decision: A McNamara-Hitch-Enthoven Anthology.* Washington, D.C.: Industrial College of the Armed Forces, 1966.

URWICK, LYNDALL F. *Leadership in the Twentieth Century.* New York: Pitman Publishing Company, 1957.

YOSHPE, HARRY B., and FALK, STANLEY L. *Organization for National Security.* Washington, D.C.: Industrial College of the Armed Forces, 1963.

Index

Acheson, Dean, 61, 144
Advanced Research Projects Agency (ARPA), 75, 83
AEC; *see* Atomic Energy Commission
Agencies, defense; *see* Defense agencies
Agriculture, Department of, 211, 220
Air Force, Department of, 5, 20–21, 23–24, 26–27, 31–32, 35, 54, 109, 129, 153, 170–72, 189, 192, 197, 201, 214, 226, 250, 328–30
Air power, 5, 16, 19, 34, 67, 268–69
Air Transport Command; *see* Military Airlift Command
Aircraft, 5, 12, 58, 166, 186, 198, 227, 269–70, 279, 297
Airlift and Sealift Forces, 137
Alaskan Command, 91
Anderson, Robert B., 314
Anti-ballistic missile; *see* Missiles, defense against
ANZUS, 150–51
Armed Forces Management Association, 178
Armed Forces Policy Council, 45, 82–83
Armed Forces Special Weapons Project; *see* Defense Atomic Support Agency
Armed Forces Staff College, 92
Armed Services Procurement Regulations, 86, 114, 237
Arms control, 90, 293–97
Arms Control, Special Assistant for, 90
Arms Control and Disarmament Agency, 220, 293–94
Arms race, 126, 155, 293, 299
Army, Department of, 4, 54, 59, 109, 128, 129, 136, 153, 172, 213–14, 239, 250, 329
Army Air Forces; *see* Air Force, Department of
Arnold, General Henry H. "Hap," 17, 20–22
ARPA; *see* Advanced Research Projects Agency
Assured destruction, 200
Atlantic Command, 91
Atomic Energy Commission (AEC), 93, 168–70, 213–14, 220
Attlee, Clement, 11

Bacteriological warfare, 296
Barbary War, 4
Berlin, 59–60, 158, 162, 165, 228–29, 262
Bradley, General Omar N., 316
Brown, Dr. Harold, 125, 197, 201, 203
Budget, 9, 26, 50, 55, 58, 61–62, 64–65, 69, 95–96, 100, 114, 121, 132, 134–39, 152–53, 164, 204–5, 210, 251–57, 288–89
Budget, Bureau of the, 44, 54, 212, 218, 252–53
Bundy, McGeorge, 104

Career development, 79
Catton, Lieutenant General Jack J., 192
Censorship, 242–44, 279
Central Intelligence Agency (CIA), 37, 40–42, 214–15, 227–28, 264, 320–23
Central Supply and Maintenance, 137
Chemical warfare, 111
Chiefs of Staff Committee, 21
Churchill, Sir Winston, 21–22, 285
CIA; *see* Central Intelligence Agency
Civic action, 161, 239
Civil and Defense Mobilization, Office of; *see* Emergency Planning, Office of
Civil defense, 213
Civil Service, 106–9
Civil War, 4–5, 18
Clifford, Clark, 287, 313
Coast Guard, 220
Cold War, 151, 245, 260, 285, 295
Collective security, 8, 86, 90, 150–52, 159–60, 273–74
Collins, Lieutenant General J. Lawton, 31–33, 38
Collins Plan, 31–33, 38
Combined Chiefs of Staff, 21–22
Commerce, Department of, 211, 220
Communications, 47, 72, 93–94, 131–32, 137, 227

337